HEADS OF THE LOCAL STATE

Historical Urban Studies

Series editors: *Jean-Luc Pinol* and *Richard Rodger*

Titles in the series include:

Heads of the Local State
Mayors, Provosts and Burgomasters since 1800

Edited by
JOHN GARRARD
University of Salford, UK

Routledge
Taylor & Francis Group

LONDON AND NEW YORK

First published 2007 by Ashgate Publishing

Reissued 2018 by Routledge
2 Park Square, Milton Park, Abingdon, Oxon OX14 4RN
605 Third Avenue, New York, NY 10017

First issued in paperback 2021

Routledge is an imprint of the Taylor & Francis Group, an informa business

A Library of Congress record exists under LC control number: 2007000575

Notice:
Product or corporate names may be trademarks or registered trademarks, and are used only for identification and explanation without intent to infringe.

Publisher's Note
The publisher has gone to great lengths to ensure the quality of this reprint but points out that some imperfections in the original copies may be apparent.

Disclaimer
The publisher has made every effort to trace copyright holders and welcomes correspondence from those they have been unable to contact.

ISBN 13: 978-0-815-38942-2 (hbk)
ISBN 13: 978-1-351-15672-1 (ebk)
ISBN 13: 978-1-138-35705-1 (pbk)

DOI: 10.4324/9781351156721

Contents

List of Illustrations

Scottish Provosts

The traditional provostship

The modern provostship

The Mayoralty in Northern Ireland

Contrasting Ways of being a Mayor in France

The Mayoralty in the Netherlands during the Occupation

The Mayoralty in Italy

Mayoralty American Style (Baltimore)

List of Maps and Tables

Map

Tables

List of Contributors

Olivier Borraz is a CNRS fellow researcher in sociology at the Centre de Sociologie des Organisations and a lecturer at Sciences Po in Paris. His fields of research are French local government, and risk regulation. In the first field, he has published Gouverner une ville. Besançon 1959–1989 (Presses Universitaires de Rennes 1988), more recently 'France: The inter-municipal revolution', in S.A.H. Denters and L.E. Rose (eds), Comparing Local Governance: trends and developments (Basingstoke, Palgrave, 2005, with Patrick Le Galès), and has directed a symposium with Peter John on 'The transformation of urban political leadership in Western Europe', in the International Journal of Urban and Regional Research, vol. 28, 1, 2004.

Mark Callanan is a lecturer with the Institute of Public Administration in Dublin, and holds a BA from University College Dublin, a Masters from the College of Europe in Bruges, and a PhD from University College Cork. His research interests include local government and comparative sub-national government, public management reform, participation, and EU governance and policy-making. He has published widely on issues of local governance in both domestic and international journals and books, and is co-editor of Local Government in Ireland: Inside Out (Dublin, Institute of Public Administration, 2003). He has also carried out commissioned research for several government departments in Ireland as well as the European Commission.

John Garrard is Senior Lecturer in Politics and Contemporary History at the University of Salford. His research and teaching lie on the borderline between history and politics. His books include The English and Immigration: A comparative study of the Jewish influx 1880–1910 (Oxford University Press 1970); Leadership and Power in Industrial Towns 1830–1880 (Manchester University Press 1883); The Great Salford Gas Scandal of 1887 (Altrincham, British Gas North Western 1988); European Democratisation since 1800 (Basingstoke, MacMillan 2000) edited with Vera Tolz and Ralph White; Democratisation in Britain: Elites, civil society and reform since 1800 (Basingstoke, Palgrave 2001); Scandals in Past and Contemporary Politics (Manchester University Press 2006, edited with James Newell).

Colin Knox is Professor of Public Policy in the School of Policy Studies at the University of Ulster, Northern Ireland. He is currently completing (with Professor Paul Carmichael) an ESRC project on Devolution and Constitutional Change with specific reference to the reform of public administration in Northern Ireland. He has a long-standing interest in the field of local government and acts an academic advisor to the Department of Environment's Taskforce on reform of the sector.

Benjamin A. Lloyd holds a Bachelor of Arts degree in Political Science from Towson University and a Master of Public Policy degree from the University of

Maryland, Baltimore County, where he focused on local government policy. He formerly served as a Policy Fellow at the Maryland Institute for Policy Analysis and Research. Ben resides in Harford County, Maryland.

Muiris MacCarthaigh is a Research Officer with the Institute of Public Administration in Dublin. He holds a PhD from the School of Politics and International Relations at University College Dublin. His most recent publication is Accountability in Irish Parliamentary Politics (Institute of Public Administration 2005) and is co-editor of Recycling the State: The politics of adaptation in Ireland (Irish Academic Press forthcoming). He is currently involved with the Comparative Public Organisation Data Base for Research and Analysis network (www.public-management-cobra.org), which is a cross-national research network on the governance of national, regional and local public sector agencies.

Anthony McElligott is Professor of History and Director of the Centre for Historical Research at the University of Limerick. He is the author and editor of a number of books on early twentieth century Germany, most recently: The German Urban Experience 1900–1945: Modernity and crisis (Routledge 2001) and, with Tim Kirk, Working Towards the Führer. Essays in honour of Sir Ian Kershaw (Manchester University Press 2003). He is currently editing The Weimar Republic (Short Oxford History of Germany Series, OUP forthcoming) and finishing another study of the republic titled, Authority and Authoritarianism 1916–1936: Rethinking the Weimar Republic, to be published by Hodder Arnold. The current chapter derives from a long term project: The Civic Nation: Germany in the Twentieth Century (Cambridge University Press forthcoming).

Irene Maver is Senior Lecturer in Scottish History at the University of Glasgow. Her research interests focus on urban Scotland, particularly the history of Glasgow. With Professor Hamish Fraser of Strathclyde University, she co-edited Glasgow, volume II, 1830–1914 (Manchester University Press 1996). She has also written a single volume history of the city, Glasgow (Edinburgh University Press 2000). She is currently researching and writing an illustrated history of Edinburgh for Edinburgh University Press.

Emmanuel Négrier is a CNRS fellow researcher in political science at CEPEL (University of Montpellier – France). His fields of research are local politics and policies in Europe, with a special focus on cultural policies and changes in metropolitan governance. He has recently published La Question Métropolitaine (Presses Universitaires de Grenoble 2005); Une Politique Culturelle Privée en France (L'Harmattan 2006); 'A French Urban Powershift? The Political Construction of Metropolization', in French Politics (Basingstoke Palgrave, n 1 2003); 'Rescaling French Urban Territories', European Planning Studies, vol. 14, 6, 2006.

James L. Newell is Professor of Politics at the University of Salford. His recent books include Parties and Democracy in Italy (Ashgate 2000); The Italian General Election of 2001: Berlusconi's Victory (edited, Manchester University Press 2002); Corruption in Contemporary Politics (edited with Martin Bull, Palgrave McMillan 2003); Italian Politics: Adjustment under Duress (with Martin Bull, Polity Press 2005) and Scandal in Past and Contemporary Politics (edited with John Garrard, Manchester University Press 2005). He is co-editor of the European Consortium for Political Research's journal of the political science profession, European Political Science, and co-convenor of the UK Political Studies Association's Italian Politics Specialist Group.

Donald F. Norris is Director of the Maryland Institute for Policy Analysis and Research and Professor of Public Policy at the University of Maryland, Baltimore County. He is a specialist in urban politics, public management, and the application, management and impacts of information technology (including e-government) in public organisations. Dr. Norris is a widely published scholar whose works have appeared in a number of scholarly books and journals. He holds a BS in history from the University of Memphis and both an MA and a PhD in government from the University of Virginia.

Cameron Ross currently holds the post of Reader in the Department of Politics at the University of Dundee. He has published widely in the field of Russian domestic politics. His most recent books are: Federalism and Democratisation in Russia (Manchester University Press 2002); Regional Politics in Russia (edited, Manchester University Press 2002), Russian Politics under Putin (edited, Manchester University Press 2004). Cameron is also editor of the journal Perspectives on European Politics and Society (Routledge, Taylor Francis). At present he is completing a book on local politics in Russia which will be published by Routledge in 2007.

Thomas J. Vicino is Assistant Professor of Urban Affairs at the University of Texas at Arlington. He earned a PhD in public policy from the University of Maryland, Baltimore County. His research examines the socio-economic impacts of suburbanisation, economic development and urban politics and planning. His recent works appear in Urban Studies and the Encyclopedia of American Urban History.

Nico Wouters holds a doctoral degree in contemporary history (University of Ghent, Belgium). He has published several books and articles on Belgian (local) authorities and administrative collaboration during World War II, and international comparisons of occupation history between Belgium, the north of France and the Netherlands. He currently works for the Centre for Historical Research and Documentation on War and Contemporary Society (Brussels), where he is one of the researchers employed by the Belgian Senate to investigate the possible responsibility of Belgian authorities in the persecution of the Jews in Belgium during the War.

Historical Urban Studies
General Edit ors' Preface

Density and proximity are two of the defining characteristics of the urban dimension. It is these that identify a place as uniquely urban, though the threshold for such pressure points varies from place to place. What is considered an important cluster in one context – may not be considered as urban elsewhere. A third defining characteristic is functionality – the commercial or strategic position of a town or city which conveys an advantage over other places. Over time, these functional advantages may diminish, or the balance of advantage may change within a hierarchy of towns. To understand how the relative importance of towns shifts over time and space is to grasp a set of relationships which is fundamental to the study of urban history.

Towns and cities are products of history, yet have themselves helped to shape history. As the proportion of urban dwellers has increased, so the urban dimension has proved a legitimate unit of analysis through which to understand the spectrum of human experience and to explore the cumulative memory of past generations. Though obscured by layers of economic, social and political change, the study of the urban milieu provides insights into the functioning of human relationships and, if urban historians themselves are not directly concerned with current policy studies, few contemporary concerns can be understood without reference to the historical development of towns and cities.

This longer historical perspective is essential to an understanding of social processes. Crime, housing conditions and property values, health and education, discrimination and deviance, and the formulation of regulations and social policies to deal with them were, and remain, amongst the perennial preoccupations of towns and cities – no historical period has a monopoly of these concerns. They recur in successive generations, albeit in varying mixtures and strengths; the details may differ.

The central forces of class, power and authority in the city remain. If this was the case for different periods, so it was for different geographical entities and cultures. Both scientific knowledge and technical information were available across Europe and showed little respect for frontiers. Yet despite common concerns and access to broadly similar knowledge, different solutions to urban problems were proposed and adopted by towns and cities in different parts of Europe. This comparative dimension informs urban historians as to which were systematic factors and which were of a purely local nature: general and particular forces can be distinguished.

These analytical and comparative frameworks inform this book. Indeed, thematic, comparative and analytical approaches to the historical study of towns and cities is the hallmark of the Historical Urban Studies series which now extends to over 30 titles, either already published or currently in production. European urban historiography has been extended and enriched as a result and this book makes another important addition to an intellectual mission to which we, as General Editors, remain firmly committed.

Richard Rodger   *University of Leicester*
Jean-Luc Pinol   *Université de Lyon II*

Acknowledgements

My thanks are due to Richard Rodgers and Mike Goldsmith for encouragement and suggestions, and to David Garrard for suggestions and additional research. Thanks also to Tom Gray and Adam Richardson at Ashgate Publishing; Chris Agius, Linda Eastham, Kath Capper and Mike Freeman at the University of Salford; Ida Glendinning and David Kett at Dundee; Morag Penny at Aberdeen; Paul Adair at Perth; the Staffs of Aberdeen, Birmingham, Blackburn, Bolton, Dumfries, Liverpool, Perth and Dundee Local Studies Libraries; and (for splendid indexing) Roger Bennett.

Acknowledgments

Introduction

John Garrard

His unremitting attention to the multiplicity of public duties ... during a year of more than average difficulties notably illustrated in the great flood and the sudden invasion of Belgian volunteers ... his catholicity of attention to the interests of all parties in the borough and generous hospitality have naturally invested his lease of power with great popularity ... when we have an efficient mayor, his (re)election ... must be an advantage, since his power to serve the community ... is augmented and he is able to carry to completion many important objects.[1]

SCHOOLBOY VOTED AS AMERICA'S YOUNGEST MAYOR
The new mayor of Hillsdale, Michigan is a man of the people, ready to listen to their every concern ... but only until 6pm. Then he has to do his homework ... the $3000 a year job is part-time. 'From 7.50am to 2.30pm, I'll be a student. From 3 to 6, I'll be the mayor of Hillsdale, working on the mayor stuff.'[2]

If we imagine a polar scale measuring for mayoral significance, these two quotations appear to reveal its opposite ends. The fact that the first derives from England where tradition holds mayors to be largely honorific at best, and the second comes from the very recent United States where mayoralty is supposedly an important position of power shows the malleability of the office in the face of time and town-size, as well as the possible deprivations visited upon it by the passage of years.

In fact it will be one the contentions of this book that mayors, provosts, burgomasters and other heads of the local state have been, and remain, important – partly because they are often powerful positions, partly because considerable symbolic significance attaches to the ceremonies surrounding them. Even the 18 year old featured above campaigned hard for the mayoralty, regarded it as significant and may even be doing the presidential 'stuff' in the not too distant future. Given all this, it is odd how little attention has been allotted to heads of the local state by historians and political scientists. As most of our contributors testify, national historiographies often contain few studies of individual incumbents and virtually none of the office in general. This neglect is evident in countries where mayors and other local heads are powerful; still more, as in countries like Britain, Ireland and Sweden, where they are supposedly impotent. Indeed, as our contributor on the Russian mayoralty discovered, even the normally prolific sources of the internet managed to produce remarkably little on mayoralty in that country.

At this stage, it is worth saying something about the chosen title of this book, since the circumstances governing its appropriateness, or otherwise, are central to the contexts in which mayors, provosts and burgomasters exist; also because it provides us with a convenient peg upon which to begin to explore comparisons between mayoralties in the

---

[1]   *Salford Weekly News*, 10 November 1867, p. 2. On the re-lection of H.D. Pochin as mayor.
[2]   *The Guardian*, 12 November 2005, p. 5.

various countries on offer here. In several senses, it is entirely proper to see these offices as heading something called a local state since they preside over sets of institutions wherein significant amounts of governmental, and even judicial, power are located and they are (like the monarchs and presidents who stand at the head of national political systems) the centres of significant allegiance-inducing ceremony. Like their national counterparts, they also preside over a bounded space – one of the things supposedly distinctive and essential to a state.[3] For these reasons, and because the idea is widely used and provides us with a reasonably attractive shorthand way of identifying the central theme, the title stands. However, in other senses of course, the term may seem questionable since municipalities are clearly subordinate authorities exercising powers, allocated or allowed them by the legislative and executive arms of the national state. Moreover, there are some powers that are central to what states are about that local authorities simply do not have, most notably in relation to defence and foreign policy, although globalisation and the emergence of the European Community has meant that municipal governments and their heads are increasingly involved in relations with others of their kind in other countries, with inter-municipal bodies and with super-national authorities. Furthermore, vibrant local government has often been seen more as an aspect of civil society, and thus as part of the desirable underpinnings for healthy liberal democratic states, than as part of a state in its own right. In this respect, municipal politics can be seen as one of the crucial locations where citizens learn democratic ways, which provides bases from which they can resist the overweening attentions of the national state, and where aspirant national politicians can receive their training.

If it is appropriate to see municipalities as part of civil society, then the ability of mayors and burgomasters to capture popular attention and allegiance, and even to wield power, is important to their democratic functionality. The charismatic success of mayors of important cities in post-war West Germany, as revealed in Anthony McElligott's chapter, almost certainly made significant contributions to citizens' ability to find a democratic pathway out of Nazism. Olivier Borraz and Emmanuel Négrier take a rather similar view of French mayors in the early decades of the Third Republic: mayoral activities are seen as important in drawing their communities into adherence to the new regime and into increased acceptance of state authority. Their links with central politics also enabled them to contribute significantly to the writing of the constitutions of both the Fourth and Fifth Republic. There seems evidence from Nico Wouters' chapter that, having shown remarkable resilience and (within the context of the local governmental culture in which they operated) remarkable ability to preserve a degree of local-governmental autonomy, during the German occupation of Belgium, mayors were important in managing the transition to a democratic regime after the War. Some of what is revealed in the chapters by John Garrard and Irene Maver may suggest to readers that English mayors and Scottish provosts were sufficiently attention-commanding and persuasively illustrative of local elite values to reinforce the attachment of working-class voters to the political system in the decades after the 1867 Reform Act. Similarly, Labour's pre-1914 and interwar fixation with mayoralty and access to mayoral office may, like its absorption

---

[3]   Michael Mann, 'The autonomous power of the state', *Archives Europeennes de Sociologie*, 25, 185 (1984), cited by Miles Ogbourne, 'Local power and state regulation in nineteenth century Britain', *Transactions of the Institute of Geographers*, N.S. 17 (1992) 217.

with Parliament, have been a factor reinforcing that party's attachment to the system. Finally, and by contrast, the far less certain fortunes of mayors in post-Communist Russia, as evident in Cameron Ross' chapter, may raise worrying questions about the vibrancy of local government, along with other aspects of civil society, and thus about the viability of some sort of Russian democracy.

Uncertainty about whether something as clearly subordinate as a municipality should be dignified into a local state is central to another crucial characteristic of the office standing at its head. McElligott sees German mayors since around 1900, even more since 1918, as caught – sometimes creatively, sometimes destructively – within the often conflicting pressures stemming from their roles as servants of the national state, agents of their political party and representatives of the people. This is because they stood at the 'fulcrum wherein state, party and people came together'. At various times, pressures from one or more of these roles have become overwhelmingly powerful. During the Third Reich and again in Communist East Germany, the force exerted by the totalitarian state and its Nazi and Communist familiars became irresistible, yet, even at such times, the third role as citizens' representative still posed choices. Even under Nazism, cries of agony from bombed German cities forced themselves to mayoral attention. For the rest of time and place – under Weimar, in at least three of the four post-war occupation zones, and in post-1949 West Germany – pressures from all three roles have been more or less in balance.

McElligott's conceptual scheme, meanwhile, provides us with a way of thinking comparatively about other heads of the local state. Unsurprisingly, the forces of party and state are perhaps least evident in those polities with supposedly weak and honorific mayoralties – particularly in England, Wales, Scotland, Northern Ireland and in the Irish Republic. Here mayoral impotence renders the office an unlikely target of pressure from the centre, while traditions of mayoral impartiality make it an improper focus for party pressure, at least so long as impartiality is perceived to be maintained. However, this simply means that pressures upon local authorities from above are channelled through Town Clerks rather than mayors and party operates through the real centres of power within councils, the Majority and Minority Leaders. Moreover, as we shall see, mayors and provosts in the past have often been altogether more activist and such incumbents have sometimes been virtual party leaders. Meanwhile, the very honour and supposed impartiality of mayoralty has periodically rendered mayoral elections the scene of bitter conflict as rival parties have contended for their place in the respectable sun.

The cross pressures involving party, state and people are much clearer in countries with 'strong mayors' – though they do not always run in one direction. Nico Wouters' chapter on occupied Holland and Belgium makes clear that even mayors from collaborationist parties like the *Vlaams Nationaal Verbond* (VNV) and Rex were obliged to balance pressures from the Nazi occupier against those from the local citizenry. Partly because of traditions of local self-government flowing from Belgium's past, they did so in ways that left surprising amounts of local autonomy and successful resistance to central authority. It seems appropriate to see the Belgian, and perhaps the Dutch, mayoralty as the crucial interlocutor between the occupying power and the occupied population.

Meanwhile, it is clear from chapter 5 that French mayors certainly stand at the apex of pressures from state, party and people – though in this case (and probably in most of the others), mayors are active agents in the deployment of power and thus pressures are exerted *by* mayors as much as they are *upon* them. Mayoral roles, like those for French local government as a whole, are built around two interrelated and interdependent sets of objectives and activities: first garnering political support by providing services to the local population, ensuring local administrative coherence and integrating parties and groups into the local political system; second, wielding influence in situations where mayoral status as agents of the national state within their localities gives them privileged access to the local representatives of that state such as prefects. Meanwhile the mayoral tendency to hold other offices (for example, seats in the Senate) has given mayors more direct influence in Paris. Wielding influence also involves establishing partnerships in order to produce and implement public policies – with the state, with business and with voluntary associations. Alongside mayors' rather proactive roles as agents of the state and representatives of the people, party was also a factor influencing mayoral activity. However, in recent years, declining voter loyalty has led them to operate in more depoliticised and cross-party ways and to garner support from segments of the population far beyond the old party client groups.

James Newell, in his chapter, takes a rather less pro-active view of the Italian mayoralty, at least until the changed circumstances apparently emerging from Law number 81 in 1993. Nevertheless Italian mayors were clearly the focus of competing pressures from state, party and people. As in Germany, and for somewhat similar reasons, the balance between these forces has varied over time. In Mussolini's extended period of dictatorship, the state and its fascist party mentor were the central influences in the lives of mayors and of the *podestas* who replaced them in 1926. However, the 1948 Constitution changed the balance between state, party and people dramatically: it legally recognised local authorities for the first time and, indeed, assumed they had general competence to act in any area not expressly prohibited by parliament. This instantly subjected the resurrected mayors to the overwhelming clientelistic expectations of their constituents. These could only be satisfied – not through the state's formal bureaucratic apparatus – but via informal party networks leading up to the centre, a location where decisions were made according to the broad tactical needs and internal dynamics of *partitocrazia* – the almost permanent governing alliance between Christian Democrats and other parties of the centre. This situation has been widely seen as constraining Italian mayors to the frequent point of paralysis – a paralysis from which they were only rescued by the 1993 law, making mayors directly elected (previously, they had been selected by local councils) and freeing them from local party constraints in a variety of other ways at a time when *partitocrazia* had been deeply discredited by massive scandals at the centre. For Newell, this has rendered mayors significantly more powerful and meant that they 'at last have become heads of their local states'.

The pressures upon mayors in Russia, as is evident in the chapter by Cameron Ross, also varied considerably over time, though within far narrower limits than in either Germany or Italy. In the USSR's highly totalitarian system, democratic centralism, 'dual subordination' effectively to party and state, *nomenklatura* and frequent career moves all ensured that Soviet mayors were purely the enforcers of state and Communist Party dictates and not community representatives at all, even to the extent that they were in Nazi Germany. The only other pressure (a formidable one) in their lives came from local factory managers who also took their orders from above. Gorbachev's reforms from the late-1980s and the subsequent collapse of the Soviet system in 1991 guaranteed the existence of local self-government for the first time and permitted its direct involvement in the appointment of local officials, including mayors. For the first time, mayoral representation of community interests was rendered conceivable and a set of clientelistic expectations found representative expression. Thereafter, the popular election of mayors notwithstanding, the future of local self-government remained uncertain, as Russian mistrust of subsidiary loyalties resurfaced, first under Yeltsin and then more decisively under Putin. With national party formations still in a rudimentary condition, mayors were forced to form their own personal parties in order to fight elections. However, in a quasi-federal system, mayors now had two state masters – with pressures emanating from both central and republican/provincial level and not from party at all. As of 2003, Ross sees mayors 'at the mercy of provincial of regional governors', to a point where their functions may become largely ceremonial.

As is hopefully already clear, mayors, burgomasters and provosts are important. This is evident in both ceremonial and executive terms. Mayoral rituals have received significant attention only in some chapters – most notably those on England, Scotland and Northern Ireland (all countries where civic heads tend to be regarded as non-partisan and largely honorific), but also in France where mayors have been consistently powerful and (until recently) altogether more party-oriented. It is clear that the ceremonial side of these offices has a variety of important functions and uses, both for the immediate participants and for broader arrays of citizens.

First, civic ceremonial is a public proclamation of various sorts of unity. In most countries (significantly not in the USSR where central hostility to any sort of local loyalty rendered mayoral ceremony inconceivable), it provides a platform from which the existence of, and pride in, urban 'community' can be proclaimed, imagined and probably reinforced. Since around 1918, such claims have become outwardly and increasingly implausible as cities have become larger, more socially and economically complex and more impersonal. However, they were persuasive until at least the early-twentieth century because urban places were sufficiently introspective for citizens to pay attention in large numbers. Connectedly, mayor making in England, Wales and Scotland at least was an occasion to publicly celebrate, or at least argue for, the essential unity and civic-mindedness of otherwise deeply divided urban political elites. Mayoral ritual could also provide occasions upon which the linkage between particular towns or cities and the broader nation could be proclaimed. In this book, this theme is most evident in France where town hall external decoration, busts of Marianne within and tricolour mayoral sashes, all became part of a conspicuous process that attempted (successfully so the authors claim) to wed urban communities to the Third Republican regime after 1871. However, similar themes are also evident in the British Isles, with mayor- and provost-led celebrations of national events like coronations and jubilees and occasions upon which visiting royals are ceremonially greeted by civic heads. Mayoral ceremony can also provide platforms from which urban values, or at least those of the dominant elites and classes, can be proclaimed with hopefully persuasive, if not (as in Scotland) always unifying, effects. Finally, as is evident in the chapters on England, Scotland and Northern Ireland by John Garrard, Irene Maver and Colin Knox respectively, mayor-making and mayoral entertainment has provided occasions upon which to mark the social and political arrival of new groups and parties – the working classes, religious and ethnic minorities, women, the Labour Party and, in Northern Ireland and even England (Liverpool), various sorts of Irish nationalist. In recent years in Northern Ireland, as Knox demonstrates, mayoral appointment has also generated an arena in which to launch experiments in power-sharing, doing so at a time when political avenues within the broader province have been blocked. Thus, 'the seemingly innocuous role of local head of state, presiding over a relatively small tier of local governance, is imbued with powerful political symbolism with wider constitutional ramifications'.

Secondly, however, mayoral ceremony has also provided occasions when various sorts of conflict could be ritually advertised, sometimes as a preliminary to ultimate settlement, sometimes not. The extensively bitter debates in many English industrial towns in the interwar years about Labour's exclusion from mayoral office, and the party's subsequent and still embittered monopoly of the mayoral chair, represent one example. The furious and highly ritualised walkout by Unionists over Sinn Fein's elevation to mayoral office in Belfast in 2001 is another. In the German-occupied Netherlands, Nico Wouters shows that mayoralty became the final bastion of 'Dutchness' and its capture by the collaborationist *Nationaal Socialistische Beweging* (NSB) led to boycotts of mayoral ceremony by municipal administrators and the disregarding of mayoral orders by citizens. In the Irish Free State, Muiris McCarthaigh and Mark Callanan note that republican prisoners were sometimes elevated to mayoral status, this becoming one of a number of ways of making out the case for a full republic.

Mayors are also important centres of executive power. In what literature there is on mayoralty, there is a frequently drawn distinction between strong and weak mayors based primarily upon their formal legal powers. Strong mayors have the ability to *veto* acts of their councils, hire and fire municipal personnel and to prepare budgets; they also tend to be popularly elected – though, as the German example demonstrates over many decades, it is perfectly possible to have strong mayors who are not popularly elected. Weak (or weaker) mayors do not have one or more of these powers and tend to be appointed by their council. In fact, although the distinction may be useful as a means of characterising the opposite ends of a polar scale, the borderlines between the two are decidedly hazy. This is because other factors besides the legal situation, such as personality, party regime and other features of the political and historical context in which the incumbent is situated, are highly important in determining actual mayoral power and effectiveness.

The argument is most explicitly explored by Benjamin Lloyd, Donald Norris and Thomas Vicino in their chapter on the American mayoralty. Their central theme is an enquiry about the effects of changes in governmental structure, particularly those engineered by the Progressives in their battles against allegedly corrupt and inefficient city administrations from the turn of the twentieth century. While the scholarly evidence about the general problem may be ambiguous as the authors say, that concerning American mayors seems fairly clear-cut. Structurally, most are fairly weak in the ways defined above. However, the real determinants of mayoral effectiveness seem to be personality, political skill and the broader economic and political circumstances of time and place: as the authors note, 'individual mayors can overcome structural weaknesses and govern strongly ... (M)ayors in structurally strong offices can fail to use their powers effectively and govern poorly'.

Although less directly focused upon the circumstances governing mayoral effectiveness and power, the other chapters provide similar conclusions at least to the point of making context and personality as important as structure. The 1993 Law, number 81, was intended to empower Italian mayors by making them directly elected and freeing them from party control in other structural ways. Its framers wished to liberate them from the paralysis imposed by *partitocrazia* at the centre, shifting party coalitions on local councils and the clientelistic expectations of their constituents. According to James Newell, the post-1993 evidence is encouraging for the reformers but also ambiguous. There are certainly signs of successful mayoral initiative as the result of this law, but equally salient in liberating mayors from at least one paralysing factor has been the discrediting and at least medium-term collapse of *partitocrazia* at the national centre. Overall, the author concludes that the reforms have given mayors:

> a set of opportunities which together constitute necessary but not sufficient conditions for them to make considerable difference to local policy-making ... (They have) helped ensure that today's mayors are more well-known, more authoritative and more central figures in public political debate than they have ever been before.

The evidence on France seems to point in similar directions, indeed making structure seem less important as a variable than in Italy. French mayors are undoubtedly powerful. In part, this stems from their legal powers. They are admittedly not popularly elected (again suggesting that this is not a necessary precondition for wielding power), but have considerable influence over recruitment to the top levels of their administrations, particularly the politically sensitive positions; in so far as they need it, they also have de facto veto power over council decisions. However, Olivier Borraz and Emmanuel Négrier argue that the real key to success is not so much their formal powers, but mayors' skill and discretion in using them, their access to central government via local prefects and multiple office-holding and their consequent ability to influence the regulatory framework within which local authorities exist. This has made French mayors very powerful figures, capable of producing considerable benefits for their areas. In the twenty-first century, mayoral authority has become more uncertain than ever before, but this is not due to any contraction in legal power. Rather it stems from the unpredictable and fragmentary character of the social and political alliances mayors need to mobilise given the fading of the old ideologically-bound party followings; it is due also to the uncertain outcomes of mayoral attempts to build support and wield influence within the ever-multiplying numbers of inter-municipal bodies and the wider networks of the European Union within which modern mayors have to work. All of this might be taken as one expression of the regionalised and globalised context wherein modern urban areas now exist.

Structural factors have certainly played an important part in determining mayoral power in Germany. Anthony McElligott, in his chapter, draws a common German distinction between *Bürgermeisterverfassung* and *Magistratsverfassung* systems of mayoralty, which seem to roughly coincide with the categories of strong and weak mayors. The legal structures, powers and constraints implied by the terms have clearly had a significant impact on the roles mayors have been able to play. However, it is clear that other factors have also been important. Wilhelmine and Weimar mayors, irrespective of their legal situation seem to have been powerful figures, with reputations and influence that extended into their region, even into national politics (again multiple office holding played a part here). Weimar's declining years saw a strengthening of mayoral positions quite independently of their formal powers as a conservative reaction set in across the Republic. During the Third Reich mayors were elevated into charismatic leading figures by the Nazi *fuhrerprinzip*, though they were also heavily constrained from above by the totalitarian state, and by their often part-time status and limited financial resources. In the aftermath of the Second World War, mayoral power was circumscribed by the Allied occupation, and the precise character of what they could do in any given zone was conditioned by varying British, French, American and Russian assumptions, derived from their own ideology and political culture, about the sort of office mayoralty should be. In 1953 and 1956, mayoral power in West Germany was legally enhanced and responsibility to the state reinforced. However, mayors' effectiveness was equally conditioned by the often-charismatic authority of particular incumbents, sometimes in response to events beyond their territorial borders like the Berlin Blockade, allowing them to achieve national and even international reputations, as well as to become key figures in the reconstruction of their cities.

In Russia, mayors have very considerable legal powers. However, this chapter makes clear that, even after the collapse of Communism, actual mayoral power has been conditioned far more by the state of politics at the national centre. It is also conditioned by power handed out by that centre to republican and provincial authorities. As already noted, mayors' fine array of legal powers in relation to their councils may not have much meaning if the reassertion of central authority denies them any sort of autonomy in their exercise.

Aside from recent actual and contemplated experiments with elected mayors, which have been clear attempts to render them identifiable centres of urban authority and leadership by legal and institutional means, heads of the local state in Britain and Ireland are legally weak. Indeed, they are endowed with few formal powers beyond the ability to preside at council meetings. In the Irish Republic, mayors have been further constrained by the existence of city and county managers – as has been the case in some American cities. Formal mayoral powers may have been somewhat augmented by the chairing of Lord Mayor's Commissions in Dublin, essentially extra-legal bodies, and of the more general and legally constituted Corporate Policy Groups (CPGs), the latter at least being seen as possible routes to some form of cabinet government amongst local authorities.

However, British and Irish heads' real situation has been somewhat more complicated than the legal picture suggests. As MacCarthaigh and Callanan note, whether the CPGs or Lord Mayors' commissions produce any augmentation of mayoral power depends upon mayoral powers of persuasion. It is also notable that Irish proposals to institute popularly elected mayors in 2001 deliberately contained no actual augmentation of legal authority, the assumption being that popular election alone and the accompanying enhancement of visibility would together be sufficient to enhance mayoral power. Meanwhile, periodically in both England and Scotland, other circumstances besides legal empowerment have combined to allow the practical possibility of substantial power for mayors and provosts. In the decades up to 1914 and even beyond, particularly in Scotland, weak party articulation within councils (a factor also influential upon mayoral power in Italy since 1993), the introspective character of urban communities and the habits of forceful governance that come naturally to substantial businessmen enabled many mayors and provosts to become powerful centres of council leadership particularly in areas such as civic improvement.

Overall, mayoralty is a socially and politically significant institution. It represents one answer to problems posed by the ever-growing size, complexity and impersonality of towns and cities. Civic heads provide a symbolic centre that can try to give meaning to notions of community in increasingly unpromising urban places. In most countries, even intermittently in Britain, they are also seen to represent a single directing centre of political authority, with power derived both from how their roles are formally defined and from the ways they manage to use a variety of political resources to expand those roles. However, they are also caught up in, and inhibited by, influences and expectations that flow from their relationships with state, party and people. In recent decades, they have also become subject to influences flowing from regions and the wider international stage. How mayors, provosts, burgomasters and other heads of local state have tried to resolve the choices and dilemmas posed by these various factors, and what has happened to them in the process, hopefully will give interest to the chapters that follow.

CHAPTER ONE

English Mayors: What are they for?

John Garrard

Traditional mayors in England and Wales seem impotent and insignificant today – apparently confined to chairing their councils and vacuously beaming their way around schools, old folks homes and myriad voluntary groups; indeed, a few towns have replaced them with directly-elected executive mayors. This image is misleading. Until recently, the mayoralty has been an important, even a shaping, force in local political and social life, perhaps even having implications for national political dispositions. It has been important for the internal dynamics of municipal councils and has had great symbolic significance for both municipalities and groups constituting the wider communities they govern. Periodically, mayors have also been influential.

Part of this importance lies in mayoralty's ambiguous position, rather akin to a monarchy open to all and the contradictions flowing from this: an office to which many aspire but others feel impelled to reject; a position with few formal powers but from which some have exerted significant leadership and upon which many others have focused to the point of near-fixation; a place where honours can be shared but also where superiority can be proclaimed and honour denied; a point of political integration and incorporation but also of stinging exclusion; and, underpinning this, a generator of municipal and civic unity, consensus and mutual 'kindly feelings', but also sometimes of bitter and enduring conflict.

Before exploring these themes, we should examine the broader and interdependent features of the changing context for mayors. For the sake of brevity, I will list them:

1. Until around 1880, even 1914, the local urban arena was intensely visible, even absorbing, to its inhabitants. So too were the local social and political elites inhabiting this arena. Thereafter, both progressively faded from view, as national images increasingly dominated popular attention. Connectedly, socio-economic leaders progressively withdrew from the local scene or faded from view.
2. Nineteenth-century municipalities were substantially autonomous of the centre. Starting in the 1870s, and accelerating after 1918 and 1945, they became evermore dependent upon national government for powers and finance. From the 1970s, under mistrustful central government guidance, municipalities also began losing functions to other bodies.
3. Until around 1914, political parties controlled municipal electoral processes, but had far less impact upon council deliberations and policies. Thereafter, with the advent of the Labour Party, party programmes and thus policy-mandates, they began dominating these too.
4. Until around 1914, local newspapers were vibrant and locally owned, providing copious and vivid vantage points upon the local scene. Thereafter,

they progressively decayed in all respects, and that scene increasingly faded from popular view, doubly so with the emergence of syndicated free sheets in recent decades.

5. Until the 1880s, economic enterprise was mostly locally owned. Thereafter, it became progressively regional, national and eventually global.

Within this context, we can now explore the constant and changing features of mayoralty. At the outset, we should note that the office has always been very burdensome, and this was one reason why some rejected nomination. In 1935, Canterbury's retiring mayor estimated he had 'almost a full-time job'.[1] In 1963, Liverpool's John Braddock looked back on a year containing 1000 engagements and 60,000 miles of travelling, while a colleague regarded matters more biblically and zoologically: 'A Lord Mayor must have the patience of Job, the wisdom of Solomon, the strength of an ox and the digestion of an ostrich.'[2] Back in 1895, Oxford's retiring incumbent wearily remembered, '18 council meetings ... 237 committee meetings ... 50 (sub-committee meetings) ... 100 attendances at the City Court, besides many meetings of the Guardians ... and (when possible) the Littlemore Asylum Visitors'.[3] Present-day mayors confirm such testimony.

Underpinning these burdens, we can identify three interconnected functions, each with considerable importance for both municipality and community and deriving much initial impetus from councils' historic preference for incumbents who were socio-economic leaders. First, mayors were periodically executive figures; second, they have always been charitable leaders; third, as heads of their local state and representatives of their town, mayors are traditionally major centres of ceremony and sociability.

The Executive Mayor

Many mayors were content with honour, impartiality and political impotence – and these characteristics have been mostly obligatory in the party-dominated context since 1945. However, in the past, councils and their heads were periodically decidedly unsatisfied with 'mere show mayors'[4] and incumbents turned their office in powerful executive directions. Many opened their terms with quasi-presidential state-of-the-union addresses. In Birmingham in 1873, Joseph Chamberlain hailed the virtues of municipally-owned utilities, sanitary and housing reform, using his three-year mayoralty as a platform from which to dramatise and successfully execute these causes.[5] Others too used their inauguration to review municipal work, indicating 'one or two matters that would receive attention in the coming months'. The speaker here, H.D. Pochin, Salford's mayor 1866-1868, sought more attention for road communications

---

[1]   *Kentish Gazette and Canterbury Press*, 16 November 1935, p. 4.

[2]   J. Maxwell Entwistle, *Liverpool Daily Post*, 21 May 1963, p. 7.

[3]   *Jackson's Oxford Journal*, 16 November 1895, p. 6.

[4]   Councillor Prentice, *Manchester Guardian (MG)*, 12 November 1845, p. 6.

[5]   E.P. Hennock, *Fit and Proper Persons: Ideal and Reality in Nineteenth-Century Local Government* (London, Longman 1973), p. 104ff.

and the borough's sanitary condition.[6] After one year, the *Salford Weekly News* praised his 'administrative ability' and recommended a second: 'When we have an efficient mayor, his (re)election must be an advantage, since his power to serve the community ... is augmented and he is able to carry to completion important objects ... more effectively ...'[7] In Banbury in 1865, Councillor Osbourne surveyed someone else's two-year incumbency, noting 'the active part the late-mayor had taken on all the great questions which had arisen ... (for example) the waterworks, railway, and other matters ... on which he stood up manfully for the interests of the town'.[8] In Margate (where executive mayors were the norm), D.T. Evans was greeted in council in 1907 as 'the right man for the right place ... If Margate ever wanted a strong man at the head of affairs, it was now ... (There was) a man-of-war lying off the town ... (perhaps) it was a compliment to the new Mayor'. At the luncheon, Mr MacFarlane agreed: 'Margate needed at its head a man with initiative such as their host, and the watchword of the borough today should be "Hustle" and "Intelligent Anticipation".'[9] In Bolton, James Scowcroft chose sanitary and poor law reform, the postal service and Sabbath observance as his favoured causes, concluding an active year by being summonsed for assaulting someone he found outside a shop during Sunday service.[10]

Some councils (Canterbury and Banbury for example) continued their predilections for strong mayors into the late twentieth century. However, such figures mostly belonged to municipal life before 1918 (though wartime emergencies sometimes revived such preferences between 1939 and 1945). Several contemporary factors rendered executive mayoralties viable, even likely, options. For one thing, the role was long legitimised by time. In their formidable survey of pre-1835 local government, Sidney and Beatrice Webb discovered executive mayors to be normal, outside that small group of municipalities whose relatively democratic constitutions rendered them too chaotic for such direction. Otherwise, amidst vastly varied local political systems, mayors invariably were formally 'invested with large and indefinite powers', 'filled a large part of town life' and had 'great power and dignity heaped upon them'.[11] Though fading somewhat after 1689, mayoral activism remained normal across virtually all municipalities before 1835. What was true of Liverpool – 'The mayor has taken the place of the Lord of the town'[12] – was evident almost everywhere else. Even in tiny Penzance, he was 'the one authority ... uniting in his person virtually every executive power'.[13]

The occurrence of such power after 1835 was rendered likely by the fact that, even more than other nineteenth-century council members, mayors were mostly economic and social leaders in their communities. Used to wielding economic and philanthropic authority, political initiative came naturally. In councils heavily laced

6   *Manchester Guardian (MG)*, 10 November 1866, p. 3.
7   *Salford Weekly News (SWN)*, 10 November 1867, p. 2.
8   *Banbury Advertizer (BA)*, 16 November 1865, p. 4.
9   *Keble's Margate and Ramsgate Gazette*, 16 November 1907, p. 4.
10   *Bolton Chronicle (BC)*, 6 November 1847, p. 4.
11   Sidney and Beatrice Webb, *English Local Government: The Manor and the Borough* (London, Longman 1908), p. 310.
12   ibid, p. 311, quoting Ramsay Muir, *History of Local Government in Liverpool* (1906), p. 49.
13   *English Local Government*, p. 410.

with such persons, activism was also permissible, even expected. They had after all originally been nominated as council candidates because of the belief that skills and understandings acquired from running large businesses transferred naturally into municipal life.[14] Local newspapers agreed: recommending a second term for one 'in the first rank of our local aristocracy' (a wealthy businessman) in 1875, *The Kentish Gazette* noted that, immediately upon first election, he had consequently become 'what a mayor ought to be, the head and leader of the local community', observing also that the important objects he had identified at his inauguration had been successfully executed.[15] Thirty years later, contemplating Sir George Collard's unprecedented and highly active ten-year mayoralty, it noted the same natural connection between socio-economic authority and political leadership. Collard was 'a gentleman of good family ... culture and ability, moving in influential circles, possessed of ample means and animated with the best desires ...'.[16]

If business-based mayors desired to lead, nineteenth-century municipal situations often presented opportunities, even urgent needs, for what they could offer. Parties dominated elections, aldermanic and even mayoral selection. However, until Labour emerged, they rarely produced distinctive policy stances, still less ones springing from ideology, and thus rarely acquired electoral mandates. Council life was consequently individualistic, competitive and factionalised; majority party leaders could rarely produce policy initiative. This might come from powerful committee chairmen in areas like finance, public utilities and public health. However, inter-committee rivalry could also produce paralysis and, whenever action was required spanning broader policy-remits or needing public attention for successful prosecution, mayors were often the only available points of leadership. Thus in Manchester in 1845, 'the work ... being divided amongst various committees ... independent of each other, and therefore needing some one directing head, that directing head they had found in the late-Mayor'.[17] However, mayors could not always find the time: Salford offered no opposition to the 1848 Health of Towns Act, because, according to the incumbent, 'the mayor must give his whole attention to these matters: almost everything devolved upon him'.[18]

Normally, co-ordination and leadership were things mayors were well-equipped to give. They had *ex-officio* seats on all council committees and (unlike their present-day counterparts) generally sat in them. Furthermore, as the socio-economically magnificent centrepieces of municipal elites already commanding public attention partly as the result of absorbed local newspapers, they were highly visible figures. Both gratified and bemused, one retiring mayor noted 'I was a sort of little king as I walked about the streets'.[19] During potential crises, local journalists tended to keep one eye cocked on the mayoral parlour. As Rochdale's 1900 Improvement Bill hit parliamentary difficulty, reporters noticed:

---

[14]   Hennock, *Fit and Proper Persons.*
[15]   *Kentish Gazette* (*KG*), 9 November 1875, p. 4.
[16]   *KG*, 11 November 1905, p. 4.
[17]   Councillor Prentice, *MG*, 12 November 1845, p. 6.
[18]   William Jenkinson, *MG*, 4 March 1848, p. 9.
[19]   Alderman Miles Ashworth, *Rochdale Observer* (*RO*), 11 November 1899, p. 6.

the mayor ... in frock coat and top hat ... rushing breathless from the town hall to get to the bank ... and catch an express to London ... A telegram had been received ... requesting the immediate presence of the [council's] Parliamentary Committee.[20]

Attention-commanding socio-economic leaders themselves, mayors were also in intimate, sometimes family, contact with others of their kind, whose consent might be crucially required for town-wide projects. Liverpool did not normally favour either mayors-of-action or two-term incumbencies, but broke both rules in 1885 with David Radcliffe. He had 'inaugurated a movement for an exhibition ... Through his energy and attention ... it promises to be a most successful effort'. In this, he had 'received ... great advantage through holding the high position of mayor'. His re-election would thus 'confer great advantage on that movement'.[21]

The final factor encouraging mayoral leadership before 1914 and even afterwards, particularly in the absence of other initiating centres, was his role as community symbol, representative and head of his local state. This was sometimes important in relation to interests within municipal borders: rival authorities like Poor Law Guardians, docks authorities, railway companies,[22] universities and local employers. Nineteenth-century Oxford mayors, as will become evident later, were crucial points of contact and negotiation with the University vice-chancellor. In 1865, Oxford's first citizen was also seen as crucial to negotiations with the Great Western Railway over the location of its new carriage works.[23] During interwar labour disputes, particularly if they were still leading businessmen, mayors sometimes became industrial conciliators, bringing contending parties together in the mayoral parlour. Mayoral activism was far more crucial during those increasingly frequent occasions when councils impinged upon the world beyond their borders – other municipalities, key economic interests and individuals, Parliament and central government. Such excursions were impelled by urban sprawl, rising populations and mass expectations of municipal services, the inter-running of public transport, the search for water and sewage-disposal sites and municipal boundary-expansion. Much of this required negotiation, particularly with other socio-economic leaders – persons whose economic interests were affected by municipal actions, who influenced the often-deferential communities that councils desired to absorb, or dominated neighbouring councils. Mayors, as heads of their local states and paramount economic leaders in close social and even family contact with others of their kind, were ideally placed to offer leadership in all these areas. Bolton's four-year incumbent, Sir Benjamin Dobson, a major regional businessman, was architect and frantic chief negotiator of the borough's major boundary expansion in 1898/1899. He was rewarded with a magnificent statue before the town hall, though this was poor compensation for the fatal attack of pneumonia that engulfed him as negotiations neared completion. Adding to

---

20   *Rochdale Times*, 25 July 1900, p. 3.

21   Alderman Rathbone, *Liverpool Mail (LM)*, 10 November 1885, p. 4.

22   Alderman Browning, *OT*, 11 November 1865.

23   See Frank Prochaska, *Royal Bounty: The Making of a Welfare Monarchy* (Newhaven, Yale University Press 1995). See John Garrard, 'Urban Elites, 1850–1914: The Rise and Decline of an Urban Squirearchy', *Albion*, 27, 4 (Winter 1995), pp. 583–621.

the strain was the fact that mayors and town clerks were central negotiators with the parliamentary committees making the crucial decisions about Improvement Acts. Such legislation embodied many of the outcomes of the foregoing sort of haggling and was the main channel through which large nineteenth-century municipalities acquired powers within and beyond their boundaries.

The Charitable Mayor

Never more than an intermittent, if nonetheless significant, phenomenon mayoral activism steadily faded from around 1918 mostly, though not entirely, vanishing in the decades after 1945. This happened quite naturally as its facilitating conditions also faded: the overlap between socio-economic leaders and municipal elites; loose party discipline inside councils; popular focus on municipal affairs and local governmental autonomy. Mayoral activism faded too as rising party feelings and the emergence of powerful majority party leaders greatly enhanced preferences for politically neutral and thus impotent council heads. In municipalities like Liverpool's, already distinguished by sectarianism-fuelled party bitterness, powerful mayors had always been rare. Now they became largely extinct.

However, a second, highly time-consuming and more enduring, area of activity and possible influence has been central to mayoral roles since at least 1835 – active philanthropy and patronage of charitable and other voluntary organisations. Here, as elsewhere, there are clear parallels with monarchy and its rising philanthropic role[24] and with similar system-preserving motivations and (perhaps) effects. Combined with the third sociable and ceremonial function, such endeavour could render mayors influential figures with persuasive consequences, as we shall see, for both present and future.

Though still strongly continuing in our own more egalitarian world, mayoral philanthropy originated as part of a much more general field of activity by economic and social elites in nineteenth-century towns, one often rendering them akin to urban squires.[25] Mayors increasingly became super-squires, the central and most visible embodiments of such elites' legitimising values. In inward-looking urban places where economic insecurity was high and governmental aid often minimal, and in the Poor Law's case deeply shaming, this role was persuasive – impacting upon both the charitably inclined and the broader population whose needs these quasi-gentry served. Mayoral philanthropy could reach spectacular proportions, particularly, and like the monarchy, from around 1880. In 1902, Rochdale's mayor, Samuel Turner, terminated his mayoralty by purchasing the Mount Fallinge estate and presenting it to the town as a park, thereby earning himself the ambivalent tribute from a colleague: 'blessed is the man who will present us with a park and leave us to spend money only on accessories'.[26] In 1876, Liverpool's mayor William Simpson

[24]   See Frank Prochaska, *Royal Bounty: The Making of a Welfare Monarchy* (Newhaven, Yale University Press 1995).

[25]   See John Garrard, 'Urban Elites, 1850–1914: The Rise and Decline of an Urban Squirearchy', *Albion*, 27, 4 (Winter 1995), pp. 583–621.

[26]   Alderman Petrie, *RO*, 7 June 1902, p. 8.

initiated a movement to supply cauldrons of Lancashire hotpot to poor families each Christmas, each sufficient for ten people. By 1895 this was a massive operation, conducted along military lines, involving 5000 dishes, 40 butchers, 120 women, 20 stewards and multiple clergymen.[27]

Two roles were involved here. First, mayors were key initiators of collective charitable responses to local problems, crises and disasters. It was the mayor who called the obligatory public meeting to launch such appeals and his name and generous contribution that stood at the head of a persuasively expanding, and newspaper-advertised, list of elite donors. In in-turned and quite deferential towns, such movements by the great and graceful were influential upon lesser citizens seeking visibly to bask in their philanthropic afterglow.

Second, mayors were, and emphatically remain, patrons of more enduring charitable and other voluntary organisations. Given the visible arenas provided by towns and cities until around 1914, such patronage could powerfully help legitimise local civil society. Consequently, local organisations fell over themselves to secure it. As more than one weary incumbent complained, 'there seemed ... a perpetual epidemic of bazaars, sales of work, at-homes and other gatherings, all for some worthy purpose ... none it seemed could be carried through without the presence of the mayor'.[28] Witness also the determined efforts of Bolton's 8500-strong Co-op in 1881, notwithstanding constant rebuff:

> They had grown so much they had the audacity to invite the mayor ... to take the chair ... Two years ago they adopted a similar course and received a note from the then-mayor stating that the Town Clerk had advised him not to take the chair. Mr Alderman Richardson ... was invited last year but did not condescend to reply, and the appeal to the newly-elected mayor had resulted in a similar manner.[29]

So much was such anxiety for patronage habitual in Liverpool by the late-nineteenth century that Lord Mayors set aside special post-election mornings for receiving and accepting civil-associational invitations. In 1905, anxious but gratified petitioners included the Hebrew Philanthropic Society, the Masons, Wesleyan Central Mission, various hospitals and the Hospital Saturday Fund.[30]

Since 1918, still more since 1945, towns and cities have become far less in-turned; their social structure is more fractured, complex and, with the increase in overseas immigration, more potentially alienated. The local arenas that urban places once provided have disappeared. The integrative impact of mayoral actions is thus probably far less powerful than in the past. Nevertheless, anxiety for mayoral patronage remains strong. Indeed, it has unwittingly provided the one influence-seeking item left in mayoral inaugural speeches today: mayors announce charitable projects or good causes they hope to advance during their incumbency. Some have even tried turning their efforts into conscious integrative policy. Bury's retiring

---

27   *LM*, 25 December 1895, p. 6.
28   Councillor S. Turner, *RO*, 13 November 1901, p. 2.
29   President, *BC*, 26 February 1881, p. 7.
30   *Liverpool Chronicle*, 11 November 1905, p. 3.

mayor in 2005 sought to give such activity a 'corporate image',[31] while Liverpool's new incumbent in 1951 (even then, and significantly, still a major local philanthropist and businessman) included within his responsibilities 'defend[ing] the rights and privileges' of "minorities however small"'.[32] Similar motivations on both sides led Oxford's mayor in 2003 to accept the Bangladesh Society's invitation to join them for 'a mild chicken korma' at the Aziz Restaurant, while also watching 'my waistline'.[33] Few of the general public may now be watching, yet mayoral patronage remains highly important to groups and organisations themselves.

The Sociable and Ceremonial Mayor

All this shades into the third area of functional mayoral activity, or pair of activities – the sociable and ceremonial. They are paired because, although partially separate and important in their own right, they contributed significantly to powerful inclusive and integrative forces that urban local authorities proved themselves capable of wielding in response to democratisation, indeed as part of that process. This is so even though this area quite often engendered conflict and embitterment in those seeking inclusion.

Mayors were fervent entertainers long before 1835. This was perhaps why Haverfordwest's corporation customarily elected 'him who had been oftenest drunk throughout the year'.[34] After 1835, every mayor was expected to be 'like a bishop, given to hospitality'.[35] This was one reason many municipalities equipped their heads with quite substantial 'salaries' and why, without such allowances, some less wealthy politicians refused the honour – as hilariously and all-too-publicly did the old Rochdale radical Edward Taylor, who, having been forcibly enrobed, enchained and virtually nailed to the mayoral chair by his determined colleagues in 1891, repaired home, ate lunch and resigned.[36]

Mayoral hospitality came in two sorts. First, mayors entertained their council colleagues, more infrequently their paid officers. After mayor-making, councillors were normally invited to lunch or an evening banquet. They were also regularly entertained over the year, rather bibulously if they were lucky: even in puritanical Rochdale, 'people could see two lamps when they went into the mayor's house and four when they came out'[37] (the Council possessed two mayoral pillars surmounted by lamps which it rather eccentrically moved for each new incumbent). In Salford, retiring mayor H.D. Pochin presented his colleagues with 'a loving cup … for your use … and that of all future mayors. I think it … very agreeable … when we drink out of the same cup and express thereby kindly feelings towards one another'.[38]

---

[31]   Councillor Barry Briggs, interview 14 June 2005.
[32]   *Liverpool Daily Post* (*LDP*), 12 November 1951, p. 1.
[33]   *OT*, 16 May 2003, p. 3.
[34]   Webb, op. cit., p. 235.
[35]   Alderman W.W. Cannon, *BC*, 13 November 1869, p. 7.
[36]   *RO*, 11 November 1891, pp. 2–3.
[37]   Councillor Sharp, *RO*, 7 December 1901, p. 6.
[38]   *SWN*, 4 November 1868, Supplement.

Pochin imbibed just once, before departing for Westminster, but his presumably grateful colleagues continued the amatory and insanitary tradition for some years. Like other things connected with mayoralty, such activities were, and remain, highly functional for the internal dynamics of small groups of often intensely divided people (councils) needing at least minimally to co-operate. Mayoral conviviality could also help incorporate otherwise alienated groups. In Liverpool in 1895, Irish Nationalist councillors greeted Lord Derby's mayoralty with hostility, but after a year even they enthused in face of what the Liberals termed his 'noble hospitality ... which commended itself to every section of the community'.[39]

Second, as this quotation implies – and here we see close parallels in both motivation and effect with what monarchy was doing – mayors entertained people within their broader communities. These included not just other socio-economic leaders (important in worlds where their co-operation and consent might well be required) but also, and increasingly, as democratisation proceeded and the late-Victorian 'gilded age' got underway, ever-widening arrays of groups and organisations. From around 1880 and in urban squirearchy's best traditions, mayoral 'at homes', tea parties, 'conversationes' and musical evenings became not only more sumptuous but also more inclusive. Groups of many lowly sorts began gaining access – tradesmen, veterans, Sunday schoolteachers, 'old folk', even 'the poor' or more frequently the least morally suspect of them, 'poor children' (in recent times this list has been extended to include women's, and multiple ethnic, groups). Thus it was that William Stephens, Salford's incumbent from 1903–1905, became known as 'the People's Mayor'[40] and Richard Mottram, an agreeably wealthy Salford brewer and mayor in the mid-1890s, embarked upon an entertainment offensive, embracing amongst others 800 'poor children', 400 'old people' and 250 Crimean war veterans. Yet Joseph Snape eclipsed both: his 1909 festivities were sufficiently spectacular to attract full-page coverage in the local press, with careful lists of all the individuals and groups invited and a headline worthy of a sedate Roman orgy: 'Three Nights of Continuous Pleasure'.[41] In Liverpool, David Radcliffe became another 'People's Mayor' between 1886 and 1888, at one point entertaining in the Town Hall some 5000 workingmen, thereby 'gratifying a section of the community not previously the recipients of such attention'.[42]

Such activity was beguiling, even for political outsiders. As noted, Liverpool's Irish Nationalists found it so. Socialists too, and this is important for what we shall say about their later attitudes towards mayoral *selection*, could be equally charmed. Witness Rochdale ILP's reactions to John Turner's magnificently hospitable and charitable mayoralty 1895–1897. Although viewing monarchy 'as a relic of barbarism ... synonymous with favouritism, robbery and extravagance',[43] mayors, leastways this mayor, were different. Welcoming, Turner's second term in 1896, *The Rochdale Labour News* commented, 'We neither admire his economic principles

---

[39]   Councillor Lynsky, *LM*, 11 November 1895 p. 5 and 27 October 1896 p. 6.

[40]   *Salford Reporter* (*SR*), 22 November 1902, p. 5.

[41]   *SR*, 11 December 1909, p. 8.

[42]   Quoted P.J. Waller, *Democracy and Sectarianism: A Political and Social History of Liverpool 1868–1939* (Liverpool University Press 1981), p. 90.

[43]   *Rochdale Labour News* (*RLN*), June 1897, p. 2.

nor (his) political party ... but we do admire a man with a big heart'.[44] Faced with his generous donation to the infirmary six months later, the paper dropped even customary reservations about capitalistic origins: 'We like you for this Mr Turner and hope others will follow.'[45] If philanthropy was seductive, even more so was hospitality, particularly when conferring status upon lowly groups:

> The mayor did a handsome thing by inviting the day School teachers ... to a reception and ball at the Town hall ... The weary humdrum life of a teacher makes an event of this kind particularly acceptable. The teachers turned up in full force and the affair was ... brilliant and refined.[46]

The *News* was still recalling this community-incorporating honour six months later:

> The teachers ... will doubtless remember his thoughtfulness ... for many years ... This may be said by many others ... privileged to enjoy his hospitality ... The Town Council need not expect to be presided over by anyone ... command[ing] more respect and admiration.[47]

These 'others' included at least one other humble group, as the paper admiringly discovered in April 1897: 'the mayor ... has eclipsed all other mayors by entertaining all the corporation employees to a number of 800. More power to him!'[48] Nor did a musical soiree escape socialist notice: 'a brilliant affair. Everybody who was anybody was there.'[49] Finally, contemplating Turner's possible knighthood, the paper became entirely mesmerised:

> It would be a pity if the town missed the opportunity of having at least one radical aristocrat. We, as socialists, are not in love with empty titles, but if there is anything to be gained by being in the fashion – let's have the fashion.[50]

If mayoral entertainment could entice, so equally (as we shall see) could its ceremonies and rituals. Most important were those annually connected with mayor-making – the fulsome nominating, supporting and acceptance speeches in council; the votes of thanks to retiring mayors; then, frequently, the mayoral lunches or banquets attended by all council members, local and even sometimes national dignitaries; sometimes a Lord Mayor's Show; and then, always until recently, processions to church, attended by all council members, salaried officers, municipal fire and police services, 'gentlemen of the town' taking the opportunity to put themselves on display, plus somewhat random assortments of voluntary society representatives. Alongside these were other occasions where mayors were central – town-hall openings, civic jubilees, ceremonial greetings for visiting monarchs and other national figures. It is important

---

[44] *RLN*, December 1896, p. 1.
[45] *RLN*, May 1897, p. 2.
[46] *RLN*, April 1897, p. 2.
[47] *RLN*, October 1897, p. 2.
[48] *RLN*, April 1897, p. 2.
[49] *RLN*, November 1897, p. 2.
[50] *RLN*, April 1897, p. 2.

for what we will say about the significance of these occasions that, until around 1914, and even later in many places, they were the focus of fairly intense public interest, attracting crowded public galleries to listen and large crowds to watch. They were part of an often otherwise grey urban world wherein ceremony and ritual of all kinds, non-mayoral as well as mayoral, occupied a central and absorbing place. It is also important that mayoral ceremony at least has now mostly lost its hold upon the public imagination.

These ceremonies had several functions, mostly intentional with the activity intended as persuasive. Central both to these functions, and the acute conflicts they periodically engendered, was the fact that mayoralty was seen as a localised version of monarchy ('the chosen of the people to preside over them, ... their king for the time being, [with] no one in front of him save the sovereign himself'),[51] but a version open to all. This was reinforced by widespread urban attachments to Smilesean self-help and myths about rags-to-riches elevation.

First, and particularly in the in-turned and middle-class-dominated municipal circumstances before 1914, mayoral ceremonies were platforms from which urban values, as interpreted by their socio-economic elites, could be persuasively proclaimed. Most important was the idea that economic, social and political elevation was open to anyone exercising appropriate self-helping and industrious virtue. Urban middle-class leaders often constituted a sort of squirearchy, with their mayor resembling a monarch, but these urban squires were supposedly products of individual achievement rather than birth. Mayor-making was particularly redolent with these notions. Whenever possible, even in market or seaside towns like Banbury or Margate where one might assume the self-helping ethic to be less vibrant than in the industrial North, even the most wealthy nominee was proclaimed to have raised himself from nothing, or at least not too much.

Furthermore, this monarch, because 'elected', was first amongst equals. In 1858, the *Rochdale Observer* said the mayoralty was 'prized as a mark of confidence, all the more valuable as coming from the social equals of him to whom it is accorded'.[52] Thus, alongside obligatory declarations from mayor-elects about their lack of ambition and the overwhelming character of the pressures to stand (obligatory precisely because mayoralty was the focus of so much ambition and its conferment the visible mark of such esteem), mayor-elects invariably proclaimed their unworthiness for office and the superior virtues of 'the many gentlemen who would have filled this office better than I ...'.[53] Even Lord Derby, magnificently hoisted into Liverpool's mayoral chair in hope of unifying the newly expanded city in 1895, managed to pronounce himself 'unworthy of office'.[54] If high-born aristocrats felt obliged to say such things, modesty was doubly incumbent upon supposedly self-made urban squires, particularly from mayors needing co-operation from council colleagues in the coming year – so much so that extravagant colleague-praising became part of the ritual:

[51] Alderman Bucknell, *OT*, 13 November 1915, p. 4.
[52] Editorial, *RO*, 13 November 1858, p. 2.
[53] Councillor J. Moore, *RO*, 10 November 1860, p. 3.
[54] *LM*, 11 November 1895, p. 5.

> If I was endowed with the combination of gifts which some of the men who surround this board possess – if for instance I had the dignity of my friend opposite ... the business ability of his neighbour ... and the geniality of the gentleman on my right ... I might think myself fit to fill the office.[55]

As this begins to imply, mayoral ceremonies were also secondly intended to celebrate and reinforce civic unity and pride: both amongst council elites – purveying the notion that councillors, though divided by party, were united by concern for the town's welfare – and thereby amongst the broader community. Thus, 'public life was sweetened on such occasions ... Throughout the length and breadth of the land ... party strife gave way to friendly feeling ... their minds were centred not on their party but on their town'.[56] This was why, wherever possible, mayoral elections were and are unanimous, extravagantly endorsed by all parties and factions; also why mayoral incumbency was often rotated amongst them; and why unanimous nominations were often suffused by frenzies of mutual thanking. Even in Liverpool, tumultuously divided as it was by party, religion and ethnicity, mayoral nominations were by 1900, political relations permitting, explicitly supported by Conservatives, Liberals, Home Rulers, Protestants and later by Labour. Here, and elsewhere, even when conflict prevented unanimity, those opposing normally explained extensively that they had nothing personal against the majority's nominee, rather vast admiration. Similarly persuasive intentions caused even contending councillors to join their 'brethren' at mayoral lunches, and at subsequent and more public church processions.

Public displays of 'kindly feeling' between councillors were of course highly ritualistic, even spurious. Nevertheless, like mayoral entertainments and similar ceremonies surrounding parliamentary Speakers, they were, and are, important for group dynamics amongst councillors who, whilst often bitterly divided by party, faction and personality, still must coexist. 'Public life' really does need 'sweetening' if they are to co-operate even minimally. Furthermore, the symbolic presentation of ultimate civic unity was also probably persuasive for groups within wider urban communities whose conflicts local politicians portrayed and represented, even if such ritual has become too invisible to have much impact now. To a substantial but declining extent, mayoral ceremony probably enhanced the ability of large, often fractious and geographically defined collections of people to imagine themselves as communities, probably with real implications for how they perceived their local governments.

Desires to promote wider communal unity and civic consciousness also led some mayors to process to one (for example Nonconformist) church in the morning and then visit another (Anglican) establishment in the evening; and induced rather more to spread their worship ecumenically during the year and invite clergymen from all denominations to mayoral ceremonies. Similar motivations have led recently expanded boroughs to draw mayoral incumbents from the new 'out-districts', rotate mayoralty amongst all the districts or, as with Liverpool and Lord Derby in 1895, to recruit some magnificent and neighbouring outsider. Desires for civic-consciousness-raising also

---

[55]   Councillor J.S. Littlewood, *RO*, 13 November 1875, p. 6.
[56]   Alderman Stephens, *SR*, 15 November 1902, p. 5.

produced mayor-making speeches linking current incumbents with sometimes long-past predecessors, and – as in Liverpool's case – mayoral processions of increasing splendour and using an ancient and magnificent mayoral coach.

The unifying effects of mayoral ceremony were greatly reinforced by the fact that, like mayoral sociability, it also provided very public ways of marking the boundaries of the respectable community, dignifying the salient forces within (and sometimes beyond) it, defining relationships between them and registering the social and political arrival of new groups. Oxford's mayor-making celebrations were very grand indeed, with the banquet (and often the church procession) sumptuously and very publicly embracing many persons: mayors from surrounding towns; prominent local landowners; MPs from town and county; sometimes national politicians pronouncing upon government policy;[57] prominent local businessmen; multiple clergymen; and normally and perhaps above all the university's Vice-Chancellor and chief officers. Moreover, as we have noted in passing, at times of conflict between town and gown, banqueting speeches became points where negotiating positions were publicly laid down – for example, over the sharing of costs of the Poor Law during the 1850s and in 1865 how the running and costs of the local police were to be shared. During the latter feasting, Oxford's Vice-Chancellor:

> made two propositions to the city: either (the university) would pay a greater proportion of the rating, in which case they must have a larger part of the representation ... or their respective properties should be assessed, and the representation should follow according to their value.

The retiring mayor, upon being thanked for his services, announced himself:

> one of those who could not consent to (earlier proposals) ... but if the University was now prepared to pay according to their assessment and to receive only a share of the representation according to that assessment ... there was no difference of opinion ... between (them).[58]

In Canterbury, meanwhile, mayoral ceremonies invariably embraced not just social and political elites, military personnel, local businessmen and landowners, but also the Archbishop or his representative, sundry other figures from the local Anglican establishment and clergy from other denominations. Such churchmen also found themselves toasted because 'they identify themselves with the public life of the city, (and) their association and co-operation are of the greatest advantage ... to their fellow citizens'.[59] From 1965, these were joined by Kent University's Vice-Chancellor, and mayoral banquets became points where the partnership between council, cathedral and university was proclaimed and celebrated. In Liverpool, major trading port as it was, mayoral election and retirement ceremonies invariably accorded very prominent places for the Consul-Generals from the many countries diplomatically represented in the city. In 1905, matters became unusually magnificent when the French Consul, on behalf of his President, explicitly reinforced the *Entente Cordiale* by bestowing the *Legion d'Honneur* upon the Lord Mayor. This gesture

---

[57] See for example, *Jackson's Oxford Journal*, 1 December 1855, p. 5 during the Crimean War.
[58] *OT*, 4 November 1865, p. 6. The University elected some councillors.
[59] High Sheriff, *KG*, 16 November 1935, p. 4.

also represented thanks for mayoral entertainment some months previously of a visiting French battleship's entire company, who had, improbably, 'fallen in love with the mayor and his wife'.[60]

However, mayoral ceremony could also register the arrival and status of *new* social groups within the politically salient community. Women householders possessed the municipal vote from 1869, voting on the same basis as men from 1928. Lady mayoresses had long supported their husbands in philanthropic and other activity, but it is significant that from the 1890s, still more from 1918, they began receiving separate and increasingly fulsome tributes in thanks given to retiring mayors and the welcoming of new ones. They also featured in mayoral newspaper photographs. By the 1920s in Liverpool, seats at mayor-making ceremonies were set aside not just for new mayoresses but also for increasingly numerous predecessors, prompting fulsome newspaper descriptions of their 'delightful costumes' (like politicians, newspapers had an eye on their female punters). By the 1960s, the city had manufactured a special chain and, alongside mayor-making, there was a parallel mayoress-making ceremony; Canterbury was acting similarly by 1975. Some mayors began paying tribute to their mothers, while Warrington's first citizen in 1937 discovered no fewer than three crucial women in his life: 'first his mother whose good life under adverse conditions still made him wonder, second the lady who introduced ... him to the church, and third his wife who had put up with him for 30 years'.[61]

From just before the First World War, some mayors actually were women. Mrs Sarah Lees for example became the very active mayor of Oldham in 1910. Widow of a local brewing magnate, and a massively philanthropic urban squire in her own right, she had fought and won the council elections at the head of a Liberal majority on a platform of civic improvement.[62] As women ascended the mayoral throne, mayoral ceremony became an important place where men and women alike could publicly explore, assure themselves about, and come to terms with, the implication of women in public life. Oxford elected its first woman in 1933, and 'the success ... attend(ing) Miss Tawney's year of office led them to believe ... the mere men on the council ... need not be afraid to repeat their action ... he [the speaker] had (therefore) risen to nominate a wife and a mother'.[63] In 1955, Councillor Mrs Johnson, thanking Banbury's retiring female mayor, observed comfortingly that 'her home duties had been done although she (was) the representative of the town'.[64] In 1965, Banbury's vicar 'thanked God that they had been given a woman' as mayor and noted a similarly female monarch in London: 'They come to give us rule, sweet ordering and decision. They are both married women and would not pretend to usurp the qualities which men can give to the world'.[65] Over in Oxford, with women as both mayor and sheriff, things had moved on a bit, if not too much. The mayor's

---

[60]   *LM*, 14 November 1905, p. 4.

[61]   Alderman Harry Sinclair, *Liverpool Echo* (*LE*), 9 November 1937, p. 4.

[62]   Pat Hollis, *Ladies Elect: Women in English Local Government 1865–1914* (Oxford University Press 1997).

[63]   Alderman Bennett, *OT*, 15 November 1935, p. 14.

[64]   *BA*, 25 May 1955, p. 12.

[65]   Reverend Eastman, *BA*, 2 June 1965, p. 1.

Labour nominator noted: 'Often direct and blunt in manner, she was nevertheless a woman whose shrewdness and sagacity revealed ... real wisdom'. Amid nervous and just possibly excited male laughter, the new incumbent said she was aware of being 'regarded as a bit of a dragon', adding 'I hope a rather friendly dragon'. Meanwhile the new sheriff 'thought of herself as militant and feminine rather than a militant feminist' and disagreed 'with those who have said to me in private that the city is in for ... matriarchal Stalinism'.[66]

Religious and ethnic minorities also began finding their way inside the mayoral pale. Liverpool elected its first Catholic (indeed Irish nationalist) in 1943; other Merseyside towns had done so considerably earlier. In 2005, both Blackburn and Manchester have elected their first Asian and Muslim mayors, the latter interestingly seeing himself as a role model for alienated Muslim youth.[67]

However, the most spectacular reactions to mayoral incumbency were evident amongst the ranks of labour. When Rochdale's Liberal elite elevated Lib-Lab Councillor Charles Redfern, secretary of the town's Operative Spinners, into first citizenship in 1913, his ecstatic followers presented him with a gold watch and silver tea-service at a specially organised tea and dance attended by some 2500 spinners and their wives. A. Holland, President of the Rochdale spinners, said this was 'probably the first time ... so many spinners had gathered together in one room'. They also heard W. Marsland, general secretary of the Spinners Amalgamation, declare this event even more significant than the foundation of the Co-operative movement in 1844, and 'one of the most progressive steps that this or any other town ... had ever taken ... a great honour to the working man'.[68] Even in 1946, the Railway Workers Federation were still sufficiently delighted at one of their members becoming Wrexham's mayor to add two pendants to the mayoral chain, thereby metaphorically incorporating themselves.[69]

If mayoral succession could produce celebration from organised workers, rejections of mayoral aspiration induced incandescent outrage, at least amongst their political leadership. Here we begin seeing how an office, so often a point of unity and unification, could also produce intense conflict. The reason for this paradox lies in another already mentioned: mayors might stand at the top of urban hierarchies, even be 'little kings', but their position was also the focus of intense ambition and theoretically open to all. Mayoral elections, though normally harmonious occasions, had long been capable of producing conflict, particularly where perceived rules of fairness were broken by majority parties deciding to monopolise the office and deny civic respectability to their opponents. When mere party division was involved, conflict could normally be ritually assuaged. However, when other sorts of division, like nationality or class, were added, this became far more difficult. Yet it is also important that rejection never led those excluded to reject either the office or the local political system it headed up. Rather, exclusion made outsiders' hearts grow fonder.

---

[66]   Messrs Ireland, Lower and Gibbs, *OT*, 28 May 1965, p. 4.

[67]   I am indebted to Melanie Tebbutt for this reported conversation.

[68]   *Rochdale Times*, 7 January 1914, p. 4.

[69]   *LDP*, 11 November 1946, p. 3.

We begin witnessing this interactive mix of bitterness and incorporation in the case of Liverpool's Irish Nationalist councillors. Their interest in mainland political baubles might be expected to be somewhat peripheral. Yet, in 1917, with the residential stability of their mass-following already creating growing interest in council policies,[70] their leader protested vigorously, as he had many times, before that 'he and his party had very strong feelings on the subject … Why were … the Irish Nationalist Party boycotted from their just rights and privileges?'.[71] In 1919, growing problems in Ireland notwithstanding, the point became yet more fervent: 'his party represented nearly a third of the population of the city, and its members were living up to as high ideals of citizenship as many others … yet they were made to appear as Ishmaels and pariahs.'[72]

If mayoral rejection could annoy Irishmen, so much greater were the effects of denying working-class Englishmen this ultimate mark of respectability. Throughout much of the interwar industrial northwest, anti-socialist majorities routinely excluded Labour from the Mayoralty. The result was incandescent preoccupation. For a start, expressions of indignation absorbed much Labour time and energy, far more than any single policy issue in towns rife with unemployment and poverty. In Ashton-under-Lyne, one of many mayoral exclusions in 1934 produced an angry two-hour debate. Similar behaviour in Salford produced two-and-a-half hours of furious contention in 1924, and an impassioned seven hours in 1928.

The content of Labour's anger was equally revealing. In 1924, contemplating yet another rejection of Labour's claims, Jim Openshaw, secretary of Salford City Labour Party, demanded: 'Are we again to see the flouting of the claims of the Labour movement to recognition? The party was well established … and means to fight for its prestige in the public life of the borough.'[73] Over in Stockport in 1930, Councillor Flowers could 'not conceive any party … with the least spark of decency or honour taking action of this character',[74] while in 1936, Councillor Baldwin complained:

> Stockport was the only town of its size and importance in which the Labour Party had not had the honour of having one of its own members (as) mayor … he was not speaking on behalf of the Labour group or a clique but on behalf of 14 of 15 thousand people … It was not playing cricket.[75]

Elsewhere in Lancashire, Councillor Davies got another insult to Labour's claims nicely into perspective in 1933 by calling it 'Ashton Hitlerism',[76] and must have taken comfort when a Conservative mayor had to retire after catching psittacosis off his parrot. In Liverpool in 1925, similar exclusiveness allegedly constituted 'a deliberate insult to the rest of the council, and a slight on the 48,000 people who

[70]   P.J. Waller, *Democracy and Sectarianism; A Political and Social History of Liverpool 1868–1939* (Liverpool University Press 1981).
[71]   Alderman Harford, *LE*, 9 November 1917, p. 3.
[72]   Alderman Harford, *LE*, 11 November 1919, p. 5.
[73]   *SR*, 2 August 1924, p. 6.
[74]   *Stockport Advertizer (SA)*, 15 November 1930, p. 5.
[75]   *SA*, 30 October 1936, p. 6.
[76]   *Ashton Reporter*, 11 November 1933, p. 8.

had voted Labour ...'.[77] This emphasis upon 'insult' and insistence upon 'the rules of the game' were constant Labour themes, apparently as persuasive to the left as to the right. In a rare moment of council unity in Stockport in 1932, only one member opposed mayoral selection from amongst the Council's Independents, Councillor Ponsonby of the ILP. He did so 'not for personal reasons but because he objected to (selecting) the mayor from any class outside the working class. The borough had been incorporated for nearly a century, but there had never been a representative of the workers in the mayor's chair'. [78]

Mayoralty's integrative effects upon Labour are also evident once it began achieving this much-desired goal. In Manchester, as elsewhere, there was delight at 'this red letter day for the workers', and certainty that:

One of the best ways of impressing our views is by convincing people that out of the ranks of the Labour movement, in spite of their lack of education, we (can) produce people who can fill the highest offices in the state as well as every other section of the community.[79]

Over three decades later in Salford, by which time Labour had monopolised the office for five years, elation remained if anything more intense: 'I decided to consecrate my life ... to the uplifting of a particular class ... If claiming the mayoralty can help them, we (will) have it now and in the future.'[80] If in 1921 Labour politicians had apparent reservations about mayoralty's 'social side' – 'the majority of our people are not very concerned about the so-called honours and dignities'[81] – by 1951, these had been replaced by embittered emulation:

It is high time ... some of our people got a look-in at functions which have been a sort of 'upper-ten' preserve in the past, and that Labour women had the chance to show ... they too can organise successful charity dances, whist drives and socials.[82]

By this time, Labour was often itself excluding other parties from both mayoral and aldermanic office. This was partly about power, even policy, but equally expressed the vengeful embitterment of inter-party council relations in the wake of earlier 'insults'. Memories were long: 'We are only carrying out the opposition's methods when I came into the council in 1935 ... they took more than their fair share then.'[83]

The mayoralty has thus had considerable importance for urban political and social life until the fairly recent past: as a periodic centre of municipal leadership; a highly visible and probably legitimising advertisement for the paternalist image of local elites; and a powerful civic symbol whose rituals and entertainments have registered the changing boundaries of respectable political life and marked the arrival and status of new constituent groups. Even as, like councils themselves, mayoralty began fading from view after 1918, its capture had great significance for local

---

[77] Alderman Robinson, *LDP*, 10 November 1925, p. 5.

[78] *SA*, 11 November 1932, p. 6.

[79] Councillor Joe Toole, *Manchester City News*, 15 November 1919, p. 6.

[80] Councillor Headon, *SR*, 6 April 1961.

[81] Jim Openshaw, 'Labour Notes', *SR*, 27 July 1921, p. 4.

[82] Unnamed Labour source, 'a moderate', *SR*, 15 June 1951, p. 1.

[83] Councillor Davies, *SR*, 6 April 1961, p. 4.

Labour politicians – many probably with youthful memories its golden age. In these respects, along with other institutions like Monarchy and Parliament, mayoralty and its ceremonies probably had significant integrative influence. This may also be true for other politically arriving groups – though women started becoming mayors after the decline of the first wave of feminism and before the emergence of the second. In recent decades, particularly with the arrival of syndicated local free-sheets, mayoral Cheshire-cat smiles are almost the only publicly visible parts of most municipalities. Indeed, with wealthy incumbents and visibility mostly gone, mayoralty lives on the edge of ridicule, as one incumbent discovered when he used the mayoral limousine to collect his dole money.[84] Yet voluntary groups still frenetically seek its patronage. Since they still think mayoralty highly important, it still is.

---

[84]   *LE*, 17 May 1979, p. 3.

CHAPTER TWO

The Scottish Provost Since 1800: Tradition, Continuity and Change in the Leadership of 'Local Self-Government'

Irene Maver

Introduction

Provosts are the Scottish equivalent of mayors, the title and office deriving from the feudal function of *prepositus*, which originated before the Reformation.[1] The provostship was inextricably bound up with the leadership of Scotland's burghs; units of civic administration that were swept away with the radical reorganisation of local government in 1975. Originating during the twelfth century, burghs evolved as mechanisms for maintaining order and encouraging urban commercial activities in the Scottish Kingdom. Provosts primarily acted as chief magistrates and presided over council meetings. In this capacity formal powers were limited and remained so even as provosts became highly visible figureheads for the civic community in the post-Reformation period.

As this chapter explains, the provostship survived the twentieth-century demise of the burghs, withstanding pressure from modernisers who regarded the office as anachronistic. However, numbers of provosts have declined since 1975. Of the 32 elected Scottish unitary authorities at the time of writing (2006), 23 have provosts, with the remaining nine opting for the more neutral office of 'convener'.[2] This compares starkly with the period immediately before municipal reform in the 1830s, when there were 66 royal burghs (those given charters from the crown) and around 100 functioning burghs of barony (those originating under baronial or landowner jurisdiction).[3] Despite amalgamations from the late-nineteenth century, on the eve of reorganisation in 1975 there were 197 burgh councils, plus the four cities of Aberdeen, Dundee, Edinburgh and Glasgow, all with their provost or lord provost.[4]

---

[1]   William Mackay Mackenzie, *The Scottish Burghs* (Oliver and Boyd, Edinburgh, 1949), p. 100; James D. Marwick, 'The municipal institutions of Scotland: a historical survey, part I', *Scottish Historical Review*, 1 (1904), pp. 127–8.

[2]   Jackie Barker (ed.), *Municipal Year Book: Public Services Directory, 2005, Vol. II* (Hemming Information Systems, London, 2005), pp. 1401–1503.

[3]   George S. Pryde, 'The Scottish burgh of barony in decline, 1707–1908', *Proceedings of the Royal Philosophical Society of Glasgow*, 73 (1948/9), pp. 44, 55–6.

[4]   British Parliamentary Papers, Cmnd 4150, *Royal Commission on Local Government in Scotland, 1966–1969: Report* [Wheatley Commission] (HMSO, Edinburgh, 1969), p. 26.

The analysis that follows considers why the provostship grew from 1800 and then contracted, despite continuing community attachment to the office. Three chronological phases are covered, commencing with Scotland's pre-1830s municipal *ancien régime*. Although there were limits to the provost's formal function, the office at that time was more than ceremonial. Incumbents often wielded power under the tight patronage system prevailing in royal burghs, especially the municipal monopoly of parliamentary elections. In consequence, provosts came to be identified with oligarchy and political ossification. This negative image was often journalistic exaggeration, but provosts were among the most readily recognisable local figureheads and thus easy targets for reformers seeking to expose the exclusive nature of burgh government. The provostship's ceremonial aspects compounded this distinctiveness and prompted ambiguous responses from critics of the unreformed system. For some ceremony represented the ostentatious display of elitism, for others it reinforced confidence in municipal institutions, but only if civic leaders respected the burgh tradition of protecting communities and nurturing the common good.

The chapter then considers the Victorian and Edwardian provostship, when burgh councils were created across Scotland to administer populous communities. Municipal reform in the 1830s radically altered public perceptions of the provost. Liberalism replaced Toryism as the prevailing political orthodoxy in the burghs and provosts were elevated into role models for such motivational qualities as enterprise, philanthropy and commitment to public service. 'Local self-government' became a virtue, with strong moral overtones, in a bid to engender urban cohesion. This related to new as well longstanding communities, which sought to create their own identities through the visible symbols of burgh government, including the provostship. In this context, tradition was often invented to reinforce municipal values on the public consciousness. There was also intense competition among towns and cities in their quest for civic legitimacy, with the provost articulating local aspirations, especially through ambitious improvement projects.

The chapter finally explores the provost's fluctuating fortunes during the twentieth century. Wider municipal democracy allowed for the emergence of women and socialist provosts, showing how the office could reflect social change while at the same time remaining a reassuring expression of urban continuity. However, during the inter-war period the virtue of local self-government was increasingly challenged by central government interventionism and the rising power of the Scottish Office. The burghs attempted, with a degree of success, to stand their ground collectively against moves towards local government consolidation. They retained authority as the voice of the local state up to the 1960s, but arguments about the integrity of the burgh system became difficult to sustain in an era of unprecedented Scottish Office strategic planning for national regeneration. In the 1975 reorganisation, burghs and their provosts were to some extent victims of state managerialism and trends towards large-scale local administration. Yet the provostship was not consigned to history. Instead, the office's historical identity was a feature of its continuing resilience, despite provosts' diminished role and detachment from their traditional burgh power-base.

The Pre-Reform Provostship

Until 1832 the royal burghs monopolised parliamentary power in urban Scotland, with the result that provosts had strong political roles under the pre-reform regime. Indeed, before the Scottish and English Parliaments were unified in 1707, each royal burgh was entitled to send commissioners to Parliament House in Edinburgh and these were usually provosts or ex-provosts. Provosts also served on the Convention of the Royal Burghs of Scotland, an organisation evolving from medieval roots as a forum for commissioners to discuss and determine matters of common concern, including trade, finance and civic administration.[5] One commentator has described the Convention as '[rivalling] the churches' general assemblies as a national body', signifying the continuing influence of the 'burgess estate' on Scottish political life during the post-Union period.[6] Unsurprisingly, the Convention had been vocally anti-Union, partly in protest against the decrease in parliamentary commissioners from 67 in Edinburgh to only 15 MPs in London.[7] Yet there was already scant democracy in the political process. Leadership in the burghs of barony usually depended on landowner patronage, while in the royal burghs a complex system of municipal self-election prevailed to maintain the protectionist ethos of the craft and merchant elites.

In the long term, political Union blurred the provost's role as the direct link between Scottish local and central government. The self-perpetuating burgess oligarchies retained sole rights to vote for urban MPs, but new circumstances limited the scope for distinctively local interests to dictate the choice of candidates. Only Edinburgh, as Scotland's capital, returned an MP in its own right and Lord Provost Sir Patrick Johnston was duly despatched to Westminster in 1707.[8] The remaining royal burghs were aggregated into groups; for example, Aberdeen formed a constituency with the smaller burghs of Arbroath, Brechin, Inverbervie and Montrose. The total electorate was 85 councillors and Aberdonians were outnumbered and often outmanoeuvred by the collective strength of the opposition.[9] The erosion of the royal burghs' political identity created a vacuum, which encouraged wealthy patrons to take the initiative in directing Scotland's parliamentary affairs. By 1800 MPs were invariably pro-government loyalists, whose position was secured by town-council votes in return for favours and influence at Westminster. Here provosts often acted as local political managers, conduits for delivering electoral support to individual patrons. For instance, Edinburgh's parliamentary representation fell into the hands of the powerful Dundas family, who came to epitomise 'Scotch Toryism' and were

[5]   Theodora Pagan, *The Convention of the Royal Burghs of Scotland* (Convention of Royal Burghs, Glasgow, 1926), pp. 18–22.

[6]   Lindsay Paterson, *The Autonomy of Modern Scotland* (Edinburgh University Press, 1994), p. 55.

[7]   Karin Bowie, 'Public opinion, popular politics and the Union of 1707', *Scottish Historical Review*, 82 (2003), p. 244.

[8]   Sir Thomas B. Whitson [and Marguerite Wood], *The Lord Provosts of Edinburgh, 1296–1932* (T. & A. Constable, Edinburgh, 1932), pp. 57–8.

[9]   David Findlay and Alexander Murdoch, 'Revolution to reform: eighteenth-century politics, *c.* 1690–1800', in E. Patricia Dennison, David Ditchburn and Michael Lynch (eds), *Aberdeen before 1800: A New History* (Tuckwell, East Linton, 2000), pp. 276–7.

implacable opponents of burgh reform.[10] According to their critics, Edinburgh's lord provosts had been transformed into puppets; indeed, the Whig campaigner, Henry Cockburn, identified the town clerks as the real municipal driving-force by 1800.[11]

Whigs were cynical about the apparent deference of Scotland's civic leaders, but one historian has seen this as merely pragmatic, arguing that they were 'practical men, open to influence, yet not devoid of objectives'.[12] There was certainly an enlightened as well as a dark side to Scottish provosts during the pre-reform period. Ironically, one of the most celebrated was Edinburgh's George Drummond, whose enduring claim to fame was instigating Edinburgh's New Town in 1752; a monumental venture, underpinned by generous municipal funding.[13] On the dark side, Alexander Riddoch of Dundee was a striking example of how longevity in office did not necessarily bring public esteem or commitment to the common good. His municipal career lasted for over 40 years from 1776, with his regime as provost characterised by cavalier burgh accounting and conspicuous lack of vision in the city's structural embellishment.[14] Riddoch's shortcomings were eventually exposed by Dundee's exasperated burgesses, although he suffered no penalty other than notoriety for his prolonged manipulation of council representation and finances.[15]

The dominance of men like Riddoch came to be identified as a glaring symptom of Scotland's municipal decadence and debate over burgh reform intensified from 1815. The controversy went beyond the royal burghs, as large burghs of barony, like Falkirk, Greenock and Paisley, had inconsistent local governance and no direct parliamentary representation. The Renfrewshire textile town of Paisley exemplified the aspirations of Scotland's rising industrial communities, striving to have their political rights recognised. Paisley had an independent council by the 1800s, whose members were determined to emulate the civic opulence of royal burghs and show that they could equal any community in Scotland. Through a quirk in the burgh constitution, Paisley's senior magistrate had never been dignified as 'provost', but after legal advice the oversight was remedied in 1812. According to leading councillors, the title reflected Paisley's 'respectability and augmented population', as did newly acquired magisterial chains of office 'in best guinea gold'.[16] There

---

[10]   Michael Fry, *The Dundas Despotism* (Edinburgh University Press, 1992), p. 335.

[11]   Henry Cockburn, *Memorials of his Times, 1779–1830* (T.N. Foulis, Edinburgh, 1910 [1856]), pp. 88–93.

[12]   Alexander Murdoch, 'The importance of being Edinburgh: management and opposition in Edinburgh politics, 1746–1784', in *Scottish Historical Review*, 62 (1983), p. 4.

[13]   Michael Hook et al., *Lord Provost George Drummond, 1687–1766* (Scotland's Cultural Heritage, Edinburgh, 1987); A.J. Youngson, *The Making of Classical Edinburgh* (Edinburgh University Press, 1988 [1966]), pp. 15–17.

[14]   Enid Gauldie, *One Artful and Ambitious Individual: Alexander Riddoch (1745–1822)* (Abertay Historical Society, Dundee, 1989); Charles McKean, '"Not even the trivial grace of a straight line" – or why Dundee never built a New Town', in Louise Miskill, Christopher A. Whatley and Bob Harris (eds), *Victorian Dundee: Images and Realities* (Tuckwell, East Linton, 2000), pp. 24–30.

[15]   Burgess Committee [of Dundee], *Remonstrance Addressed to Provost Alexander Riddoch* (privately printed, Dundee, 1818).

[16]   Robert Brown, *The History of Paisley from the Roman Period down to 1884, Volume II* (J. and J. Cook, Paisley, 1886), p. 154.

was irony in this approach, as the town was a centre of radicalism, with a relatively enlightened civic leadership. For instance, William Carlile, who served as provost between 1816 and 1822, was proprietor of Paisley's first substantial thread-works and a forthright free-trade Whig.[17]

Meanwhile, Whigs vigorously attacked the Tories' patronage network in the royal burghs. Tradition here was identified with reaction and even some liberal Tories were uneasy about the power monopoly. In 1822 Tory John Galt gave fictional substance to concerns in his classic satirical novel *The Provost*. Galt captured the contemporary climate in his wry evocation of Provost James Pawkie and his domain of Gudetown, based on the author's hometown of Irvine in Ayrshire.[18] Outwardly genial and obliging, Pawkie's overarching ambition was to attain 'discreet dominion' over the community; a position he achieved by shrewdly exploiting the vanity and venality of council colleagues.[19] Satire was also used by the increasingly assertive Scottish press. The *Scots Times*, founded in Glasgow in 1825, relentlessly lampooned the city's magistrates and their trappings of office.[20] Cocked hats and gold chains, along with the lord provost's velvet court dress, were depicted as outmoded symbols of the eighteenth century. Yet the attack was misleading, as in reality Glasgow was a model of civic probity. Notwithstanding the council's Tory leadership, in 1819 Edinburgh's pro-reform *Scotsman* newspaper praised Glasgow's businesslike approach to administration.[21] Particularly impressive was the lord provost's £40 claim for personal expenses during 1818, which contrasted strikingly with his Edinburgh counterpart's claim for £1,000.

To be fair, Edinburgh's chief magistrate had distinctive status in Scotland. In 1667 King Charles II had formally granted the title 'lord provost' to emphasise the city's pre-eminence in the hierarchy of Scottish burghs.[22] Glasgow's provost was more frequently referred to as 'lord provost' after 1715, reputedly as a reward for the city's loyalty to the Hanoverian regime during the Jacobite rebellion.[23] However, this was a courtesy title, not universally applied until the nineteenth century. Edinburgh's lord provost had additional responsibilities, notably as High Sheriff and Lord Lieutenant. He invariably chaired the Convention of Royal Burghs and served as privy councillor, advising the monarch.[24] Glasgow's lord provost did not become a privy councillor until 1912, allowing him (and later her) to claim the prefix of 'The Right Honourable'.[25] The

---

[17]   Sylvia Clark, *Paisley, A History* (Mainstream, Edinburgh, 1988), p. 43.

[18]   Ian A. Gordon, 'John Galt', in Christopher A. Whatley (ed.), *John Galt, 1779–1979* (Ramsay Head Press, Edinburgh, 1979), pp. 19–30.

[19]   There have been numerous editions of *The Provost* since 1822.

[20]   *Scots Times*, 16 July 1825.

[21]   *Scotsman*, 16 January 1819.

[22]   Marguerite Wood (ed.), *Extracts from the Records of the Burgh of Edinburgh, 1665 to 1680* (Oliver and Boyd, Edinburgh, 1950), pp. 243–5.

[23]   George Eyre-Todd, *History of Glasgow, Vol. III: from the Revolution to the Reform Acts* (Jackson, Wylie and Co., Glasgow, 1934), p. 89.

[24]   William Blackwood (publisher), *The New Statistical Account of Scotland, Vol. I: Edinburgh* (Blackwood, Edinburgh, 1845), p. 708; David Keir, *The Third Statistical Account of Scotland: The City of Edinburgh* (Collins, Glasgow, 1966), pp. 282–6.

[25]   *Glasgow Herald*, 6 November 1912.

provost's ceremonial function was particularly evident in Edinburgh because the city had been the seat of Scotland's monarchy and pre-1707 Parliament. This heritage was visible in 1830, with the elaborate pageantry surrounding King William IV's accession. Lord Provost William Allan led a procession of civic and legal dignitaries from the old Parliament House, to read the royal proclamation from four strategic points in the city.[26] Borne before him were Edinburgh's municipal symbols, a mace of Scots silver and a sword sheathed in velvet. Robes and official dress enhanced the spectacle, the knights wearing the decorations of their respective orders and a host of functionaries suitably liveried and uniformed.

Allan embraced a theatrical role in 1830, vividly demonstrating the provost's responsibilities as community figurehead. Yet, at the same time, tensions over the desirability of burgh reform put pressure on municipal leaders. Lord Provost Robert Dalglish of Glasgow, proprietor of Scotland's largest calico-printing firm, voiced the resentment of the city's industrial elites at their marginalisation from the parliamentary power base. At a council meeting in March 1831 he proposed a unanimously approved resolution, welcoming the Whig government's reform proposals as a boon to Glasgow's mercantile and manufacturing interests.[27] Conversely, in 'High Tory' Edinburgh, Lord Provost Allan's loyalty to the Dundas regime rendered him a hate figure during the 1831 general election. Councillors had voted narrowly to return Robert Adam Dundas as the city's MP, with Allan claiming during the debate that the working classes were being 'deluded' by promises of reform.[28] On leaving the council chambers he was confronted by an angry crowd which pursued him with inimitable Edinburgh insults. He was also pelted with assorted debris, including, as the *Scotsman* reported, 'a large fish'.[29] The blows were not severe, but the outrage was clearly directed at the lord provost because, as figurehead of the community, he had acted against its wishes on a particularly emotive issue.

Reform in 1832 ended the municipal monopoly of parliamentary elections in urban Scotland and to some extent redistributed constituency representation to reflect changing demography. In the first open general election later that year, reformers triumphed in all but one of the 23 urban constituencies; thereafter Liberalism remained virtually unchallenged in the burghs up to the 1880s. In 1833, a series of enactments fundamentally altered Scotland's local government and municipal leadership. The self-election system was replaced by a degree of public accountability via the £10 male property franchise, while mechanisms were introduced for the creation of new administrative entities, the parliamentary and police burghs. For every new burgh there had to be a figurehead; the provost's importance was thus reinforced, albeit in a different political context than before. The era of Liberal-dominated 'local self-government' was instituted, with the steady advance of burgh autonomy as communities sought effective town management.

---

[26]   *Scotsman*, 30 June 1830.
[27]   Robert Renwick (ed.), *Extracts from the Records of the Burgh of Glasgow, Vol. XI, 1823–1833* (Glasgow Corporation, Glasgow, 1916), pp. 416–17.
[28]   *Scotsman*, 4 May 1831.
[29]   *Scotsman*, 13 July 1831.

The Victorian and Edwardian Provostship

According to one 1904 calculation, 14 parliamentary burghs and over 119 police burghs had been created in Scotland since 1833.[30] The former were populous, usually industrial, towns, which from 1832 could return their own MPs. Recognising that their existing municipal constitutions might be 'defective', legislation was passed the following year authorising council structures that mirrored the royal burghs.[31] Particularly sweeping changes occurred in the port of Leith, a burgh of barony that since 1636 had been under the suzerainty of neighbouring Edinburgh.[32] The 1820s witnessed an epic clash of political wills between port and city, with Leith's business elites adopting a pugnaciously pro-reform stance in their determination to take control of their own economic destiny. In 1833 parliamentary burgh status gave Leith an independent town council, along with its first provost. Adam White, a wealthy Baltic merchant and free-trade Liberal, embodied the port's commercial and political aspirations in this new civic role. One early official duty was to write an effusive address to William IV, on behalf of Leith citizens, pointedly celebrating their 'emancipation from the yoke of feudal Vassalage'.[33]

Police burghs were another post-reform novelty, although as with parliamentary burghs, old structures were initially adapted to meet contemporary needs. The first general legislation in 1833 related only to existing burghs, whose inhabitants desired to establish elected boards of commissioners to oversee policing and environmental control.[34] Crucially, boards had taxation powers, unlike contemporary town councils. The 1850 Police of Towns (Scotland) Act extended local government to 'populous places'; communities with no previous municipal governance, whose residents sought police-burgh status to fund arrangements for basic services like street lighting, cleansing and drainage.[35] The great champion of Scottish police burghs was Provost William Lindsay of Leith, a ship-owner and former lawyer, whose sense of mission had been spurred by his hometown's post-reform municipal autonomy.[36] He was also a dedicated sanitary reformer, informing the *Scotsman* in 1859 that police burghs represented the most efficient means of securing the regenerative power of cleanliness for urban areas.[37] Lindsay's legal expertise and Liberal political networks

---

[30] Mabel Atkinson, *Local Government in Scotland* (Blackwood, Edinburgh, 1904), p. 74.

[31] William IV, cap 77, *An Act to Provide for the Appointment and Election of Magistrates and Councillors for the Several Burghs and Town of Scotland which ... are not Royal Burghs* [28 August 1833], p. 1.

[32] Mackenzie, *Scottish Burghs*, p. 84.

[33] James Campbell Irons, *Leith and Its Antiquities*, Vol. II (privately printed, Edinburgh, 1898), p. 252.

[34] R.M. Urquhart, *The Burghs of Scotland and the Burgh Police (Scotland) Act, 1833* (privately printed, Winchester, 1985), p. 13.

[35] R.M. Urquhart, *The Burghs of Scotland and the Police of Towns (Scotland) Act, 1850* (privately printed, Winchester, 1987), p. 16.

[36] Irons, *Leith*, Vol. II, pp. 531–4; R.M. Urquhart, *The Burghs of Scotland and the General Police and Improvement (Scotland) Act, 1862* (Scottish Library Association, Motherwell, 1991), pp. 13–19.

[37] *Scotsman*, 25 June 1859.

proved instrumental in securing amending legislation in 1862, with emphasis on public health provision. Up to 1892, when this enactment and its 1850 predecessor were repealed, 87 'populous places' had been erected into police burghs.

Initially, these new burghs were not envisaged as traditional civic entities, hence the prosaic use of 'senior magistrate' rather than 'provost' to describe their presiding officer. Yet over time their leaders became ambitious, particularly if the burghs were expanding towns in search of a distinctive identity. Though senior magistrates had no legal claim to call themselves 'provost', the term conferred gravitas and suggested a sense of history to fledgling communities, whether their character was middle-class residential or working-class industrial. According to one Glasgow journal in 1875, George Browne – Crosshill's senior magistrate – 'loves and affects to be called *Provost* Browne'.[38] Crosshill was a small, middle-class 'mushroom' burgh, so-called because of its sudden emergence on Glasgow's southern fringes. Elsewhere the historical record could be adjusted to legitimise the senior magistrate's inflated status. For instance, the Dunbartonshire shipbuilding boom-town of Clydebank adopted the Lindsay Act in 1886, and shipyard-owner James Rodger Thomson immediately entered collective memory as the first 'provost'.[39]

Because of environmental responsibilities, police-burgh leadership tended not to be overtly political. However, non-partisan appearances were often deceptive. Crosshill became a police burgh in 1871, partly to ensure it remained outside Glasgow and thus did not divert Liberal votes from the marginal Renfrewshire constituency.[40] The Midlothian town of Dalkeith was yet another political creation as a police burgh. Here the struggle was personalised between grocer and radical Liberal, Alexander Mitchell, and wealthy landed magnate and Conservative, Walter Francis Montagu-Douglas-Scott, fifth Duke of Buccleuch. Originally a burgh of barony, Dalkeith never had an autonomous council, instead being governed by a nominated board of 12 trustees, with successive Dukes serving as baron-bailie. Mitchell single-mindedly sought to free the town from feudalism; democratic local self-government, he argued, formed the bedrock of British liberty and prosperity.[41] Dalkeithers were split down the middle about adopting the Lindsay Act and Mitchell even launched his own newspaper to convince them of the cause. In 1878 the burgh came into being, with the veteran Mitchell embodying the triumph of Liberal progress as the town's first provost.

Mitchell's political stance was intertwined with adherence to religious nonconformity. He was a United Presbyterian, an evangelical denomination encouraging civic activism as a vehicle for missionary outreach. The electoral reforms of the 1830s had made municipal office more accessible to Protestant dissenters, who brought strong moral earnestness to burgh affairs. In 1843 publisher Adam Black became Edinburgh's first dissenting lord provost; a symbolic victory

---

[38]   *The Bailie*, 10 February 1875.

[39]   Carrick Watson, 'The town and its politics', in John Hood (ed.), *The History of Clydebank* (Parthenon, Carnforth, 1988), p. 24.

[40]   Glasgow City Archives CO1/7/5. 'Printed letter in opposition to the City of Glasgow Extension Bill, 21 December 1869', not paginated.

[41]   Alexander Mitchell, *Political and Social Movements in Dalkeith from 1831 to 1882* (privately printed, Dalkeith, 1882), p. 170.

demonstrating that the pre-reform Tory orthodoxy had been conclusively reversed.[42] As city treasurer from 1833, Black had endeavoured to unravel Edinburgh's tangled municipal finances, consciously cultivating an image of puritan austerity. The old regime's pageantry was drastically curtailed; Black even talked of dismissing the two functionaries who carried the ceremonial sword and mace before the lord provost. Upon becoming provost Black made no secret of his abhorrence of robes and chains of office and very publicly refused a knighthood in 1848. Even relatively solvent burghs adopted a sober attitude to civic ceremonial during the 1830s and 1840s, although they generally stopped short of dispensing with magisterial gold chains. Glasgow's post-reform councillors in 1833 saw them as an 'honourable badge' and 'necessary distinction'.[43]

There were evidently 'honourable' qualities to the post-reform provostship itself. While some incumbents may have reshaped the office to reflect their own politico-religious beliefs, provosts generally personified responsible and active citizenship. During his five years as Edinburgh's civic chief, Adam Black visibly demonstrated that less was more in terms of reclaiming the authority of the provostship and proving that the old citadels of burgess and feudal elitism had been breached. Here, Scottish provosts were little different from their mayoral equivalents south of the Border. Although the mayorality could be bitterly contested, 'no one questioned the institution itself or even seriously queried its ceremonial trappings'.[44] John Garrard has placed this in the context of Labour's mayoral aspirations during the 1930s, but the same could be said about Scotland a century earlier. Thus, Paisley councillors may have baulked at purchasing extra gold chains for a new magistrate in 1833, but radicals still coveted the provostship.[45] In 1841 the election of John Henderson, a radical journalist, was greeted with mixed feelings by fellow Chartists, some seeing him as forsaking principles in pursuit, ultimately, of parliamentary ambitions.[46] This division revealed the tensions between 'moral' and 'physical' force Chartism, with Henderson's espousal of municipal respectability indicative of the institutional route to political power favoured by the former camp.

However, urban Scotland was not entirely a Liberal one-party state from the 1830s. Personalities rather than politics often dictated the choice of provost, as was evident in 1842 when Major (later Sir) Hugh Lyon Playfair was elected provost of St Andrews. A retired army officer and veteran of India, the formidable Playfair undertook the structural improvement of this ancient royal burgh with military

---

[42]   Alexander Nicholson (ed.), *Memoirs of Adam Black* (Adam and Charles Black, Edinburgh, 1885), p. 126.

[43]   John Tweed (publisher), *Biographical Sketches of the Hon. the Lord Provosts of Glasgow* (Tweed, Glasgow, 1883), p. 6–7.

[44]   John Garrard, 'The mayorality since 1835', in Alan O'Day (ed.), *British Political Institutions since 1832* (Edwin Mellern Press, Lampeter, 1995), p. 5.

[45]   Brown, *Paisley*, Vol. II, p. 155–6.

[46]   See Edward Polin's satirical poem, 'John Henderson my jo', in Tom Leonard (ed.), *Radical Renfrew: Poetry from the French Revolution to the First World War* (Polygon, Edinburgh, 1990), pp. 164–5.

precision.[47] In some respects he was a small-scale throwback to Lord Provost Drummond of Enlightenment Edinburgh, in others he foreshadowed the vogue for 'Haussmannized' urban redevelopment, inspired by Parisian example during the 1850s and 1860s. Playfair had an authoritarian streak and was no friend of political reform, yet he cajoled or bullied wealthy St Andrews residents into raising funds to help fulfil his project. His ambitions for the town were not always appreciated; in 1911 one local critic wrote, 'A good deal was done under his imperious rule that would have been better left alone'.[48] Nevertheless, Playfair represented a growing trend in nineteenth-century Scotland; the direct involvement of individual civic leaders with major urban improvements, in furtherance of the municipal modernising mission.

The association of provosts with the landscape became more frequent from the 1850s, as post-reform retrenchment gave way to interventionism in efforts to resolve social problems arising from precipitant urban growth. Provosts represented both the virtues of benevolent individual action and the collective good of the community, while the personalised nature of specific projects meant that citizens could readily identify with them. Provosts could also be projected as non-partisan figureheads, aiming to reconcile communities and engender class cohesion. Provost Lindsay of Leith was thus celebrated as a hero of the sanitary revolution. In the 1850s Robert Stewart, a wealthy ironmaster and Glasgow's lord provost, was lauded for securing parliamentary sanction to initiate the city's controversial Loch Katrine water scheme.[49] In Edinburgh, publisher William Chambers became lord provost in 1865 specifically to oversee the clearance and restructuring of the deteriorating Old Town.[50] His conciliatory presence at the head of a council notorious for its combative and divisive politics made him one of Scotland's best-known nineteenth-century civic leaders.

Yet images of pro-active, public-spirited provosts could provoke a backlash, especially from taxpayers who were expected to subsidise civic initiatives. In 1866 Lord Provost John Blackie, junior, was sensationally defeated in Glasgow's municipal elections, after an acrimonious contest over city improvements.[51] His opponent alleged that Blackie's slum-clearance plans constituted little more than a grandiose vanity project, aimed at bettering Lord Provost Stewart's water scheme.[52] In 1902 Samuel Chisholm suffered a similar fate in Glasgow, ostensibly over proposals to borrow £750,000 to fund municipal housing.[53] The intensity of the attack was generated not only

---

[47]   Rev. Charles Roger, *History of St Andrews, with a Full Account of the Recent Improvements in the City* (Adam and Charles Black, Edinburgh, 1849), pp. 163–72; Ian Edward Wareham, 'Sir Hugh Lyon Playfair', in *Oxford Dictionary of National Biography* [hereafter *Oxford DNB*], http://www.oxforddnb.com/view/printable/22365 (02/08/2005).

[48]   James Maitland Anderson, *Handbook to the City and University of St Andrews* (W.C. Henderson, St Andrews, 1911), p. 10.

[49]   Tweed, *Lord Provosts of Glasgow*, pp. 145–51.

[50]   Richard Rodger, *The Transformation of Edinburgh: Land, Property and Trust in the Nineteenth Century* (Cambridge University Press, 2001), pp. 431–3.

[51]   Irene Maver, 'Glasgow's civic government', in W. Hamish Fraser and Irene Maver (eds), *Glasgow, Vol. II: 1830 to 1912* (Manchester University Press, 1996), p. 460.

[52]   *Glasgow Herald*, 6 November 1866.

[53]   Irene Sweeney, 'Local party politics and the temperance crusade: Glasgow, 1890–1902', in *Journal of the Scottish Labour History Society*, 27 (1992), pp. 55–6.

by Chisholm's policies, but his outspoken radical Liberalism. Above all, Chisholm's faith in the redemptive power of alcohol prohibition divided the community and rallied his enemies. He was by no means the first ardent teetotal provost – Dundee's George Rough laid claim to that distinction in 1853 – but many Glaswegians felt Chisholm had ventured too far in his zeal to transform the moral as well as social fabric of the city.[54] Significantly, the young Chisholm had served a grocery apprenticeship in Dalkeith under co-religionist Alexander Mitchell, demonstrating the importance of personal connections for motivating future civic leaders.

By the time of Chisholm's provostship, the office's status had risen in Scotland and the Edwardian period literally represented a golden age, at least in terms of public visibility. The continuing saga of Paisley's gold chains illustrated this; the provost had acquired an imposing new set in 1882, after complaints that 'especially in London, he was thrown entirely into the shade by the insignia of office displayed by other Chief Magistrates'.[55] Decorative lampposts represented another gleaming status symbol and most burghs eventually succumbed to the practice of placing lamps prominently outside their provost's residence. In Glasgow the lamps were a feature of the urban landscape from at least the 1820s.[56] However, in the seaside burgh of North Berwick, East Lothian – marketed as 'the Biarritz of the North' – they were a gift from the local gas company in 1905.[57] Meantime, the people of Edinburgh had recovered their affection for ceremonial, helped by their belief that the city's lord provost was not just Scotland's premier civic head, but the second citizen of the British Isles. Keen rivalry had developed with Dublin from the 1860s over which city officially came after London according to royal precedence. The Edinburgh lord provost and Dublin lord mayor embodied the legitimacy of competing claims and Edinburgh's resourceful town clerk, James D. Marwick, produced a weighty volume aiming to prove the former's superior credentials.[58]

Scotland's burgh hierarchy became further cause for competitiveness, especially over the use of the term 'lord provost' in relation to major cities. Dundee's appropriation of the title provoked heated controversy within the Convention of Royal Burghs, eventually resolved in 1892 when the Scottish Secretary ruled in the city's favour.[59] In addition to Edinburgh and Dundee, the title was formally recognised for Aberdeen, Glasgow and Perth. More generally, the Convention's membership was becoming less exclusive, with the admission of parliamentary burghs in 1879 and police burghs in 1895. By the latter date Govan and Partick, two shipbuilding police burghs contiguous to Glasgow, were among the ten most populous Scottish communities, well ahead of prestigious royal burghs like Perth and Stirling. The

[54]   P.T. Winskill, *The Temperance Movement and Its Workers: A Record of Social, Moral, Religious and Political Progress, Volume III* (Blackie and Son, London, 1893), pp. 41–2.

[55]   Brown, *Paisley*, Vol. II, p. 156.

[56]   Renwick, *Records of the Burgh of Glasgow*, p. 157.

[57]   *Fourth Statistical Account of East Lothian: Parish Volume*, http://www.el4.org.uk/parish/n.berwick.php (25/1/2006).

[58]   [James D. Marwick], *Precedence of Edinburgh and Dublin: Proceedings in the Privy Council* (Edinburgh Town Council, 1865).

[59]   Alexander M. Munro, *Memorials of the Aldermen, Provosts and Lord Provosts of Aberdeen, 1272–1893* (privately printed, Aberdeen, 1897), pp. ix–x.

quest for equal status was finally achieved under legislation of 1900, which fully integrated municipal and police administrations and recognised all town councils as having the same corporate identity.[60] Crucially, senior magistrates could legitimately call themselves 'provosts', complete with traditional ceremonial regalia.

The Twentieth-Century Provostship

In November 1913 the *Glasgow Herald* reported on a major municipal development, headlined 'First Lady Provost in Scotland'.[61] Lavinia Malcolm had been unanimously elected to the civic chair of Dollar in Clackmannanshire, a small police burgh created only in 1891.[62] Malcolm was politically progressive and had been Scotland's first female councillor in 1907, after legislation allowed women to stand in municipal elections. Malcolm's family had a tradition of civic activism. Her grandfather, John Kynoch, served as provost of Forres, Morayshire, between 1848 and 1855, while her husband, schoolteacher Richard Malcolm, had been Dollar's senior magistrate during the late 1890s. Her ideological background was staunch Liberal and United Presbyterian; as provost she represented the continuation of the radical ethos of local self-government. Yet Malcolm's success was untypical, and owed more to her personal standing in Dollar than her gender. Only from the 1930s did women councillors begin making headway as provosts, and only in 1960 was Jean Roberts of Glasgow elected as the first female lord provost.

Labour provosts, like Roberts, were a phenomenon that emerged after 1918. While Labour councillors increased steadily from 1900, the provostship depended on promotion through magisterial ranks and goodwill from fellow councillors; commodities generally difficult for socialists to attain. Moreover, cross-party anti-socialist groupings under the label of 'Moderate' were beginning to emerge in the council chambers. Assorted Liberals, Unionists and Conservatives, as well as the non-aligned, collaborated to safeguard ratepayers from the supposed danger of Labour control, using the slogan of 'non-party politics'. Despite the growth of anti-socialism, there were socialist sympathisers among the pre-war provosts. As far back as 1893, Paisley's Robert Cochran had chaired Keir Hardie's first political meeting in the town.[63] Cochran, a former Chartist and provost during the 1880s, represented a direct link between Paisley's old and new radical traditions. Glasgow's lord provost from 1911, Daniel Macaulay Stevenson, was the grandson of a pioneering trade unionist.[64] Although an active Liberal, Stevenson demonstrated support for the Fabian brand of socialism by serving as president of the Society's Glasgow branch during the 1900s.

---

[60]   Urquhart, *General Police and Improvement Act, 1862*, p. 437.

[61]   *Glasgow Herald*, 11 November 1913.

[62]   Janet Carolan and Leah Leneman, 'Lavinia Malcolm', in *Oxford DNB*, http://www.oxforddnb.com/view/printable/55608 (27/10/2004).

[63]   Catriona M.M. Macdonald, *The Radical Thread: Political Change in Scotland. Paisley Politics, 1885–1924* (Tuckwell, East Linton, 2000), p. 135.

[64]   Irene Maver, 'Sir Daniel Macaulay Stevenson', in *Oxford DNB*, http://www.oxforddnb.com/view/printable/36286 (23/09/2004).

Fabian arguments underpinned Stevenson's enthusiasm for municipal socialism, or 'civic co-operation' as he called it. Glasgow had become famous (and controversial) for the array of public utilities and services accumulated since the 1850s and Stevenson argued there should be no limits on these.[65] While the city remained the focus of national and international attention, there were also smaller burghs projecting themselves as models of municipal socialism. Kirkintilloch, a Dunbartonshire police burgh close to Glasgow, acquired a reputation for civic experimentation in eclectic spheres like banking, cinemas, restaurants and animal husbandry.[66] Thomas Gibson, Kirkintilloch's provost from 1918, belonged to the Independent Labour Party (ILP) and heralded the arrival of avowedly socialist provosts.[67] After the war, electoral reform opened the municipalities to increased Labour representation and boosted chances of overall control. The process was slow and socialist provosts were uncommon during the 1920s, with Labour councillors tending to form the minority group against their Moderate opponents. One notable exception was Clydebank, where a highly organised and popularly supported rent strike brought Labour to power in 1924 and returned Samuel Macdonald as the town's first socialist provost.[68]

Despite Labour's 1931 general election debacle, and the damaging ILP split the following year, socialist provosts steadily consolidated their position during the 1930s. Housing and unemployment were burning municipal issues and many voters saw Labour as a more attractive option than the Moderates and their cost-obsessed campaigning. Glasgow's first Labour lord provost, John Stewart, was elected in 1935. A veteran of Keir Hardie's pioneering Scottish Labour Party, Stewart was chosen because he was the longest-serving Labour councillor.[69] Like Hardie, he was a pacifist and refused to wear the ceremonial military uniform required of lord provosts in their capacity as Lord Lieutenant. Otherwise Stewart adhered to civic tradition, conspicuously appearing in the standard robes and gold chains, and accepting the knighthood automatically offered to the city's lord provosts after their three-year term. Elsewhere, Dalkeith, Darvel, Greenock, Kilsyth, South Queensferry and Turriff were among the disparate group of burghs claiming the novelty of a Labour provost. In 1934 Keir Hardie's son-in-law, journalist Emrys Hughes, was elected provost of the Ayrshire mining community of Cumnock and Holmhead.[70] The following year Hughes stood down to make way for his wife, allowing Nan Hughes to find an outlet for her political talents as Labour's first female provost.[71]

Hughes, another pacifist, suffered agonies of conscience after war was declared in 1939. She could never reconcile her commitment as wartime provost with deeply held

[65] D.M. Stevenson, 'Preface', in [John Lindsay], *Municipal Glasgow: Its Evolution and Enterprises* (Glasgow Corporation, 1914), p. 2.

[66] Thomas Johnston, *Memories* (Collins, London, 1952), pp. 21–30.

[67] E.J. Thurston (publisher), *Scottish Biographies, 1938* (Thurston, London, 1938), p. 277.

[68] *Scotsman*, 4 September 1925.

[69] *Glasgow Herald*, 8 November 1935 and (obituary) 30 May 1948.

[70] *Scotsman*, 10 November 1934.

[71] Caroline Benn, *Keir Hardie* (Hutchinson, London, 1992), p. 411; Helen Corr, 'Agnes Paterson Hardie [Hughes]', in *Oxford DNB*, http://www.oxforddnb.com/view/printable/50060 (23/09/2004).

convictions. The First World War had been equally traumatic for Daniel Macaulay Stevenson, although he dutifully exercised his responsibilities as Glasgow's lord provost. An ardent internationalist, with German family connections, after retiring as provost Stevenson became active in the Union of Democratic Control, a forum for Liberals and socialists to campaign for a negotiated peace.[72] Patrick Dollan, the city's Labour lord provost from 1938, had been imprisoned in 1917 for refusing conscription.[73] Yet Dollan, a journalist, was determined to fulfil his leadership role during the second conflict; indeed, his organising zeal was sometimes criticised for being too controlling. A motivating factor was Dollan's Irish Catholic ancestry. In Scotland provosts and Protestantism were closely identified and religious sectarianism was rife in interwar municipal politics.[74] The election of a Catholic, David McKay, as Dunfermline's provost in 1933 provoked one die-hard Protestant councillor to vocally dismiss the decision as 'a farce'.[75] While Dollan was anxious not to create divisions as wartime lord provost, he was also committed to representing a significant section of Glasgow's population hitherto excluded from the prime municipal honour.

During the inter-war period, municipal structures had been radically altered by the 1929 Local Government (Scotland) Act. Thomas Johnston, erstwhile Kirkintilloch magistrate and leading Scottish Labour politician, was blunt in his assessment that local government had been 'County Councilled', to the detriment of the burghs and other smaller units of administration.[76] He also dated the rise of the professional local politician from this time, claiming that centralisation of powers in county councils diminished grass-roots community involvement. However, there had been longstanding criticisms of Scotland's fragmented local government system, with Fabian socialist Mabel Atkinson arguing in 1904 that many burghs were too small for cost-effective administration.[77] Centralisation was already apparent, with Glasgow annexing its ring of nine 'mushroom' burghs and Edinburgh reabsorbing Leith in 1920. Arguments about the unnecessary duplication of resources cut little ice with most of Leith's 80,000 inhabitants, but Edinburgh's Lord Provost, Sir John Lorne Macleod, convinced Parliament of the need to enhance the city's 'position and prestige'.[78] The 1929 Act aimed to encourage such economies of scale, with the new category of 'small burghs' – those with 20,000 people or less – shorn of major functions.

The Act's centralising tendencies would have been stronger, had not the Convention of Royal Burghs fought ferociously to preserve the integrity of the prevailing system. Eventually 36 amendments were made to the original Bill, allowing burghs to keep services like council housing. Leading the Convention's vanguard was Sir Henry Keith, son of a Hamilton provost and himself provost of the Lanarkshire burgh from

[72]   Irene Maver, *Glasgow* (Edinburgh University Press, 2000), p. 167.
[73]   Irene Maver, 'Sir Patrick Joseph Dollan', in *Oxford DNB*, http://www.oxforddnb.com/view/printable/40305 (23/09/2004).
[74]   Tom Gallagher, 'Protestant extremism in urban Scotland, 1930–1939: its growth and contraction', in *Scottish Historical Review*, 64 (1985), pp. 143–67.
[75]   *Scotsman*, 11 November 1933.
[76]   Johnston, *Memories*, p. 21.
[77]   Atkinson, *Local Government*, pp. 74–8.
[78]   [Andrew Grierson], *Reconstruction Problems: Local Government in Edinburgh and District* (Edinburgh Corporation, 1919), p. 5.

1904 to 1908.[79] Keith was a Conservative and thus opposed to his political confrère, Sir John Gilmour, the Scottish Secretary and key figure in promoting the reorganisation. However, Keith could rely on considerable cross-party support. Alexander MacEwen, Liberal provost of Inverness, argued that the Highland region was too extensive to be administered under monolithic county council control.[80] Scottish Labour politicians regarded the counties as inherently more conservative than the burghs. The onslaught on local self-government was seen above all as an attack on Scottish institutions by an English-dominated Westminster government. As part of a Convention deputation to Gilmour in 1928, Keith asked: 'Why single out the Scottish burghs for degrading ... why were the English burghs [sic] left untouched?'[81]

The campaign against the 1929 Act had more complex political motivations than defending small burghs, but the Convention's emphasis on upholding civic tradition and burgh autonomy helped to rally popular support. That the Convention was still the collective voice of Scotland's provosts and ex-provosts, totalling some 200 representatives, influenced attitudes to the proposed legislation. Mabel Atkinson may have described provosts as akin to constitutional monarchs, 'he reigns, but does not govern', but in their role as Convention commissioners, provosts expressed burgh opinion, which throughout 1928 and 1929 was outspoken.[82] The Conservatives certainly regarded Scottish local government reorganisation as a vote loser in the 1929 general election.[83] However, the new Labour government did not repeal the legislation, despite continuing disquiet among the party's Scottish MPs. As support for Home Rule grew with the onset of Depression, the newly knighted Sir Alexander MacEwen cited the imposition of local government reform as a major reason for seeking the restoration of an Edinburgh-based Parliament.[84] In November 1932 MacEwen and Keith helped found the Scottish Self-Government Party, which two years later became part of the new Scottish National Party.[85]

In 1928 Sir John Gilmour tried placating his Convention critics by fatefully stating: 'The history and dignity of the royal burghs would not be touched; they stood and would stand for all time'.[86] Yet the argument against Scotland's local government structures continued. In 1942 James E. Shaw, who had helped draft the 1929 legislation, attacked 'vested interests' for undermining the 'symmetry' of the original proposals.[87] Shaw's vision for post-war Scotland was radical, suggesting that local government should be administered as one entire area, with elections based on six regional constituencies to ensure proportionality of representation. This

---

[79]   Thurston, *Scottish Biographies*, p. 396.

[80]   *Scotsman*, 4 October 1928.

[81]   Quoted in the *Scotsman*, 4 October 1928.

[82]   Atkinson, *Local Government*, p. 48.

[83]   James Mitchell, *Governing Scotland: the Invention of Administrative Devolution* (Palgrave, Basingstoke, 2003), p. 116.

[84]   Sir Alexander Malcolm MacEwen, *The Thistle and the Rose: Scotland's Problem Today* (Oliver and Boyd, Edinburgh, 1932), p. 80.

[85]   *Scotsman*, 1 November 1932.

[86]   Quoted in the *Scotsman*, 4 October 1928.

[87]   James E. Shaw, *Local Government in Scotland: Past, Present and Future* (Oliver and Boyd, Edinburgh, 1942), pp. 27–8.

was only one of several unfulfilled blueprints for reconstruction, but the Scottish Office's emphasis on large-scale and long-term planning generally favoured local government consolidation. Ironically, those gleaming urban testimonies to post-war Scottish modernism, the New Towns, soon sought their own burgh identity, complete with provosts. In 1963 and 1968 East Kilbride and Cumbernauld respectively were added to the roll of the Convention of Royal Burghs.[88] However, their life was short. In 1966 the Labour Government established a Royal Commission into Scottish local government and its Report three years later was unequivocal: 'The structure is no longer right, and … needs to be reformed'.[89]

The rationale underpinning reform was to achieve 'a less fragmented structure, capable of strategic planning in co-operation with the centre and able to exploit economies of scale'.[90] Labour's Scottish Secretary, William Ross, and his civil servants had little regard for historical sensibilities in pursuing national development policy. Lord Wheatley was more sensitive about local democracy and tradition, but his commission still opted for sweeping rationalisation. It recommended a two-tier system, with 65 local councils emerging under the 1975 legislation. The new authorities were divided according to regional, district and island functions and the 201 burghs and 33 county councils disappeared as administrative units. This time the Convention of Royal Burghs was less united than in the 1920s; there were too many disparate viewpoints among the large burghs, small burghs and cities. Moreover, there was broad recognition that the prevailing system was unsatisfactory, especially given the complex relations between burghs and county councils. One complaint from large burghs was the inordinate time spent by elected representatives (including provosts) in liaising with the counties, an obstacle that deterred suitable candidates from standing for municipal office.[91]

Some also regarded the provost's role as incompatible with wide-ranging local government rationalisation. In 1983 it was claimed: 'Those who bemoan the disappearance of the "Provost" often appear unaware of the limited powers which the small burghs possessed'.[92] The Wheatley Report tried circumventing anxieties about disappearing provosts: 'A burgh does not necessarily cease to be a burgh because it is no longer a self-contained unit of local government'.[93] This response was intended to allay the fears of certain Borders towns, where the ceremonies of common ridings were deemed inoperable without provosts, magistrates and councillors.[94] A flamboyant

---

    [88]   'Memorandum by East Kilbride Town Council', in *Royal Commission on Local Government in Scotland: Written Evidence, 22* (HMSO, Edinburgh, 1968), pp. 3–5; Urquhart, *General Police and Improvement Act, 1862*, p. 438.

    [89]   *Royal Commission on Local Government: [Wheatley] Report*, p. 1.

    [90]   Michael Keating and Arthur Midwinter, *The Government of Scotland* (Mainstream, Edinburgh, 1983), p. 96.

    [91]   'Memorandum by the Large Burghs Committee of the Convention of Royal Burghs', in *Royal Commission on Local Government in Scotland: Written Evidence, 2* (HMSO, Edinburgh, 1968), p. 96.

    [92]   Keating and Midwinter, *Government of Scotland*, p. 101.

    [93]   *Royal Commission on Local Government: [Wheatley] Report*, p. 263.

    [94]   'Border Burghs Convention', in *Royal Commission on Local Government: Minutes of Evidence, 17* (HMSO, Edinburgh, 1968), pp. 3–12.

celebration of civic pride and community identity, common ridings derived from the traditional 'perambulation of the marches', which aimed to protect burgh boundaries from outside encroachment. In examining Selkirk's common ridings, anthropologist Gwen Kennedy Neville notes that local autonomy had particular resonance in the wake of Borders regionalisation, or 'Texanization' as one ex-provost described it.[95] Deprived of traditional provosts, 'honorary' provosts were informally elected to oversee common ridings. In this capacity, Selkirk's provost still appears annually in traditional regalia, as an expression of historical continuity in the administratively defunct royal burgh.

The new 1975 councils showed mixed reactions towards the provostship. Out of 65 local authorities only 21 retained provosts, while 24 opted for 'chairmen' and 20 (including the regions and islands) preferred the old county council designation of 'convener'.[96] The four city councils, which objected to losing functions (and prestige) to the regions, doggedly retained their lord provosts. One irony about Wheatley's reorganisation was that the 1970s witnessed unprecedented electoral support for the Scottish Nationalists. Yet the intensity of debate over parliamentary devolution diverted attention from the legacy of local self-government identified with burghs and their provosts. Indeed, as Graeme Morton has observed, analysts of Scottish nationalism often overlook the civic factor, even though the royal burghs had direct links with the pre-Union governance of Scotland.[97] A further irony was that the 1975 reorganisation did not endure. Local government was streamlined in 1996; an exercise described by one critic as a 'structural gerrymander' to favour the Conservative-controlled Scottish Office.[98] From 1975 Labour had become entrenched within Scotland's councils, and reorganization was an attempt by John Major's Government to blunt the party's influence, as with Greater London Council abolition in 1986. Of the 32 new unitary authorities, 23 opted to call their conveners provosts or lord provosts; a rehabilitation of the office in some respects, but still well short of the Victorian and Edwardian golden years.

Conclusion

At the start of the new millennium the provostship has largely shed its political identity and the function is ceremonial, with incumbents acting as civic figureheads and ambassadors. While most provosts are still politically aligned, and all depend for election on the votes of fellow councillors, they are expected to mute their partisanship. Throughout their term of office provosts embody the all-embracing

---

[95]   Gwen Kennedy Neville, *The Mother Town: Civic Ritual, Symbol and Experience in the Borders of Scotland* (Oxford University Press, 1994), pp. 43–4.

[96]   John Knox and Eban Wilson, *Scotland '78: the Scots' Yearbook* (Wilson and Knox, Alva, 1977), pp. 30–36.

[97]   Graeme Morton, 'Civil society, municipal government and the state: enshrinement, empowerment and legitimacy, Scotland, 1800–1929', in *Urban History*, 25 (1998), p. 367.

[98]   Ronan Paddison, 'The restructuring of local government in Scotland', in Jonathan Bradbury and John Mawson (eds), *British Regionalism and Devolution: The Challenges of State Reform and European Integration* (Jessica Kingsley, London, 1997), p. 112.

common good of their community, echoing a traditional key feature of the burgh system, albeit in a context discouraging the strong and often outspoken personalities of the past. Instead, the local authority's political voice tends to be the council's majority party leader.

This does not mean that provosts have become detached from controversy. From 2003 there was a bitter power struggle between the Conservative and Labour groups on South Ayrshire Council, where the parties were evenly represented with 15 councillors apiece. The legitimacy of the Labour provost, including the privilege of placing the traditional decorative lampposts outside his home, became contested territory, with the Conservatives winning out after taking legal action towards the end of 2005.[99] The affair had echoes of the nineteenth rather than the twenty-first century. Yet this was a relatively rare example of the perpetuation of the provost's symbolic authority. According to one commentator, the dualistic nature of Scottish heads of local state since 1975, based on the provost/convener and party group leader, has had the effect of fragmenting overall responsibility and clouding perceptions of local leadership.[100] Moreover, there is reluctance to reconnect the ceremonial and political roles in an executive provost. So far Scotland has conspicuously not followed England and Wales, where legislative changes in 2000 allowed communities to opt for popularly elected mayors, heading cabinet-style executives within councils.[101]

---

[99]   Glasgow *Evening Times*, 6 January 2006; *Scottish Mail on Sunday*, 22 January 2006.

[100]   Gerry Stoker, 'The leadership role in local government', in *Scottish Affairs*, 25 (1998), pp. 121–4.

[101]   Allan McConnell, *Scottish Local Government* (Edinburgh University Press, 2004), pp. 83–9.

Symbolism or Substance? The Mayoralty in Northern Ireland

Colin Knox

Introduction

The role of mayors and other council chairs in Northern Ireland's local government has attracted little attention from historians or political scientists. The literature has been dominated by research on the 'high politics' of the 'troubles', including detailed speculation over the conflict's party-political aspects.[1] Indeed, Northern Ireland's local government, with some notable exceptions,[2] is largely under-researched because of the emasculated nature of councils. The Local Government Act (Northern Ireland) of 1972 stripped local authorities of key functional responsibilities in response to a litany of sectarian practices aimed at consolidating the hegemonic Unionist state from the 1920s. In 1973, core public services (education, housing and social services), typically delivered by local government in the rest of the United Kingdom, were vested in appointed boards accountable to British ministers under 'direct rule' from Westminster. Hence, the role of the mayor/chair in local government is largely symbolic but hugely significant in a province where symbolism is pervasive in the form of flags, emblems, parades, anthems and paramilitary paraphernalia marking out republican and loyalist territories.[3] Yet, as one political initiative after another failed to 'solve' Northern Ireland's constitutional crisis, local government became the only forum for expressing the political views of elected representatives. The role of the mayor/chair became pivotal to the emergence of power-sharing (or 'responsibility-sharing' as unionists

---

[1]   A. Aughey, and D. Morrow (eds), *Northern Ireland Politics* (Longman, London 1996); A. Aughey, *The Politics of Northern Ireland* (Routledge: London, 2005); P. Bew, H. Patterson and P. Teague, *Between War and Peace: The Political Future of Northern Ireland* (Lawrence and Wishart: London, 1997); P. Dixon, *Northern Ireland: The Politics of War and Peace* (Palgrave: Basingstoke, 2001); R. Wilford (eds), *Aspects of the Belfast Agreement* (Oxford University Press 2001).

[2]   P. Carmichael and C. Knox, 'Towards a New Era? Some developments in governance in Northern Ireland', *International Review of Administrative Sciences*, Vol. 65 (1): pp. 103–16, 1999; D. Birrell and A. Hayes, *The Local Government System in Northern Ireland* (Institute of Public Administration: Dublin, 1999); C. Knox, 'Northern Ireland Local Government', chapter 27: pp. 460–74, in M. Callanan and J. Keogan (eds), *Local Government in Ireland: Inside out* (Institute of Public Administration: Dublin, 2003).

[3]   L. Bryson and C. McCartney, *Clashing Symbols* (Institute of Irish Studies, Queen's University: Belfast), 1994; B. Rolston, *Drawing Support: Murals and transition in the North of Ireland* (Beyond the Pale Publications: Belfast, 2003).

preferred to call it). This, in turn, offered a model for proportionality (the d'Hondt allocation of committee chairs[4]) and arrangements for cross-community consent in the devolved Northern Ireland Assembly from December 1999.[5]

This chapter attempts three tasks. First, it explores the context of the debate about the mayor/chair's constitutional position and role in Northern Ireland local government since 1898, while emphasising the most recent period since 1972. Second, it points to the importance of the mayoralty despite local government's functional unimportance in the Province, by exploring how the election of one high-profile republican Mayor (Alex Maskey) to Belfast City Council, a bastion of unionist power and supremacy, offered wider potential for power-sharing arrangements. Finally, in the light of the current major review of local government, it discusses what the future offers for mayors/chairs in Northern Ireland.

Background

Local government in Northern Ireland is the product of the Local Government (Ireland) Act 1898, which in turn derived from the 1888 and 1894 legislation for England and Wales. First, the 1898 Act established a two-tier system of local government wherein county boroughs (the six largest towns: Dublin, Cork, Limerick, Waterford, Belfast, Londonderry) and county councils formed the upper tier and urban and rural districts the lower tier. Second, the public health functions of the Poor Law guardians in rural areas were transferred to rural district councils. Third, the Act rationalised local government boundaries, eliminating overlapping jurisdictions. Fourth, a simplified rating system, based on a single assessment for all local government purposes, was introduced. Finally, the Act extended the local government franchise to include all adult male ratepayers, thereby rendering the new county councils as *foci* of growing nationalist agitation for the separation of Ireland from the United Kingdom. Overall, this legislation established the local government structure obtaining in Ireland at the time of the establishment of the Irish Free State and devolved government of Northern Ireland.

When the 'free state' was created in 1920, Northern Ireland's devolved government consisted of six counties, which formed the administrative state. Within the six counties the local government framework comprised two county boroughs, six county councils, ten boroughs, 24 urban districts and 31 rural districts; a total of 73 local authorities, serving (by 1966) around 1.4 million people. This ranged from Tandragee Urban District Council, with 1,300 inhabitants, to the city of Belfast

---

    4   The d'Hondt system, also known as the highest average method, is named after Victor d'Hondt, a Belgian lawyer. The principle of the system is that seats are won singly and successively on the basis of the highest average. The method requires that the number of seats each party gains in the Assembly is divided initially by one, and thereafter by one more, than the number of seats won until all the seats are decided.
    5   T. Hadden, 'Constitutional Provisions', chapter 6: pp. 49–58, in R. Wilson (ed.), *Agreeing to Disagree? A Guide to the Northern Ireland Assembly* (The Stationery Office: Belfast, 2001).

CHAPTER THREE

with 407,000.[6] Elections were held triennially and all councils except rural districts had rating functions. They fulfilled the same roles as their British counterparts except for protective services like police and civil defence. The post-1920 period witnessed several controversial changes wherein 'the invincibility of the Unionist local government system was carefully constructed and maintained'.[7]

The first of these was the 1922 Local Government (Northern Ireland) Act. This replaced proportional representation (PR) with simple-majority elections; enabled the redrawing of electoral divisions and ward boundaries once PR had been removed; and altered the franchise by incorporating property ownership as a qualification for the vote. In short, the mechanisms for Unionist hegemony were established, or as O'Dowd et al. put it:

> While Britain and the Irish Republic had been democratising local government, the Unionist Government was consolidating its grip on local politics by fixing ward boundaries, by distributing votes to the propertied, and by disenfranchising the propertyless ... The abolition of PR and the reconstruction of wards and the franchise meant that, for rural and county councils, elections were hardly necessary. The only question for Unionists to resolve was who was chosen to serve on the local council.[8]

Growing recognition of the inadequacy of local government machinery to provide services efficiently became apparent from 1940 onwards. Loughran noted that it 'has not made any considerable contribution to the development of Northern Ireland since the war'.[9] This is evidenced by the growth of *ad hoc* statutory bodies and the removal and centralisation of local government functions (hospitals, fire, electricity and housing). Pressure for reform eventually surfaced in the 1960s from two complementary sources. First, the Northern Ireland government at Stormont started campaigning to modernise the system from March 1966, and remedy its defects – mainly the multiplicity of small local authorities with small rateable bases and hence limited financial resources. Of the 73 councils, 27 had fewer than 1,000 people and 46 had rateable values where one penny produced less than £500.[10] Many councils were therefore neither administratively nor financially viable. Second, there was ongoing dissatisfaction with gerrymandered electoral wards and the restricted franchise, helping produce the disturbances of 1968. Local politics were dominated by sectarian considerations. Unionists controlled a disproportionate share of local authorities with disproportionately large majorities – few councils changed hands at local elections. Buckland noted, 'local government remained an outstanding grievance, with Unionist majorities bolstered by discriminatory housing practices,

---

[6]   D. Birrell and A.S. Murie, *Policy and Government in Northern Ireland: Lessons of Devolution* (Gill and Macmillan: Dublin, 1980).

[7]   L. O'Dowd, B. Rolston and M. Tomlinson, *Northern Ireland: Between Civil Rights and Civil War* (CSE Books: London, 1980), p. 98.

[8]   ibid, p. 100.

[9]   G.F. Loughran, 'The Problem of Local Government in Northern Ireland', *Administration*, Vol. 13: pp. 35–8, 1965.

[10]   D. Birrell and A.S. Murie, *Policy and Government in Northern Ireland: Lessons of Devolution* (Gill and Macmillan: Dublin, 1980).

carefully drawn electoral areas and the persistent refusal to adopt the British practice of one man (*sic*), one vote'.[11] Minority-community grievances about housing and employment helped motivate the 1968 civil rights protest and the subsequent outbreak of civil disturbances.

Local government history until and during the 1960s is best characterised by the Town Clerk of Downpatrick Council who subsequently became a permanent secretary and Ombudsman for Northern Ireland. Recounting his time in local government, he wrote:

> Majorities were winners: they took the spoils and held the field. Councils were 'won' or 'lost', positions so well entrenched, heads so well counted that change rarely took place. Offices were not shared, committees, where they existed, were dominated by majorities; minorities knew their place and took the crumbs with as much grace as possible.[12]

Hayes relates the story of a veteran nationalist councillor who, finding himself in hospital with a minor ailment, joked to the nurse when she removed the bedpan, 'I've been on the council for 20 years and that's the first motion I've ever had carried!'[13] However, the invincibility of the Unionist-dominated local government system, carefully constructed from 1922 onwards, was about to be threatened. Until then, the role of elected council chairs was simply to hold the party line, reaffirm majoritarianism and share the spoils of a political system buttressed by gerrymandering and a restricted franchise. Yet, even within Northern Ireland's highly insular and sectarian *milieu*, the qualities or competencies of a chair were important:

> While officials are there to serve all members and no single party, the chairman is the key figure, both in the procedures and in ensuring the efficient disposal of the public part of the business. His (*sic*) personality too will have a great bearing on the way ... members behave – amicably or with animosity, and since he is often the public face of the council, it helps if it is a restrained and dignified one.[14]

A series of reforms initiated by the Stormont government in November 1968 modernised local government structures, reformed the franchise, including abolishing the company vote, introduced a points system for housing and established a Parliamentary Commissioner for Administration. Michael Farrell described these as 'too little, too late; ... enough to outrage loyalists without satisfying the civil rights movement at all'.[15] By October 1969 local government had been stripped of its responsibility for housing and a decision made to create a centralised housing agency (the Northern Ireland Housing Executive). In December 1969, the Minister of Development (with overall responsibility for local government) initiated a review chaired by Patrick Macrory.

---

[11]   P. Buckland, *A History of Northern Ireland* (Gill and Macmillan: Dublin, 1981), p. 116.

[12]   M. Hayes, *Minority Verdict: Experiences of a Catholic Public Servant* (Blackstaff Press: Belfast, 1995), p. 23.

[13]   ibid., p. 23.

[14]   ibid., p. 40.

[15]   M. Farrell, *Northern Ireland: The Orange State* (Pluto Press: London 1976), p. 248.

The Macrory Report (1970) divided services into regional (requiring large administrative units) and district (suitable for small areas) services. The Stormont parliament was to take responsibility for regional services and district councils would administer district services. Macrory recommended establishing 26 borough or district councils and establishing appointed boards to decentralise the administration of centrally provided health and education services. The recommendations were subsequently passed into law under the Local Government Act (Northern Ireland) 1972. Macrory's proposals were however overtaken by Stormont's abolition in 1972 and the imposition of 'direct rule' from Westminster.

Outline Map of Northern Ireland; District Council Areas

Map 3.1   Local Government in Northern Ireland
Source: Map by Conal Kelly – CAIN website.

Local Government since 1973: Emerging Consensus?

The most significant changes introduced by the 1972 Local Government Act (Northern Ireland) were new local government boundaries (see Map 3.1), universal adult suffrage and the replacement of simple plurality voting by proportional representation (the single-transferable-vote). The new district councils came into operation in October 1973 and have remained largely unchanged since then, although a major review of public administration is currently underway which will reform local government once more.[16]

The allocation of powers to local authorities was confined to providing a limited, and outwardly uncontroversial, range of services: refuse collection and disposal, leisure and community services, street cleaning, parks and tourism. Some 582 councillors now represent 1.68 million people in Northern Ireland. Councils have four main functions – ceremonial ones associated with civic leadership; the direct provision of the public services; a representative role where councillors are appointed to a number of public bodies; and a consultative role whereby government departments responsible for functions like planning, roads, water and conservation engage with councils about service provision within their areas.

Under the provisions of the 1972 Act, councils were initially designated as 'district councils' but they could be granted city or borough status in certain circumstances. As section 2 puts it, 'a council may, in pursuance of a special resolution of the council, submit a petition to the Governor praying for the grant of a charter designating the district of the council a borough'. The two largest councils – Belfast and Derry – retained their city status, whilst Armagh was granted it by royal order in March 1995 and Lisburn and Newry attained theirs in 2002. Fourteen other councils have obtained borough status either because of charters applying in their area before 1973 or through petitions for new charters since 1973. The title for the head of the council is determined by the council's status. Hence district councils have chairpersons; city and borough councils a mayor; and Belfast City Council a Lord Mayor. City and borough councils may designate up to one quarter of their councillors with the ceremonial title of 'alderman'. The typical role of the Mayor is described by Lisburn City Council thus:

> As first citizen of the city, the Mayor will actively lead on all matters of civic life, take responsibility for chairing council meetings, undertake the management of the full council, and positively represent the City of Lisburn and its residents to the wider community both domestically and internationally.[17]

In spite of councils' radically reduced powers since 1973, local government has been the focus of revitalised electoral competition. In 1973 there were 1,222 candidates for 526 seats compared to the previous local government election (1967) where a majority of seats were uncontested. The political composition of councils also reflects the PR electoral system, there being relatively few where one party has an overall majority. Minority parties also have greater representation.

Notwithstanding its innocuous powers, local government became immersed in wider constitutional controversy when, in the 1985 elections, 59 Sinn Féin councillors, representing the political wing of the Provisional Irish Republican Army, secured seats. Unionists perceived Sinn Féin's electoral strategy (the infamous mantra of the 'ballot box and armalite') as a threatening new dimension in local government and marked their displeasure by disrupting its operation. Some councils

---

[16]   Office of the First Minister and Deputy First Minister, *The Review of Public Administration in Northern Ireland: Further Consultation* (RPA: Belfast, 2005).

[17]   Lisburn City Council (2005), 'Mayor', http://www.lisburncity.gov.uk.

adjourned business and all 18 Unionist-controlled local authorities refused to carry out normal duties. Varying degrees of conflict ensued, with occasional fist-fights in council chambers over the presence of Sinn Féin. Disruption was superseded by a hard-line campaign against the Anglo-Irish Agreement of November 1985. All Unionist councils adjourned in protest, refusing to levy district rates. The courts ordered several indicted councils to resume normal business and set a rate. The local government sector had, by this stage, become embroiled in a constitutional protest of defiance against the Agreement, well beyond its remit, and clashed variously with central government and the courts. Fines were imposed by the high courts against recalcitrant councils (Belfast and Castlereagh, for example) and legal censure against others (Lisburn, Antrim and Coleraine). Confronted by such set-backs, support for the protest dwindled and, from early-1988, it petered out.[18]

The 1989 local government elections marked a turning point in council chambers, with a degree of moderation appearing not unrelated to the decline in representation from the political extremes. Dungannon District Council is credited with leading the way through an experiment in responsibility- or power-sharing. It established a special committee, which passed a resolution recognising 'responsibility as an important step which might help us to develop trust in the community'.[19] It was agreed that the chair's position would be rotated, every six months, between council members 'who deplore violence and seek to pursue political progress by political means'. This effectively excluded Sinn Féin from responsibility-sharing, while the Democratic Unionist Party refused to partake on principle. The rotation of the chair effectively alternated power between the main unionist (UUP) and nationalist (SDLP) blocs at that time. Given unionist fury about wider political developments in the Province, Dungannon's decision to rotate the chair must be viewed as a major step forward in relations between unionists and nationalists.

Other councils followed suit in the wake of the 1989 elections. Eleven local authorities appointed chairs, mayors and deputies from both political traditions. The power-sharing trend continued following the 1993 local elections, with 12 councils participating and, according to one observer, an upbeat mood emerging about its longer-term prospects:

> There may be some hope in Ulster's new councils. The Ulster Unionist Party, Alliance and the SDLP have expressed varying degrees of enthusiasm for 'partnership', code word for sharing the main positions of authority ... There are several local councils where a combination of these three parties can form the critical mass necessary to take control and to blur the orange/green divide. A growth in power sharing would to a great deal to change the mood music of Ulster politics and to build trust between parties, which is the necessary precursor to a larger accommodation.[20]

---

[18]   M. Connolly and C. Knox, 'Recent Political Difficulties of Local Government in Northern Ireland', *Policy and Politics*, Vol. 16 (2): pp. 89–97: 1998.

[19]   C. Knox, 'The Emergence of Power Sharing in Northern Ireland: Lessons from Local Government', *Journal of Conflict Studies*, Vol. XVI (1): pp. 7–29: 1996: 9.

[20]   L. Clarke, 'Extremists hold the line in a tribal poll', *Sunday Times*, 23rd May, 1993: 4.

Power-sharing councils (see Table 3.1 at the end of this chapter) were not, however, havens of tranquillity and co-operation. Controversy flared over many issues, causing fundamental divisions between the parties. During 1992–1993, for example and in proper power-sharing spirit, the SDLP elected DUP Councillor William Hay as mayor of Derry City Council. During his tenure, Hay refused to meet with both the (then) Irish President, Mary Robinson, and (then) Taoiseach, Albert Reynolds. The SDLP claimed that Hay had failed in his mayoral duty to represent the wishes of Derry's majority. Divisions also emerged in Newry and Mourne Council when the nationalist council chair proposed a motion condemning road traffic delays caused by army checkpoints in South Armagh (locally known as 'bandit country'). Despite a policy of co-operation, unionists could not support such a motion. In the same council area, however, all political parties, except Sinn Féin, condemned the bombing of a local hotel by the IRA and the killing of a British soldier.

Minor partners in power-sharing arrangements were sometimes more cynical about the use of council chairs to maintain a facade of harmony. As one Ulster Unionist councillor put it:

> Derry City Council has always been portrayed nationally and internationally as a shining example of how nationalists will treat unionists and, in reality, it is quite different. It is *not* a power-sharing council. In all committees and meetings there is an SDLP majority. So no matter who chairs a meeting or who is the mayor, the SDLP still control the council and on every issue they operate a strong party whip. If unionists were in power we would probably be doing the exact same thing.[21]

Whilst rotating the chair or mayoral position up to this point appealed to middle-ground parties, power-sharing of whatever hue was anathema to the DUP who argued it was contrary to the principle of majority rule in a democracy. Sinn Féin's position was dictated by what advantages the party gained from specific power-sharing arrangements.

Symbolism Matters

The role that the chair, mayor or lord mayor played in local government, as explored thus far, characterises the wider political *milieu* within which this governmental tier has existed. From 1922 onwards, local political heads reinforced unionist hegemony to such an extent that local government became a core grievance in the civil rights movement of the late-1960s. Tomlinson highlights the symbolic importance of Belfast Corporation in strengthening unionist supremacy: 'Protestant bourgeois patronage, operating through the local government system on the basis of carefully concocted electoral districts and restricted franchise, was well fortified against political and economic forces for change'.[22] With reorganisation in 1972/1973, not least through boundary reorganisation and changes to the voting system,

---

21   R. Dallas, Author's interview with Councillor R. Dallas (UUP), Derry City Council, 1996.

22   M. Tomlinson, 'Relegating Local Government', in L. O'Dowd, B. Rolston and M. Tomlinson, *Northern Ireland: Between Civil Rights and Civil War* (CSE Books: London, 1980), p. 101.

unionist dominance decreased. Although local government's diminished functional importance made the role of chair, mayor or lord mayor less significant, what happened in councils became a barometer of the wider political process. With the imposition of Westminster direct rule in 1972, British governments presided over a series of failed initiatives attempting to restore devolution to Northern Ireland. This involved giving constitutional guarantees to unionists about their position within the United Kingdom and delivering some sort of power-sharing arrangements between Catholics and Protestants within an all-Ireland framework.[23] The 1972–1973 power-sharing executive; the 1975 constitutional convention; the 1980 talks-about-talks; the 1982 rolling devolution and the Northern Ireland Assembly; the 1985 Anglo-Irish Agreement; the Brooke/Mayhew party talks; the Hume/Adams peace plan; the 1993 Joint Declaration and the 1995 Framework Documents: all testify to initiatives which raised hopes and foundered. In the meantime local government was the only democratic forum around. Even since the historic Belfast (Good Friday) Agreement in 1998, political and administrative stability have proved elusive. With the Northern Ireland Assembly now suspended (since October 2002) for the fourth time, local government remains in place, albeit emasculated in form.[24]

The key contribution, which heads of state at local-government level have made, is to embed the principle of power-sharing that has been pivotal to the Belfast Agreement. Hence, what had been happening in local government for some time, presided over by chairs, mayors or lord mayors, became the blueprint for a devolved Northern Ireland Assembly. Legislative Assembly members (MLAs) are elected by PR (STV). The election of the chair and deputy-chair of the Assembly, main committees, and the power-sharing executive are made on the basis of proportionality using d'Hondt. Key decisions are taken on a cross-community basis (either through parallel consent or weighted majority). As one leader-writer put it at the beginning of the 2001 local government elections:

> Some council chambers, most notably Belfast City Hall, once earned a reputation for being sectarian bearpits. But tensions have eased and local government has played its part in changing the face of Northern Ireland politics. Although mayoral rotation has not worked everywhere, many councils blazed a trail for the peace process by demonstrating that power-sharing can be a reality.[25]

The contribution by councils to 'working' power-sharing at local level has been hard fought, and not without major controversy in some authorities which cling to the vestiges of majoritarianism and unionist domination. This is particularly true where Sinn Féin is vying for the post of chair, mayor or lord mayor, the political symbolism of which is simply too much for die-hard unionists to accept. The case is

---

[23] W. Harvey Cox, 'The Northern Ireland Talks', *Politics Review*, Vol. 3 (2): pp. 28–32, 1993.

[24] C. Knox and P. Carmichael, 'Devolution – the Northern Ireland way: An exercise in "creative ambiguity"', *Environment and Planning c: Government and Politics*, Vol. 23 (1): pp. 63–83, 2005.

[25] N. McAdam, 'Vote early and vote twice – the general election will not be the only show in town on polling day', *Belfast Telegraph*, 18th May: 1, 2001.

best illustrated by Sinn Féin's success in securing the post of Lord Mayor of Belfast for the first time in its history.

Belfast City Council – Mayoral Symbolism Writ Large

The 1997 local government elections were a turning point in the politics of Belfast City Council, by far the largest local authority in Northern Ireland. The mainstream unionist parties lost control, thereby producing the city's first elected nationalist Lord Mayor. Sinn Féin and the Ulster Unionist Party secured most seats (13 each) and the Alliance Party held the balance of power.[26] A century of unionist control of Belfast City Council ended when Alban Maginness, an SDLP barrister, secured the post with support from Sinn Féin and the Alliance. Although Sinn Féin held the largest number of nationalist/republican seats, neither the SDLP nor the Alliance would support a republican candidate without an IRA ceasefire. Sinn Féin reasoned that the symbolism of the first nationalist lord mayor was so momentous that they supported Maginness. Ulster Unionist councillor Jim Rodgers was elected unopposed as deputy Lord Mayor. In what was seen as one of Unionism's most potent institutions, Belfast City Council, power-sharing shuffled in. In accepting the mayoral chain, which ironically (given its unionist 'ownership') bore the Irish inscription 'Eireann Go Brea' (Ireland forever), Lord Mayor Maginness avoided the temptation of triumphalism:

> Tonight, the political mould has been broken. Its fracture does not mark a defeat of one tradition by another, nor is it a victory. Rather, it signifies a bold step towards the creation of a partnership amongst the political traditions in this divided city. A partnership in which there is neither victory nor defeat but the triumph of tolerance.[27]

This magnanimous approach contrasted sharply with the more resolute response from Gerry Adams, Sinn Féin president, who welcomed the election of a nationalist Lord Mayor by commenting 'the days of unionist domination are over forever and Sinn Féin is absolutely determined to ensure … they will never return'.[28] The first powerful test of mayoral symbolism for Mr Maginness came when he participated in a wreath-laying ceremony at the Cenotaph outside Belfast City Hall to commemorate the fallen at the Battle of the Somme where soldiers of the 36th Ulster Division were killed. Maginness had not previously attended the ceremony, claiming the political climate was not amenable to his being there. He was joined by his Dublin counterpart, Mr. Brendan Lynch. The symbolism was potent. This was the first time a nationalist Lord Mayor had led the procession at the ceremony and also the first time a Dublin Lord Mayor had attended. The DUP accused Mayor Maginness of 'blatant hypocrisy', arguing 'we can conclude that nationalists were dragged into this event out of embarrassment rather than … civic duty and true respect for those

---

[26]   In the 1997 local government elections to Belfast City Council: unionists/loyalists won 25 seats (UUP 13; DUP 7; PUP 3; UDP 1; Unionist 1); nationalists/loyalists won 20 seats (Sinn Féin 13; SDLP 7); and the Alliance Party won 6 seats.

[27]   S. Breen, 'Belfast elects nationalist Lord Mayor', *Irish Times*, 3rd June: 8, 1997.

[28]   ibid., p. 8.

who laid down their lives'.[29] Maginness, although overtly inclusive, started chipping away at the British traditions associated with the post of Lord Mayor. He opted not to toast the Royal Family in keeping with tradition at his inaugural dinner and removed the Union Flag from the Lord Mayor's parlour in a bid, according to Maginness, to depoliticise the office of Belfast's First Citizen.

The 2001 local elections witnessed a further increase in nationalist/republican representation on Belfast City Council, with Sinn Féin becoming the largest political party.[30] The Alliance, still holding the balance of power, joined the SDLP and republicans in June 2002 in electing Alex Maskey, Belfast's first Sinn Féin Lord Mayor. Maskey, a senior provisional republican and anti-monarchist, first elected to City Hall in 1983 where he attended his first meeting wearing a bullet proof vest, was an abhorrent figure to unionists. The support of the three Alliance councillors was the crucial, but by no means certain, ingredient securing his mayoral election. One observer captured the tension thus:

> Unionists stared sullenly across the floor of the chamber on the Alliance benches. From Sinn Féin benches the questioning glances towards Alliance reflected republican anxiety that the trio would recant at the eleventh hour and plead 'not guilty' to the charge that they were handing the keys of unionism's citadel to the 'Provo Pariah'.[31]

Unionists reacted to Maskey's election by walking out after this hugely historic and symbolic decision was taken, and refusing to propose anyone as Deputy Lord Mayor. They justified this refusal by arguing that it gave credibility to the city's first republican mayor. Maskey appealed to unionists, beneath portraits in Belfast City Hall of Queen Victoria and King Edward VII, symbols of the British establishment and repugnant to republicans, to 'judge me on what you see me doing and saying'. The DUP said the election was 'a night of shame for the city, a night of sadness for those who have suffered at the hands of the IRA over the last 20 years'.[32]

The civic leadership expected of Belfast's republican Lord Mayor was soon tested. Maskey attended the General Assembly of the Presbyterian Church in Ireland with some 1,200 delegates. Here, the Moderator welcomed 'the chief citizen of Belfast ... to a Christian assembly ... where we are in the business of trying to understand each other, to dialogue with each other'. The DUP accused Irish Presbyterians of 'giving cover to Maskey who is stained by the blood of innocents'.[33] Maskey then faced the same dilemma as the first SDLP Lord Mayor in commemorating the Somme. Republicans have traditionally refused to attend wreath-laying ceremonies, arguing

---

[29]   S. Wilson, cited in G. Moriarty: 'SDLP mayor joins Dublin counterpart in commemorating Somme dead', *Irish Times*, 2nd July: 9, 1997.

[30]   In the 2001 local government elections in Belfast, the unionists/loyalists won 25 seats (UUP 11; DUP 10; PUP 3; UDP 1); the nationalists/loyalists 20 seats (Sinn Féin 14; SDLP 9); and the Alliance 3.

[31]   B. McCaffrey, *Alex Maskey: Man and Mayor* (Brehon Press: Belfast, 2003), p. 148.

[32]   N. McCausland, cited in G. Moriarty 'Maskey elected Lord Mayor of Belfast', *Irish Times*: 6th June: 10, 2002.

[33]   P. McGarry, 'Maskey welcomed at annual church assembly', *Irish Times*, 11th June: 17, 2002.

they are closely associated with the British military establishment. Following internal party discussions and dissent, the republican Lord Mayor laid a wreath at the Cenotaph during the Somme anniversary after which he said 'this is a major step for republicans and nationalists on this island. I hope the initiative will be seen at face value and as a positive gesture'.[34] The Lord Mayor followed this event by laying a wreath at a ceremony in Belgium in memory of those from the island of Ireland (north and south) who died on the Somme.

On the wider front, Maskey's mayoral tenure was helped by the IRA's unprecedented public apology to the families of 'non-combatants' killed by the paramilitary group during the 'troubles' and a restatement of its commitment to the peace process. Maskey also held a high-profile meeting with John White, a member of the Ulster Political Research Group, the main conduit for the views of the Ulster Defence Association (UDA), a paramilitary group which had tried, and almost succeeded in, assassinating him. The meeting had been arranged to defuse escalating sectarian tensions in Belfast and was described as a triumph of political necessity or expediency over mutual loathing.[35]

In an office where symbols matter, Maskey had promised the Alliance Party, in return for their support in his election, that he would not strip the Lord Mayor's parlour of its unionist paraphernalia and replace them with trappings of republican history. Instead, he placed a tricolour (the flag of the Irish Republic), presented to him by a former IRA prisoner at a civic ceremony, alongside the Union flag, photographs of Queen Elizabeth, Prince Phillip and the late-Queen Mother. He justified this as a move towards equality and respect for the two traditions in Northern Ireland where both flags had a place in the mayoral parlour. Maskey also held a City Hall reception (ironically boycotted by unionists) for members of the old soldiers' charity, the Royal British Legion. In a further attempt to represent both traditions, the Lord Mayor explored the possibility of meeting the Duke of York who was to participate in a Royal Irish Regiment ceremony where he was Colonel-in-Chief. For a high-profile republican like Maskey, meeting a British Royal invited anger from his grassroots. In an attempt to balance civic leadership with his political and ideological beliefs, he tried to negotiate the conditions of the meeting, particularly to ensure what he described as 'no British military symbolism'.[36] He could not meet with someone in British military uniform given his implacable opposition to everything the British monarchy stood for. According to Maskey, the British, at the last minute, changed the Prince's schedule from a private civic reception to a public event with military overtones, making the Lord Mayor's attendance impossible.

Strategically, Sinn Féin had carefully considered plans for Maskey's mayoral role. The party explained:

> We wanted to use Alex Maskey as a kind of ambassador, following on from the success of Martin McGuinness and Bairbre de Brún (former Sinn Féin Assembly Ministers). We

---

[34]   A. Maskey, cited in S. Breen 'Maskey lays wreath for victims of Somme', *Irish Times*, 2nd July: 5, 2002.
[35]   G. Moriarty: 'When expediency triumphs over loathing: SDLP mayor joins Dublin counterpart in commemorating Somme dead', *Irish Times*, 14th August: 4, 2002.
[36]   McCaffrey, *Alex Maskey*, p. 158.

wanted to prove to unionists that they would be under no threat whenever Sinn Féin was in power, whether that was in Belfast or in a united Ireland.[37]

Handing over the chain of office in June 2003, Maskey called on all future mayors to sign a pledge of office compelling them to represent all the people of Belfast and give a written commitment to reach out to both communities and restore international confidence in a city whose image was synonymous with sectarianism. The outgoing Lord Mayor remarked: 'the City Hall didn't burn down as some unionists had predicted and, hopefully, the efforts I made to reach out to unionists can be built and strengthened by myself and others in the years ahead'.[38] Sinn Féin had now 'worked' two symbolically important political institutions – Stormont and Belfast City Hall. Detractors found it difficult to criticise their commitment, those within Sinn Féin and the IRA saw it as an integral part of implementing the internal arrangements (strand 1) of the Belfast Agreement.

Conclusions: Beyond Symbolism

The potency of mayoral symbolism and how this has been used in the wider political process in Northern Ireland goes well beyond the functional importance of local government as a democratic entity. Creating power-sharing arrangements is the most obvious manifestation of how the role of chairs and mayors has been hugely influential. This is not confined to Belfast. Several Northern Ireland councils now engage in power-sharing, a practice which, they argue, originated from rotating the chair/mayor's position between local political parties well before it became integral to the principles of devolved government in the shape of the Northern Ireland Assembly. Former SDLP Deputy First Minister, Mark Durkan, claimed that Derry City Council was where power-sharing between unionists and nationalists first operated. He described the city as a 'trailblazer' and said Derry 'has a great track record and great potential. So much of the thinking that inspired the Belfast Agreement was tried and perfected in this city over many years. We are pace setters and we must continue to be'.[39]

Not only has learning been transferred upwards to the Assembly, but increasingly councils have adopted more formalised power-sharing arrangements than previously existed. The d'Hondt system of proportional representation was adopted by the Northern Ireland Assembly to allocate seats in the executive, and appoint committee chairs and deputy-chairs. Several councils have now adopted this process as their *modus operandi*, although a few remain recalcitrant. Lisburn City Council, for example, the second largest council area in Northern Ireland, which gained city status in 2002, is accused of excluding nationalists from all key positions and refusing to adopt any form of power-sharing arrangement. This has prompted the Department of Foreign Affairs (in Dublin) to monitor the allocation of offices in response to

---

[37]   J. Gibney, cited ibid, p. 158.

[38]   A. Maskey, cited ibid, p. 211.

[39]   M. Durkan, 'Derry is the city that sets the pace', *Belfast Telegraph*, 9th March: 1, 2002.

a complaint from Sinn Féin.[40] Recently, invitations to Lisburn City Council's mayoral banquet excluded Sinn Féin councillors at the behest of the DUP mayor. Under pressure from council officials, his decision was overturned but he remained unapologetic: 'If it was down to me, there would be no Sinn Féin members there. It is certainly not a U-turn by me. I had been given to understand that the invitations to the mayoral banquet were at the Mayor's discretion. I was later informed this is not the case'.[41] The Mayor pledged to hold a toast to the Queen during the banquet to rebuff Sinn Féin's inclusion.

These vestiges of political exclusivity, exercised through the election of the chair/mayor of local authorities, raise two general issues. First, debates about the possibility of directly elected mayors/chairs in the Northern Irish context have been mostly rejected as divisive and likely to compound sectarianism. For example, in a debate in Derry City Council on the merits of having a mayor directly elected by the public every four years, the (then) DUP mayor (Mildred Garfield) argued she would be the city's last unionist mayor if the proposal became a reality. Given Derry's large nationalist majority, it is highly likely that a public vote would displace existing power-sharing arrangements to rotate the mayoralty between parties with a nationalist/republican first citizen. This would do little to foster harmony and good relations in the city.

Second, local authorities are now part of a wider review of public administration currently underway. Initiated by the Northern Ireland Assembly in 2002, this has continued despite the on/off nature of devolution. It has recently launched final proposals for consultation which stress that whatever form of local government emerged would need 'to be underpinned by a range of statutory safeguards on the operation of councils if confidence and trust in the new arrangements were to be achieved'. The statutory arrangements, the review argued, 'should provide a framework of checks and balances under which councils would conduct their business and ensure equality and fairness in decision-making'.[42] These proposals, it appears, are an oblique acknowledgement of the merits of power-sharing where it has happened voluntarily between political parties keen to built trust at local government level, but also recognition that such principles have not been universally applied. As the review envisages returning greater powers to local government, then 'equality and fairness in decision-making' become yet more important, not least because of the history of local government malpractice before 1973. The proposed new safeguards would undoubtedly include reference to the election of the chair, mayor or lord mayor of local authorities and a more detailed explication of his/her civic leadership role.

What the Northern Ireland case illustrates is that the seemingly innocuous role of local heads of state, presiding over a relatively small-scale tier of governance, is

---

[40]   Lisburn City Council comprises: 13 UUP members; five DUP members; two independent unionists; three SDLP members; four Sinn Féin members; and three Alliance Party members.

[41]   C. Calvert, 'Sinn Féin for Lisburn mayoral banquet', *Belfast Telegraph*, 12th October: 1, 2004.

[42]   Office of the First Minister and Deputy First Minister, p. 47.

Table 3.1   Council Mayors/Chairs – 2005/2006

Council	Mayor/ Chairperson	Deputy Mayor/ Chairperson
Antrim Borough Council	Drew Ritchie (UUP)	Samuel Dunlop (DUP)
Ards Borough Council	Terry Williams (DUP)	Angus Carson (UUP)
Armagh City and District Council	John Campbell (SDLP)	William Irwin (DUP)
Ballymena Borough Council	Tommy Nicholl (DUP)	James Alexander (DUP)
Ballymoney Borough Council	Cecil Cousley (DUP)	Ian Stevenson (DUP)
Banbridge District Council	Jim McElroy (DUP)	Patrick McAleenan (SDLP)
Belfast City Council	Wallace Browne (DUP)	Pat Convery (SDLP)
Carrickfergus Borough Council	David Hilfitch (DUP)	Eric Ferguson (UUP)
Castlereagh Borough Council	Tommy Jeffers (DUP)	Geraldine Rice (AP)
Coleraine Borough Council	Timothy Deans (DUP)	Maura Hickey (SDLP)
Cookstown District Council	Patsy McGlone (SDLP)	Ian McCrea (DUP)
Craigavon Borough Council	George Savage (UUP)	Robert Smith (DUP)
Derry City Council	Lynn Flemming (SF)	Mary Hamilton (UUP)
Down District Council	Carmel O'Boyle (SDLP)	Eamonn McConvery (SF)
Dungannon and South Tyrone Borough Council	Francie Molloy (SF)	Norman Badger (UUP)
Fermanagh District Council	Stephen Huggett (SF)	Gerry Gallagher (SDLP)

Larne Borough Council	John Mathews (AP)	Rachal Rea (DUP)
Limavady Borough Council	Michael Coyle (SDLP)	Marian Doherty (SF)
Lisburn City Council	Jonathan Craig (DUP)	Trevor Lunn (AP)
Magherafelt District Council	Sean Kerr (SF)	Paul McLean (DUP)
Moyle District Council	Oliver McMullan (SF)	Price McConaghy (IND U)
Newry and Mourne District Council	Pat McGinn (SF)	Michael Carr (SDLP)
Newtownabbey Borough Council	William DeCourcy (DUP)	Lynn Frazer (AP)
North Down Borough Council	Roberta Dunlop (DUP)	Tony Hill (AP)
Omagh District Council	Michael McAnespie (SF)	Paddy McGowan (IND)
Strabane District Council	Brian McMahon (SF)	Charlie McHugh (SF)

imbued with powerful political symbolism, with wider constitutional ramifications. In the absence of any other democratic forum for long periods since 1973, local government became a laboratory for power-sharing arrangements, which were later to form the whole edifice of the Belfast Agreement. How chairs, mayors and lord mayors played out their respective roles at the local level influenced the prospects of securing a workable power-sharing Assembly with major functional responsibilities. In short, the part played by local heads of state in the Northern Ireland context has been disproportionately significant in the wider political and constitutional arena and well beyond a civic leadership role in relatively powerless local councils.

CHAPTER FOUR

The Mayoralty in the Republic of Ireland

Muiris MacCarthaigh and Mark Callanan

Introduction

Whilst Irish local government can be traced back to Norman times, amongst the public at large, it remains one of the least understood facets of Irish government.[1] Partly, this is because of the lack of systematic research on public-policy development at sub-national level, partly due to the complexity of the system, entwining elements of Norman, Anglo-Saxon and even American local government into its operation. A consequence of this lack of research has been that some of the oldest and most familiar elected positions of authority have never received detailed study. The Mayoralty is the most significant casualty here, which is yet more remarkable given, for example, that Dublin has had a Mayor since the early thirteenth century. Also, while there is no study of the progression of mayors to national politics, many parliamentarians have served as mayors earlier in their careers. Indeed, at the time of writing the Prime Minister or *Taoiseach* (Bertie Ahern) was Lord Mayor of Dublin in 1986 and a Cabinet colleague (Micheál Martin) was Lord Mayor of Cork in 1992.

In this chapter, we trace mayoralty's origins and development through the centuries before detailing the consolidation of the modern Mayor's role during the nineteenth and twentieth centuries. Particularly interesting here are the recent proposals regarding directly elected mayors and what we refer to as a nascent cabinet-style model of political executive in local government. These proposals generated short-lived debate over the Irish mayoralty, with some advocating stronger Mayors, others favouring the status quo. Thus far, the latter camp has triumphed, although the question remains unresolved.

Readers should note that several different terms apply to the position of 'first citizen' at Irish local level. The expression used in law is *Cathaoirleach* (literally meaning 'chairman' in the Irish language). Even in English, this expression is used day-to-day to refer to the position in many local authorities, although others use terms like 'Chairperson', 'Mayor' and in specific cases 'Lord Mayor'. With this in mind, we begin by tracing mayoral development in the early medieval period in Ireland.

---

[1]   Nonetheless, there are several relevant studies. Desmond Roche, *Local Government in Ireland* (Dublin, Institute of Public Administration, 1982) still provides detailed analysis of the legal basis for Irish local government; while Neil Collins' 1987 study *Local Government Managers at Work* (Dublin, Institute of Public Administration, 1987) is useful for understanding the role of county and city managers. However, for more recent developments, the chapters in Mark Callanan and Justin F. Keogan (eds) *Local Government in Ireland; Inside Out* (Dublin, Institute of Public Administration, 2003), p. 17 are very useful.

The First Irish Mayors

As elsewhere in Europe, Mayoralty's origins in Ireland lie in Norman attempts at public administration in municipal areas. The twelfth-century invasion of Ireland saw the rationalisation of towns and Mayors' emergence as 'chief executive officers' of the King and his barons, along with courts and councils.[2] At the local level, the representative of central legal authority was the county 'high sheriff', who executed the law and supervised parliamentary elections. His legal duties were conducted in conjunction with local magistrates. Sheriffs also selected 23-member 'grand juries' for each county, whose function was to perform local judicial and later administrative functions (including taxation). The Lord Lieutenant appointed the sheriffs, although there was always suspicion of political involvement in such appointments.[3]

Administratively, early-medieval Ireland was divided into townlands, parishes, baronies, counties and provinces. As parishes were little used, townlands became the smallest unit of local governance and were grouped to form baronies. These were themselves sub-units of the county and counties combined to form provinces. The county and province boundaries largely survive to this day, although contemporary provincial boundaries have sporting rather than administrative significance. The 'county' was the principal administrative unit outside urban areas. However, towns tended to emerge independently of counties, thereby producing administrative overlaps continuing to this day.

Towns were presented with royal charters conferring self-governing privileges and requiring them to elect a Mayor (also sometimes known as a provost, portreeve or sovereign). The Mayor, along with his clerk and other officers, formed the town's senior management and controlled its judicial, military and economic affairs. A quasi-representative assembly held some legislative powers and acted in conjunction with the mayor. However, the electorate was traditionally limited to the propertied and business classes.

While smaller towns were closely connected with county administration, particularly the High Sheriff, larger towns had greater independence, manifested in the fact that such towns enjoyed their own court sittings. Relatively speaking, the Mayoralty was a significant position of authority and holders were endowed with various duties. A principal function was to protect civil liberties. However, over time, and when necessary, Mayors in different municipal towns also undertook other occasional administrative duties, such as coroner, clerk of the markets, corporation treasurer, keeper of the jail, town clerk, Parliamentary returning officer or even county clerk of the peace. In this regard, the Mayor could be seen as chief officer in an urban administration. Commonly, mayors also supervised weights and measures – thus ensuring Irish medieval economic life was to some extent regulated.

Mayors could also enter the judicial sphere, presiding over certain courts like Petty and Quarter Sessions. During such occasions, the town clerk acted as Court Clerk. This

---

    [2]   Richard Haslam, 'The Origins of Irish Local Government', in Callanan and Keogan, *Local Government in Ireland*, p. 17.

    [3]   Virginia Crossman, *Local Government in Nineteenth Century Ireland* (Institute of Irish Studies: Queen's University Belfast, 1994), p. 7.

practice underlined the close relationship between the Mayor's administrative and judicial functions, also common in other Norman-influenced systems. Indeed, before 1974, mayors in England and Wales were also Justices of the Peace while in office.

The honour of having a Lord Mayor was first bestowed on Dublin. The office of Mayor was created in 1229, following Henry III's charter, empowering Dublin's citizens to elect such an officer. The first Town Clerk, whose role was to prepare legal documents and keep the electoral register, was also appointed with the first Mayor. The Mayor presided at quarterly meetings of the Dublin City Assembly, which became primarily concerned with issues of trade like weights and measures and ferry services.

The members of Dublin City Assembly were elected by the freemen, who themselves all belonged to the city's trade guilds. The Assembly met once every quarter and consisted of the Mayor (later Lord Mayor), two Sheriffs, 24 Aldermen, 48 Sheriffs' Peers and 96 Commons. The Lord Mayor and Aldermen formed the Upper House of Dublin City Assembly and in the mid-fifteenth century began meeting separately. The Sheriffs, Sheriffs' Peers and Commons formed the Lower House and met separately from the early-eighteenth century onwards. The Assembly was abolished by the 1840 Municipal Corporations Reform (Ireland) Act and was replaced by Dublin City Council from November 1841.[4]

The office of Mayor in Dublin was elevated to Lord Mayor in 1665 and incumbents were ex-officio members of the Irish Privy Council. However, new regulations in 1672 required that future Lord Mayors of Dublin receive the approval of the Lord Lieutenant,[5] the monarch's representative in Dublin. In 1760, constitutional changes to the City Assembly included a provision that the city's Lower House or 'common council' approve the successful Lord-Mayoral candidate before he assumed office.[6] As of 2005, the capital has had 336 mayors, only five of which have been women. Cork City had its first provost appointed in 1199 during the reign of King John and the title Mayor was not used until 1273. In 1900, along with Belfast, the City acquired its first Lord Mayor.

The Mayor in Nineteenth Century Irish Local Government

The nineteenth century was a tumultuous one for the Irish Mayoralty, as well as local government more generally. The 1800 Act of Union had abolished the Irish Parliament in Dublin, and a reduced number of Irish MPs now took seats at Westminster. The decrease in the number of parliamentary constituencies saw many corporations and corporate boroughs abolished.[7] Furthermore, as the century progressed, the development of new institutions began eroding Mayoral authority at the local level.

---

[4]   We are grateful to Mary Clark and Padraic O'Brien in the Dublin City Archives for this information.

[5]   Also known as the Viceroy.

[6]   http://www.dublincity.ie/your_council/history/0060_office_of_lord_mayor.asp.

[7]   Crossman, *Local Government in Nineteenth Century Ireland*, p. 4.

The new institutions included bodies of elected 'commissioners' who took over local functions like water provision and street lighting. Similarly, following a Commission of Inquiry in 1836, the 1838 Poor Relief (Ireland) Act was introduced. This divided the country into Unions, each administered by a Board of Guardians under the overall control of the Poor Law Commissioners in Dublin. By 1851, 130 Unions were established. The Guardians also emerged to manage workhouses, public health and housing issues. Commissioners could hold office for three years and be re-elected. However, as Crossman notes, the existence of town commissioners did not guarantee proper municipal administration and an 1878 parliamentary committee report on local government in towns noted that, in some Irish towns, the commissioners had abdicated their functions.[8]

In rural areas, the grand jury was the most important local body and continued to hold the power to set rates known as the 'cess'. Attempts at regulating this system of local taxation tended to fail and by the early-nineteenth century allegations of grand-jury corruption were rife.[9] Although local authorities in England and Wales were reformed by the Municipal Corporations Act, 1835, it took another five years before the Municipal Corporations (Ireland) Act, 1840 similarly reshaped Irish local governance. The 1840 legislation followed an 1835 Royal Commission report who had concluded that complete reform was required.[10] The Act abolished all existing municipal corporations, reconstituting only 10 as borough councils, including Dublin, Cork, Limerick and Belfast.[11] Such bodies also lost powers of appointment, which were given to the Lord Lieutenant. In terms of the Mayoralty, the Act created in each new urban authority a corporate body consisting of mayor, aldermen and councillors.

The revamped local authorities began assuming new functions in the fields of taxation, public health and poor relief in consequence of the 1840 Act. However, as local authority responsibilities expanded, there was no corresponding increase in those of Mayors, who remained largely ceremonial. Some towns had no local authority following the abolition of their corporations. However, they regained a form of local authority under the 1854 Towns Improvement Act.

The 1840 Act added further administrative layers to an increasingly chaotic local government system, which failed miserably to deal with the catastrophic famine of 1840–1845 and its consequences. As Crossman indicates, local government was a source of significant grievance amongst the Irish Catholic majority during the nineteenth century.[12] Members of the Protestant gentry held almost all positions of authority at local level and resultant dissatisfactions fuelled mass movements for reform headed, amongst others, by Daniel O'Connell. In 1841, following the

---

[8]   ibid., p. 69.

[9]   Roche, *Local Government in Ireland*, p. 30.

[10]   Crossman, *Local Government in Nineteenth-Century Ireland*, p. 77.

[11]   The others were Londonderry/Derry, Drogheda, Kilkenny, Sligo, Waterford and Clonmel. Wexford was incorporated in 1845 after petition to the lord lieutenant, a procedure provided for under the Act.

[12]   ibid., p. 1.

franchise extension under the 1840 Act, O'Connell became Dublin's first Catholic Lord Mayor since Terence McDermott in 1690.

If the century's first half was characterised by the inefficiency and corruption of the grand jury system, the second saw significant expansions in local governmental responsibilities. Furthermore, the push for Irish Home Rule was not halted by proposals for local government reform in 1884, which were rejected. As central government in London presented local authorities with increasing numbers of duties, significant overlap in functions emerged, resulting in the 1898 Local Government (Ireland) Act. As before, the Act adapted to Irish purposes an earlier English counterpart, namely, the 1888 Local Government Act.

The 1898 Act radically reformed the system of rural local governance areas so that it resembled structures in England and Wales. As Knox points out in his chapter, the Act effectively introduced a two-tier system of local government, with county boroughs and county councils as the upper tier and urban district, rural district councils and town commissioners as the lower one. However, in cities and towns, existing structures, including the Mayoralty, hardly changed. The Act mainly sought to transfer grand jury powers in the counties to representative county councils. These consisted of a Chairperson (rather than Mayor) and councillors. Six cities (including two in what was to become Northern Ireland) were made county boroughs where corporations had almost all the functions of a county council as well as those of a borough corporation.[13] Also, the Act created new Urban District Councils (UDCs), with marginally fewer powers than borough councils.

Heads of borough councils retained the title of Mayor, while the UDCs had 'chairmen'. In terms of rating, all powers to strike a rate were given to the county councils. The 1898 Act also extended the local franchise to all those eligible to vote in parliamentary elections and the new councils elected in 1899 were more representative of the Catholic population than ever before. These elections were also the first in Ireland where women (albeit over 30 years of age) had the right to vote.[14]

It should be recognised that, as the nineteenth century progressed, elections for local authority offices became the norm, although the franchise was limited to male property owners, with a yearly rate of at least £10. Positions as town commissioners, poor law guardians and municipal councillors began being occupied by nationalist Catholic politicians and, fuelled by growing agitation for political independence from the United Kingdom, local elections took on a nationalist flavour. Throughout this period, the mayoralty remained an indirectly elected position, held for one year at a time.

Mayors from the Irish Free State to the Present

Local government played an important part in the Irish War of Independence 1919–1921, as the various authorities transferred their allegiance from the Local

---

[13] Roche, *Local Government in Ireland*, p. 45.

[14] Pauric Travers, 'A Bloodless Revolution: The Democratisation of Irish Local Government 1898–1899', in *County and Town: One Hundred Years of Local Government in Ireland* (Dublin, Institute of Public Administration, 2001), p. 15.

Government Board[15] to the subversive Irish parliament – Dáil Éireann. In fact, the idea had been mooted that the General Council of County Councils, still one of the representative bodies for local authorities at national level, would be suitable as the new Irish parliament. However, a Westminster-style bicameral legislature was created instead. The 1921 Treaty establishing the Irish Free State partitioned the island of Ireland, with six counties and two county boroughs (cities) being incorporated into the new entity of Northern Ireland. In the remaining area of 27[16] counties and four county boroughs,[17] the perception that local government, a vestige of British authority, could not be trusted to act responsibly informed official thinking. In any event, a subversive Dáil Department of Local Government was established in 1920 to replace the British system of local government oversight.

The 1920 local election had seen Sinn Féin and their Labour allies win handsomely over the nationalist Irish Party. In this election, the mayoralty was used to publicise the republican cause, and also the imprisonment of prominent republicans. For example, a Sinn Féin candidate, Thomas Kelly, had actually been elected Lord Mayor of Dublin in 1920, but as the candidate was in prison in Britain, Alderman O'Neill (see below) was re-elected to the post. Similarly, the Mayor of Clonmel was in prison when elected in 1920. In Cork City, great controversy surrounded the Lord Mayor's office in 1920, when the incumbent Tomás MacCurtain was killed during the Irish War of Independence. His successor, Terence McSwiney, was arrested later that year and jailed in Britain where he died following an attempt to force-feed him during a hunger strike.

After the 1922–1923 Civil War, the Mayor's position, though comparatively powerless, continued to provide a useful platform for making such symbolic as well as political statements. Knox in chapter 3 identifies a similar phenomenon in Northern Ireland during the period of the 'Troubles', particularly with the election of Belfast City's first Sinn Féin Mayor in 2002.

As with political offices throughout the new State, competition for the position of Mayor became a site of both compromise and contention. For example, in January 1922, contests occurred in many municipal authorities, including over city Lord Mayors. In Dublin City, Alderman Laurence O'Neill was elected for the sixth consecutive time, stating he did not belong to a political party and would be a Lord Mayor 'of the city and the citizens as a whole'. A supporter noted that:

> In addition to the discharge of his duties in a way becoming the dignity of his office, Mr O'Neill had been most successful with regard to labour troubles, and had brought the contending parties together in a manner [that I doubt] anyone else in Dublin could have done.[18]

Another councillor praised him for being 'a genius for settling strikes … the greatest man for settling strikes the country had ever seen'. However, much bitter debate surrounded mayoral elections elsewhere during this period preceding the Civil War.

---

[15]   The Local Government Board acted as a central co-ordinating and grant-aiding organisation.

[16]   Tipperary County had been divided in 1838 into two 'ridings' or county areas.

[17]   Dublin, Cork, Limerick and Waterford.

[18]   *The Irish Times*, 31st January 1922, p. 5.

For example, in Sligo Corporation, a Republican Labour candidate defeated a Free State Labour councillor for the position, stating that the only legitimate government in the State was the 'Republican Government'.[19]

The Irish Free State's violent birth and the subsequent 1922–1923 Civil War had profound centripetal effects on government and administration. Garvin argues local Government was regarded as 'a British invention, expensive, anti-national, and incompetent' and the new Dublin government sought to assert control from the centre.[20] Consequently, Irish local concerns have been traditionally transmitted through national rather than local representatives; a phenomenon facilitated by an electoral system encouraging clientelist-style politics. Garvin also noted that the newly independent Free State government proceeded to create one of the most centralised systems in Europe, observing this to be 'a characteristic outcome of revolution; successful revolutionaries like to keep the reins of power in their own hands'.[21]

Troublesome local authorities were dissolved and commissioners appointed to run their affairs. Kerry County Council was dissolved in 1923, followed by Cork and Dublin Corporations in 1924. In fact, a 'Greater Dublin Commission' was established in 1924 which recommended a much smaller number of councillors be elected, and that the position of Lord Mayor disappear, along with his 'Swordbearer, his Macebearer, and his Marshall'.[22] Presumably, this was because of their close association with British monarchy. However, these somewhat radical recommendations were not implemented immediately and the title Lord Mayor remains in use today.

The Free State government abolished the Rural District Councils established by the 1898 Act, along with Boards of Guardians. While the Irish Privy Council was abolished upon independence in 1922, the 'Right Honourable' title used by its members was retained by the Lord Mayor in Dublin. However, with the new administration seeking to establish control over the fledgling State, 20 local authorities had been replaced with commissioners by 1925, including Dublin and Cork. A Local Appointments Commission was also established in 1926 to prevent nepotism or malpractice in local public sector recruitment.

By 1940, 11 boroughs existed in the Free State. Eight had survived since 1840 (Dublin, Cork, Limerick, Drogheda, Kilkenny, Sligo, Waterford and Clonmel), while Wexford had gained this status in 1845 and Acts of the Oireachtas[23] had granted it to Dún Laoghaire (1930) and Galway (1937). In these local authorities, 'corporations' existed comprising the citizens, the Mayor, and the elected representatives. However, in counties and urban district councils, the 'corporation'

---

[19]   *The Irish Times*, 31st January 1922, p. 5.

[20]   Tom Garvin, *1922: The Birth of Irish Democracy* (Dublin: Gill and Macmillan, 1996), p. 90.

[21]   Tom Garvin, 'The Dáil Government and Irish Local Democracy 1919–1923', in M. Daly (ed.) *County and Town: One Hundred Years of Local Government in Ireland* (Dublin, Institute of Public Administration, 2001), pp. 33–4.

[22]   Eunan O'Halpin, 'The Origins of City and County Management', in *City and County Management: A Retrospective* (Dublin: Institute of Public Administration, 1991), p. 9.

[23]   The Irish law-making body, comprising the two Houses of Parliament and the Office of the President.

consisted of the elected council alone, including the Chairperson.[24] The distinction between borough corporations and urban district councils was largely ceremonial, the borough earning the right to use the title of 'mayor' for the chairperson of the elected council. Interestingly, in terms of protocol at ceremonial occasions in Dublin city, the Lord Mayor takes precedence over the *Taoiseach* (Prime Minister), but not over the President, the directly elected head of state.

However, more importantly for mayors and other chairpersons in the new State, by the 1930s a new system of management, adapted from the US model, had emerged. It introduced a completely new entity, and the county or city manager became a legally constituted part of Irish local governmental life. An account of the situation of Mayors and chairs in Ireland would be incomplete without referring to this rather unique position, regarded by one commentator as 'perhaps Ireland's major invention in the field of government'.[25]

There is a legal separation of powers within modern Irish local government between the responsibilities of elected councils and those of the manager. Formally, the manager has extensive legal powers of decision-making. Local authority decisions are divided into reserved and executive functions. The law clearly defines those of elected members as 'reserved functions'. Any other responsibility, not so designated, is automatically deemed an 'executive function' – and thus belonging to county/city managers or their nominees from amongst the local authority's staff.

Reserved functions include adopting annual local authority budgets, borrowing money, making or revoking local bylaws, adopting local development plans or schemes of letting priorities for public housing. Essentially, the intention was to clearly delineate elected members' responsibilities to determine the 'policy framework' for the local authority. County/city managers must operate within this framework established by the elected representatives, from administrative matters such as determining planning applications, to allocating local authority housing. The manager must also advise the council and thus has a right to attend all meetings, although he/she cannot vote.

Unlike US city managers, who are hired (and can be fired) by elected members, Irish local councils are not involved in recruiting county or city managers – this is carried out on a non-political basis through a central, independent agency. However, for mayoral elections, special procedures exist. All candidates for Mayor must be proposed at the outset of the local authority's annual meeting, with the candidate getting the least number of votes being eliminated at each stage until there are only two left.[26] If there is a tie, a decision is taken by lot – rare but not unknown.

The Mayor's role and local authority powers generally did not alter significantly before the 1990s. However, the 1991 Advisory Expert Committee Report on Local Government Reform (the so-called 'Barrington Report'),[27] was a landmark for Irish

---

[24]   Roche, *Local Government in Ireland*, p. 72.

[25]   Basil Chubb, *A Source Book of Irish Government* (Dublin, Institute of Public Administration, 1983), p. 150.

[26]   Roche, p. 116.

[27]   Barrington Report, *Local Government Reorganisation and Reform – Report of the Advisory Expert Committee* (Dublin: Stationery Office, 1991).

local government. Although some of the more important recommendations were not accepted by central government, many found their way into subsequent legislation and the 1996 Government White Paper, *Better Local Government*, which has been progressively implemented since then.

Interestingly, one recommendation was to continue with the election of Mayor by the elected council,[28] but extend the term of office from one to three years, renewable for the final two years of the council's life. The main motivation was apparently to increase mayoral visibility, the report arguing that the extended term:

> would have the effect of greatly enhancing the role of the Mayor or chairperson to correspond with the proposal for a greater local government role generally and should help to encourage wider interest and participation in local government.[29]

However, this recommendation was not implemented due to opposition from many local councillors who preferred to retain the system of annually elected Mayors, which allowed for the office to be distributed amongst more members (see also the discussion on proposals for directly-elected mayors below).

The Contemporary Mayor

In order to appreciate the Mayor's role in the contemporary Irish Republic, we should describe the current shape of local government. As of 2005, the structures include:

- *29 County and 5 City Councils.* Both have similar ranges of functions. Before 2002, city councils were known as county borough councils. The county and city councils are legally the primary units of local government, and together cover Ireland's entire territory;
- *75 Town and 5 Borough Councils* – These have lesser functions than counties and cities, and do not cover the country's entire area. In 2002, these had replaced urban district councils, boards of town commissioners and borough corporations.

Since 1999, local government has been formally recognised in the Republic's written constitution, including the stipulation that local elections are held every five years. However, the Irish Republic is traditionally regarded as highly centralised, certainly compared to most other European Union countries, with its local government generally possessing a narrow range of functions.[30] Local authorities in most EU countries provide at least some services, notably social services, education and

---

[28] Two members of the committee however argued in favour of local authorities introducing an elected 'chief executive', either by local council decision, or citizens' initiative from 5 per cent of electors.

[29] Barrington Report, 1991, p. 41.

[30] See for example Mark Callanan, 'Where Stands Local Government?', in Callanan and Keogan (eds) *Local Government in Ireland*), pp. 475–501; John Loughlin (ed.), *Sub-national Democracy in the European Union* (Oxford University Press, 2001), p. 65 and 79; and Neil Collins and Aodh Quinlivan, 'Multi-level governance', in J. Coakley and M. Gallagher (eds), *Politics in the Republic of Ireland*, (London, Routledge, 2005), p. 389.

healthcare, which in Ireland are provided either by central government departments or state agencies operating within state-determined policy parameters.

Nevertheless, Irish local authorities still provide some key public services, including social housing, waste management, roads and traffic, planning and development, water supply and treatment, libraries, parks and leisure facilities, promoting local arts, fire services. They have also had a 'general competence' since 1991 and some have quietly acquired enhanced roles in areas like social inclusion, heritage and conservation, childcare, environmental awareness and providing broadband infrastructure in rural areas.[31]

In terms of the mayoralty, currently all local councils annually elect the Chairperson (the Cathaoirleach) or Mayor from amongst their members. The 2001 Local Government Act, in consolidating a plethora of previous legislation into one statute, declared that Dublin and Cork would use the title Lord Mayor, while other city and borough councils would call their chairpersons Mayors. County and town councils would continue to use the Irish language title of *Cathaoirleach* (literally Chairman), but under the 2001 Act could adopt the more internationally recognised title of mayor. Quite a number of county and town councils have taken this option, although many still use the title *Cathaoirleach*, which remains the phrase used in law.

Legislation in 1994 disbarred national parliament members from becoming Mayors, while Ministers and Ministers of State had been barred altogether from local council membership since 1991.[32] Since 2003, members of the national parliament cannot consecutively hold office as local councillors (the so-called 'dual mandate').

The Mayor is generally considered a ceremonial position in the Irish Republic. Councillors do not see their mayor as having a policy-making role – the office carries few of the executive responsibilities often evident elsewhere in Europe. Indeed, many accounts see county/city managers as the main sources of policy initiation.[33] Mayors can take initiatives in some restricted areas, but usually this must be followed by council agreement. For example, they can *propose* to confer a civic honour on an individual, but the full council must make the decision. Other examples would include rights to information in certain circumstances or to call meetings. For example:

- Mayors may request information from county/city managers about any local authority activity;
- Mayors may call special council meetings, either on their own initiative or after a request by five or more council members;
- If the local authority administration has to incur additional expenditure in emergencies (for example to minimise a threat to public health) beyond that authorised by the council's annual budget, the Mayor must be informed and given

---

[31]   Tony Larkin, 'Coping with Complexity: Implications of the transition from local government to local governance for management styles', *Administration*, 2004, 52, 1, 15.

[32]   Liam Kenny, 'Local Government and Politics', pp. 103–22 in Callanan and Keogan (eds) *Local Government in Ireland*, p. 114.

[33]   Neil Collins (1987), p. 68; Basil Chubb, *The Government and Politics of Ireland* (London: Longman 1992), p. 278; Collins and Quinlivan, 'Multi-level governance', pp. 390–91.

details 'without delay' and council members told at the next practicable meeting;
- The provisions on declarations of interest, and ethics and standards in public office, provide that in cases of possible contraventions by municipal employees these are brought to the county/city manager's attention. But where the potential miscreants are elected members or indeed managers, the matter is referred to the Mayor, who may initiate an investigation, disciplinary procedures, or refer the matter to the Director of Public Prosecutions.

Mayors in Practice

As noted, councils elect their Mayors annually, normally in June. While there is nothing legally preventing consecutive re-election, this is unusual even though it sometimes happens. As Kenny points out, even on the relatively rare occasions where a single party controls a council, the mayoralty 'is rotated among party members with one taking the chair for a year at a time'.[34] However, rotation has only become the norm the last 25 years or so. Prior to that, it was quite common for a member to hold the position for several years at a time. While no research has been conducted, there may well be a relationship between this development and the advent of chair and Mayoral allowances in local authorities, although it must be noted that the financial rewards are modest. Another possible reason is that holders of the office of Mayor can expect relatively high levels of media coverage and earning the title can represent a useful staging post for those with ambitions of entering national politics.

In practice, coalitions are usually the norm in local councils and the Mayoralty is usually rotated between participating parties which tend to display tight discipline during such annual mayoral elections. However, discipline over policy issues in Irish local government is arguably less tightly enforced than at national level and issues pertaining to individual electoral areas can cause shifting voting patterns and internal party divisions. Nevertheless, the Mayoralty is usually allocated along party rather than geographical lines and party seniority provides an advantage.

In Dublin, a recent development has been the establishment of a 'Lord Mayor's Commission' to address particular issues of concern. Such Commissions have no legal underpinning and their success depends on Mayoral persuasion. Their work is legitimised by the Lord Mayor's ceremonial status as the city's civic head. Issues examined so far have included crime and community policing, local government financing and housing. The perceived success of these initiatives depends on whether the issue can grab the public eye. Dublin has also instituted a Lord Mayor's Award, recognising the work of those making special contributions to the community. However, it remains the case that Mayoral influence relates more to the incumbent's ability to pursue his/her agenda rather than any formal powers.

---

[34]   Liam Kenny (ed.), *From Ballot Box to Council Chamber: A Guide to Ireland's County, City and Town Councillors 2004–2009* (Dublin: Institute of Public Administration and General Council of County Councils, 2004), p. 15.

The Mayor and Nascent Cabinet Structures in Irish Local Government

As well as chairing council meetings, mayors also preside over meetings of smaller groupings known as Corporate Policy Groups (CPGs). CPGs consist of the Mayor and chairs of council committees in key service areas – the Strategic Policy Committees (SPCs). These committees contain a mix of councillors and nominees from local stakeholders, community and voluntary groups, although elected councillors always chair them.[35] SPC chairmanships are distributed according to party strength, tending to ensure that most parties on the council are represented within the CPG, which usually consists of five or six members.

The CPG's work is supported by the county/city manager. The 1996 White Paper on local government reform stated that CPGs would link the work being done by council committees, have specific roles in preparing annual budgets, the five-year corporate plan of the local authority (coinciding with the electoral cycle) and generally provide forums where policy positions can be agreed for submission to full council.[36] CPGs were established in each county and city council during 1998–1999, offering Mayors the chance to further involve themselves in policy formulation and implementation.

Subsequent legislation in 2001 enabled CPGs to request their manager to report on any matter related to local authority functions. In such cases, Mayors can direct managers (and their staff) to cease for up to three months any act relevant to the subject being reported on until the next council meeting. A survey in 2002 of county and city managers found that a majority felt that the CPG, chaired by the Mayor, was starting to act as a forum for direction on council priorities, discussing progress and informing members on key policy issues.[37] A separate review in 2004 found that in practice, CPGs meet in advance of council meetings, amongst other things to discuss the issues, problem areas and points of conflict likely to arise – the overall impression being that the grouping mostly acts as a 'sounding board'.[38] However, even though it has not yet fully developed into this role, Callanan[39] argues this was a clear attempt to introduce 'cabinet-style' formations into local government – possibly evolving into stronger political executives in the future, given the trend in local government internationally to strengthen political executives either through elected mayors or cabinet-based systems.

---

[35]   For further details see Institute of Public Administration (2004), *Review of the Operation of Strategic Policy Committees* (Dublin: Institute of Public Administration); and M. Callanan, (forthcoming), 'Institutionalizing Participation and Governance: New Participative Structures in Local Government in Ireland', *Public Administration*, pp. 83–4.

[36]   Department of the Environment (1996), *Better Local Government – A Programme for Change* (Dublin: Stationery Office), p. 19; Justin F. Keogan, 'Reform in Irish Local Government in Callanan and Keogan (eds), *Local Government in Ireland*, p. 90.

[37]   Richard Boyle, Peter C. Humphreys, Orla O'Donnell, Joanna O'Riordan and Virpi Timonen, *Changing Local Government: A Review of the Local Government Modernisation Programme*, CPMR Research Report No. 5 (Dublin: Institute of Public Administration 2003), pp. 34–5.

[38]   Institute of Public Administration, *Review of the Operation of Strategic Policy Committees*, (Dublin, Institute of Public Administration, 2004), p. 37.

[39]   Mark Callanan, 'Local and regional government in transition', in N. Collins and T. Cradden (eds), *Political issues in Ireland today* (Manchester University Press, 2004), pp. 64, 75.

A New Departure? – Proposals for Political Leadership at Local Level

The Mayoral powers outlined above are modest compared to other jurisdictions. However, Irish local government has not been immune to debates about strengthening local government executives evident elsewhere in Europe and beyond.[40] In this regard, the original provisions of the Local Government Act 2001 are particularly interesting. They provided that, from 2004, county and city council chairpersons would be directly elected by the local population, and hold office for five years. Mayoral elections would occur on the same day as those for local councils, and Mayors could not hold office for more than two consecutive terms (10 years). This reform would not apply to town and borough councils, which would still annually elect their Mayors.

The initiative was very much seen as coming from the then Minister responsible for local government, but was not overwhelmingly welcomed by local or indeed national politicians. One curiosity was that the legislation proposed no additional powers for Mayors, despite their being directly elected and serving much longer terms. The provisions generated much comment in the national parliament. One Senator remarked:

> In theory it is a great idea to have someone who, with the mandate of the people, is given the role to serve as chair of the county or city council for five years. Unless that office is given some powers of initiative or enabled to cope with the executive powers of the manager, it is an empty role.[41]

However, the Minister behind the initiative, Noel Dempsey TD, argued the enhanced mandate would in itself make the position stronger, explicitly highlighting examples from other countries. He argued direct election would increase mayoral accountability and visibility, and that incumbents would be able to draw on:

> powerful democratic legitimacy to speak and negotiate on behalf of the whole community with influence well beyond any formal powers and with the capacity to bring together the various elements of local governance. Experience elsewhere bears this out if the opportunities being presented are grasped and acted upon in a spirit of collaboration for the common good.[42]

It was also argued that the position would provide a personification for county and city councils, and give local authorities more visible presence in their areas, given that Mayors would serve longer terms – the implicit suggestion being that many citizens were unaware of who their Mayor was. Less frequently cited, though perhaps equally important, was that mayors, elected 'at large', could be a voice for

---

[40]   See for example Peter John (2001), *Local Governance in Western Europe* (London: Sage, 2001), chapter 7; Herwig Reynaert, Kristof Steyvers, Pascal Delwit and Jean-Benoit Pilet (eds), *Revolution or Renovation? Reforming Local Politics in Europe* (Brugge: Vanden Broele 2005), chapters 2 and 3; Bas Denters and Lawrence E. Rose (eds), *Comparing Local Governance: Trends and Developments* (Basingstoke: Palgrave Macmillan 2005), various contributions and chapter 15.

[41]   Senator Kathleen O'Meara, *Seanad Debates*, 10 July 2001, Vol. 167: col. 1362.

[42]   *Dáil Debates*, 8 March 2001, Vol. 532: col. 833.

city- or county-wide issues and cut across traditional rivalries, or fiefdoms, based on personality in individual wards or electoral areas.

To some extent, the concept of directly-elected mayors in the 2001 Act was an attempt to redress the balance between elected members (local government's political dimension) and county/city managers (its administrative dimension). This process had begun with legislation in 1955, giving new powers to elected councils over their administrations and continued with other changes in the 1990s to introduce fixed-term contracts for county/city managers. The 2001 Act was arguably a further shift in this direction. While the Mayor was given no new powers, the creation of a full-time position, with a five year long direct mandate from the electorate must be seen as modifying (or at least disturbing) the traditional council-manager relationship. Other changes in the Act, including the provisions on the Corporate Policy Group, though less high profile, heralded a similar shift.

Despite this, some national and local politicians clearly lamented the potential passing of an honorific role that could be distributed to 'deserving' local elected members. One Senator, during the Bill's passage, commented:

> the idea of direct election is not agreeable to 90 per cent of elected members ... local communities elect the people whom they believe are capable. The people concerned select their chairman, deputy-chairman, deputy-mayor, mayor and lord mayor ... It has allowed for individuals to be honoured by their own for one year to act in an honorary position representing their cities or counties ... It is one of the greatest honours that a local elected member can receive. This Bill would mean that this system would end. Are we replacing these individuals with people who have more responsibility or authority? The answer is no, we are not.[43]

The local government representative associations had proposed that Mayoral candidates should be outgoing members of their councils, or have served five years there, before being eligible. This proposal resulted from widespread perceptions that mayoral elections could effectively turn into 'beauty contests' between local celebrities or sports stars, or become dominated by campaigners on single-issues like incinerators or local hospital closures. However, restricting the field of candidates was thought to carry constitutional difficulties and therefore not included. Thus the Mayoralty would be open to all interested candidates. Indeed, for some contemporary elected members, the extended five-year term of office was almost as significant as the enhanced democratic status direct election would bring.[44]

The 2001 provisions did produce some debate on the merits or otherwise of elected mayors. A public event organised jointly by statutory and community organisations in 2003, presented some of the advantages and disadvantages. The prevailing view was that because the position changes every year, the mayoralty does not have much public visibility. Some supporters of direct election argued the Mayor would thereby acquire both influence and visibility, as well as greater continuity from the five year term. The argument was also that open elections would be preferable to 'back-room' deals between parties. Furthermore, given the general

---

[43]   Senator Fintan Coogan, *Seanad Debates*, 10 July 2001, Vol. 167: col. 1343.

[44]   Mark Callanan, 'Directly Elected Mayors: To be or not to be?', *Local Authority Times*, 2003, 7, 4.

media interest in personalities, it was argued that it might generate greater interest in local politics. On the other hand, given experience in other countries, the prospect of former wrestlers or football mascots being elected was cited! It was also pointed out that many successful European cities like Barcelona have had dynamic Mayors who were not directly elected.[45]

A straw poll of 600 people in Dublin found 89 per cent favoured directly-elected Mayors, although only 55 per cent felt they should have decision-making powers and 40 per cent felt mayors should be figureheads for the city.[46] In the event, the proposal for directly elected Mayors, while passed into law in 2001, never came to anything. Subsequent legislation in 2003 effectively repealed the provisions before their projected implementation in 2004.

Several reasons may be suggested why the concept was abandoned. The initiating Minister had moved to another portfolio following national elections in 2002 and his successor was less committed to the concept. Many continued arguing that the existing system worked well and required no change. Crucially, both local councillors and national parliamentarians were united in discomfort at the idea of creating a position that, to all intents and purposes, would produce high-profile spokespersons for local areas. Furthermore, many national politicians were concerned that directly elected Mayoralties could become effective platforms for local politicians to raise their local profile, rendering themselves competitors for seats in the national parliament at future elections. In addition, the prospect of single-issue or 'personality' candidates dominating the process was not regarded as a positive development by local and national politicians.[47]

Kenny[48] also identifies several other factors leading to this decision. He noted that while some local politicians welcomed the opportunity to invigorate local government, many regarded it as depriving them of a chance to fill a much-coveted position from within the council chamber. Ultimately, the initiative was abandoned, but perhaps only temporarily. The concept of directly elected Mayors retains popularity amongst several Irish political parties, as evidenced by their manifestoes from the most recent local elections.[49] That said, while formally party policy, it is clear that even within these parties opposition to the idea remains.

The main opposition party, Fine Gael, has proposed that directly elected Mayors be piloted in the five city councils. Under these proposals, the Mayors would hold office for five years and work alongside local cabinets appointed by council majority parties or coalitions. Every cabinet member would have a portfolio and be responsible for taking

---

[45]   ibid.

[46]   ibid.

[47]   Richard Boyle, Mark Callanan, Tony McNamara, Michael Mulreany, Anne O'Keeffe, Joanna O'Riordan and Tim O'Sullivan, 'Review of Developments, Structure and Management in the Public Sector 2003', *Administration*, 2003, 51, pp. 4, 18.

[48]   Kenny, Liam, 'Local Government and Politics', pp. 103–22 in Callanan and Keogan (eds) *Local Government in Ireland*, p. 116.

[49]   Fine Gael, *Local Elections 2004* (Dublin: Fine Gael), p. 14; Labour Party, *New Councils: Labour's Plan to Reform and Remap Local Government* (Dublin: The Labour Party 2004), p. 13; Green Party – Comhaontas Glas, *Manifesto 2004: European and Local Elections* (Dublin: The Green Party), p. 13; Progressive Democrats – An Páirtí Daonlathach, *Local Elections Manifesto 2004* (Dublin: Progressive Democrats), p. 23.

executive decisions. Under such a system, 'the Mayor would be the political leader of the community, proposing policy for approval by the Council and spearheading cross-portfolio initiatives as well as initiatives in co-operation with other local authorities'.[50] While these ideas continue being debated, a more immediate potential avenue for strengthening political leadership in Irish local government is clearly contained in the Corporate Policy Group structures introduced in 1999.

Conclusions

The Irish Mayoralty remains comparatively powerless and largely ceremonial, particularly in the cities. While high sheriffs overshadowed the original town Mayors, today's Mayors must negotiate with county or city managers to progress their agendas. There has been remarkable consistency to the mayoralty in Ireland insofar as it has always been indirectly elected and subject to strong central control. It also remains true that incumbent Mayors must work hard to achieve visibility, given the lack of formal powers.

That said, recent years have seen a debate on strengthening political executives – the idea of directly elected Mayors particularly catching the public eye. However, perhaps the best prospect of strengthening political executives in Irish local government lies with the cabinet format, the structure (if not the powers) for which already exist in the nascent form of CPGs, chaired by traditional Mayors. Following the repeal of legislation on directly elected mayors in 2003, it is tempting to conclude that the idea has slipped off the agenda for the medium term. However we should not discount the possibility of the concept resurfacing in the future. Nevertheless, Irish experience shows proposals to augment the Mayoralty can encounter considerable opposition, not least from those already holding local *and* national political office.

---

[50]   Fine Gael, *Local Election*, p. 14.

CHAPTER FIVE

The End of French Mayors?

Olivier Borraz and Emmanuel Négrier

When comparing European local government heads, we customarily classify French mayors as representative of the strong-mayor type, compared to the weak mayors of northern European countries.[1] This rests on the strong influence French mayors wield, not because of their actual powers, but their degree of discretion in using these powers and their personal access to central government where they can negotiate specific measures and aid for their commune. The changes produced by the 1982–1983 Decentralisation Acts have not altered this classification, although they have contributed to significant changes in the style adopted by French mayors.[2] More recently, the 'inter-municipal revolution', which has swept across the country and seen the multiplication of institutions of cooperation between communes, has apparently reinforced mayoral status in the largest cities;[3] but could actually presage a significant change in the role of French mayors.[4] To assess the depth and meaning of such a change, we must review French mayoral history. We limit our historical analysis to the period after the 1884 Municipal Act, because this Act signals the birth of modern French local government. A general competence clause was granted to communes, which, although mostly symbolic (most powers actually rest with central government), influenced nonetheless day-to-day local government activity. The Act also provided for mayors to be elected by municipal councils (themselves elected by universal suffrage) and not chosen by State representatives anymore. In other words, communes were given political autonomy, an important decision in a centralised country whose authorities had been engaged since the Revolution in extending the State's realm to all parts of the Nation and were clearly hostile to any emerging intermediary body.

When studying French local government, observers have often assumed mayoral centrality without always providing sufficient evidence. Undoubtedly, mayors are important figures and, through multiple office-holding, can wield

---

[1]   E.C. Page and M.J. Goldsmith (eds), *Central and Local Government Relations: A comparative Analysis of West European Unitary States* (London, Sage 1987).

[2]   W. Genieys, X. Ballart and P. Valarié, 'From "Great Leaders" to Building Networks: The Emergence of a New Urban Leadership in Southern Europe?', *International Journal of Urban and Regional Research*, 28.1 (2004), pp. 183–99.

[3]   F. Baraize and F. Négrier, *L'invention politique de l'agglomération* (Paris, L'Harmattan, 2001).

[4]   O. Borraz and P. Le Galès, 'France: The Inter-municipal Revolution', in B. Denters and L.E. Rose (eds), *Comparing Local Governance. Trends and Developments* (London, Palgrave 2004), pp. 12–28.

influence far beyond their formal powers. Furthermore, they have often played determinant roles in their commune's development. Finally, mayors remains the most popular figures in the French political system, ones to whom people easily look for answers to their problems. Yet, all this only highlights what is already most evident: too rarely do analyses go beyond this first impression to actually describe how mayors have established a power base and exercised their influence since the late-nineteenth century. Moreover, numerous other aspects of local government are simply not addressed: French municipal government is based on a complex system of representation often overlooked by observers, over-eager to focus on the mayor as an easy explanatory variable.

Reinterpreting the role and power of mayors does not imply reassessing their influence, but rather describing a position more complex than is often acknowledged. In recent years, a new generation of scholars has produced analyses offering new perspectives on French local government. They highlight particularly the conditions under which mayors could build positions of authority and exercise influence within national politics. These conditions are best explored by realising that local government, as a political institution, is built around two sets of objectives: gaining political support and wielding political influence. As we shall see, these objectives are important to both the role and position of the mayor.

Building political support encompasses three types of activity: providing services to the population; integrating political parties and groups; aggregating the urban population. The first refers to the mayor and council's capacities to ensure sufficient internal coherence within local administration to provide collective goods and amenities. The second implies mayoral capacity to build political alliances and win elections. The third concerns local government's ability to represent urban society in the diversity of its social and interest groups.

Wielding influence relates to two processes: centre-periphery relations and policy-making. The first is linked to the mayor's status as agent of the State, along with the close ties established over the years with its local representatives, and his/her privileged access to central government through multiple office-holding. The second concerns local government's capacity to establish partnerships in order to produce and implement public policies. Apart from the State, which remains a major player at the local level, this capacity extends to business, local chambers of commerce, voluntary associations and other governmental levels.[5]

These two sets of objectives are evident throughout modern local governmental history. By achieving them, mayors have gained the necessary resources to exercise local authority. Furthermore, these objectives are intimately related in the day-to-day exercise of local leadership. Building partnerships with the State or private interests can produce greater political support; aggregating urban society can provide the resources necessary to influence other government levels. Nonetheless, local government must always find an equilibrium between building support and wielding influence. Mayors intent on gaining popular support, without engaging in policy partnerships, would rapidly see their position weakened. Similar risks would

---

    5   O. Négrier, 'The Changing Role of French Local Government', *West European Politics*, 22, 4 (1999), pp. 120–40.

result from negotiating with other partners the resources necessary to engage local policies while being careless about representing the interests of the local population. Interestingly enough, adjustment between these objectives is often achieved through symbolic postures and policies that are characteristic of French mayoral authority. As we shall see, these relate to decorum (the town hall's architecture, the mayor's sash, the bust of Marianne as embodiment of the Republic), rhetoric (the mayor as a mediator between his constituency and the State, the mayor as builder or entrepreneur) or decisions aimed at enhancing the city's wealth and status (urban development, sports, culture, economic development).

The equilibrium found between the two sets of objectives, although specific to each local situation, nevertheless presents some general features varying over time. Three periods can be observed. Between the end of the nineteenth century and the Second World War, the major characteristics of local government were established around mayors as local leaders influential within the State. During the next period from the beginning of the Fourth Republic to the end of the twentieth century, local government came under great pressure but stabilised the preceding characteristics into an entrepreneurial model achieving official recognition in the 1982 Decentralisation Act. In the late-twentieth century, a new level of local government has emerged, exerting strong pressure on communal authorities and their capacity to produce policies. Meanwhile, growing electoral and social fragmentation has affected the conditions under which political support is achieved. These changes have shifted power towards presidents of the new inter-municipal bodies.

We will limit our analysis to large and medium-sized communes. Given the multiplicity of communes (more than 36,000) and the fact that the vast majority have very few inhabitants (75 per cent have a population under 1,000, 98 per cent under 10,000), local government in small and very small communes has a very limited role. Today, there are roughly 250 communes with a population over 30,000: this represents one third of the French population. The fact that total numbers of communes have hardly changed over the last 100 years, even though reforms have sought to reduce them, clearly indicates local officials' enduring capacity to protect their interests within a centralised State.

Learning to Govern 1884–1939

In 1884, the Third Republic was still under construction, both as a political regime and an institutional framework promoting a Republican model within a centralised Nation-State. This context of institution-building was favourable to municipal development: the national regulatory framework within which urban authorities organised themselves and tackled issues was still incomplete, leaving important manoeuvring-space for politicised mayoral leadership. More surprisingly, mayoral influence on the building of a new national political regime also appears to have been very important: not only did they manage to negotiate laws and decrees favourable to local government; they actually helped consolidate the regime.[6]

Building Political Support through Politicisation

Politics played a decisive role in forming municipal government. The 1884 Municipal Act provided a legal framework rapidly seized by emerging political parties.[7] In this process of institutionalisation, mayors gained prominent roles, being simultaneously heads of municipal councils and administrations and local representatives of the State. But perhaps more decisive was their capacity to assemble and manage electoral coalitions.

Local government's politicisation results from the coincidence between the implementation of the Municipal Act and the emergence of political parties. This emergence, in turn, results from a late industrial revolution combined with the growth of an urban population. The emergence of a working class, legally authorised in 1884 to found trade unions and the consolidation of a petty-bourgeoisie, with its own organisations and forms of sociability, fostered the creation of a variety of political groupings, struggling to aggregate sufficient followers to gain control of municipal governments.[8] This in turn encouraged the upper classes to form their own parties. This had various effects. First, political pluralism: for the first time, different ideas, representations and values co-existed about managing urban affairs. Second, polarisation: the political spectrum came to represent conflicting social classes: in the more industrialised cities, parties mirrored opposition between labour and capitalists; in the more commercial or administrative centres, the conflict opposed petty-bourgeoisie and aristocracy. Third, after a period of intense political fragmentation between socialists (themselves initially divided between different small parties), radicals, republicans, opportunists and conservatives, the dynamics of electoral competition every four years progressively saw strong political parties being consolidated across the political spectrum.

The emergence of political parties and electoral competition marked, in turn, a process of differentiation between urban society and a political sphere progressively gaining autonomy as a distinct field, with its own rules and agenda. This can be observed on three accounts.

First, mayors were no longer chosen by the State from amongst social leaders. They were elected amongst candidates representing contrasting political programs. In other words, mayors came to represent something more abstract than social status: ideas and values, issues and commitments. Second, mayoral success depended on their capacity to combine different political groupings, representing different social and interest groups, into winning coalitions and later to keep these coalitions working during the

---

[6]   P. Le Lidec, *Les maires dans la République. L'association des maires de France, élément constitutif des régimes politiques français depuis 1907* (unpublished PhD, Université de Paris 1 Panthéon-Sorbonne 2001).

[7]   R. Lefebvre, 'Le socialisme français soluble dans l'institution municipale? Forme partisane et emprise institutionnelle: Roubaix (1892–1893)', *Revue Française de Science Politique* (2004), pp. 237–60.

[8]   M. Agulhon, *La République au village* (Paris, Plon 1970).

term of office. Third, if local officials were previously embedded in social activities and networks defining their position (clubs, freemasonry or religious movements, local newspapers), the new elites, particularly on the left, undertook to organise urban society according to their needs. Thus, socialist municipalities encouraged and often financed trade unions, voluntary associations and cooperatives. Through these, they hoped to attract resources and support for their actions and re-election.

In so doing, the political sphere began imposing its own representation of social classes and conflict on the city's social fabric and defining its own agenda. Politics was no longer an extension of local society; it aspired to organise urban society within municipal government. Mayors were key figures in this process and thereby acquired visibility.

Mayors also undertook to organise administrations fit to answer the multiple issues and demands addressed to them. During the late-nineteenth century, they often sought to build a political clientele by recruiting in large numbers. But as socialists abandoned dreams of revolution for more reformist policies after the 1905 strikes failed, they felt the need to recruit qualified personnel to provide more efficient services and amenities. After World War I, municipal governments became more bureaucratised, albeit more limitedly than State administration.[9] This evolution is highly significant, since it marks the introduction of professional recruitment practices into what remains a political organisation, in line with the depoliticised attitude adopted by mayors regarding the management of urban affairs starting in the 1920s.

Gaining influence through depoliticisation

Because of the relatively weak regulatory framework within which municipal governments started managing urban affairs, local authorities undertook a series of policy-initiatives related to urban planning, transportation, lighting, water, hygiene, housing and welfare. Such interventionism was not specific to France, but observable across Europe and often promoted by socialist municipalities. It focused on public utilities and services addressed to the working classes and the poor. Municipal activism became a trademark of left-wing cities; but more moderate, even right-wing, cities undertook similar actions.

After the First World War, these policies came under severe criticism from the *Conseil d'Etat* (the highest administrative court), concerned to limit municipal expansion in order to protect State prerogatives and the freedom of commerce and industry. During the same period, central government undertook to codify local governmental organisation, prerogatives and resources: for example personnel in 1919 and utilities in 1926. Scholars often argue this marked a process of re-centralisation.

---

[9]   J-C. Thoenig, 'La politique de l'Etat à l'égard des personnels des communes 1884–1939', *Revue Française d'Administration Publique*, n. 23 (1982); B. Dumons, G. Pollet and P-Y. Saunier, *Les élites municipales sous la IIIème République. Des villes du Sud-Est de la France* (Paris, CNRS-Editions, 1997); E. Bellanger, 'Administrer la «banlieue municipale». Activité municipale, intercommunalité, pouvoir mayoral, personnel communal et tutelle préfectorale en Seine banlieue des années 1880 aux années 1950', (Unpublished PhD, Université de Paris 8 Vincennes-Saint-Denis, 2004).

Yet, the State often regulated urban affairs using existing rules and practices: in other words, it extended to all communes rules and practices already used in some cities. Meanwhile, mayors played active roles in this process of codification. Through parliament, government and professional associations, they directly participated in the production of laws and decrees that concerned local government.[10]

To understand the nature of the 'Republican compromise' negotiated between local and national elites, two traits of the French system must be explained: multiple office-holding[11] and the need to strengthen a centralised Republican regime.

French mayors could (and actually still can) hold several political mandates, amongst which those of deputy or senator were the most prized because they gave them a professional status, salary (mayors receive a limited allowance), political resources useful to reinforce their local position, and direct access to central government. Such positions were all the more valuable in a regime where power lay mostly in parliament. From this period we see the emergence of mayoral preferences for parliamentary over presidential systems, because the former give them more influence. Furthermore, mayors could sometimes hold governmental positions. This enabled them not only to help their communes, but more significantly to defend their own interests – for example, extending their term of office from four to six years in 1926.[12]

The second trait is complementary. Because central authorities needed to consolidate a State as yet unable to affirm its authority over the entire Nation, mayors were important allies. Working with rather than against them offered central authorities the possibility of affirming this authority, preserving public order and achieving national unity. Mayors accepted these objectives and promoted them within their constituencies, but in exchange for advantages and influence over how national regulation was implemented. More generally, they achieved a clear recognition by central government of their political influence.

In consequence of these two traits, mayors came to depoliticise their behaviour. Not only did they agree to work together nationally, whatever their political affiliations, to defend their collective interests, but they also developed a local consensual rhetoric, casting aside partisanship for 'the common good'. This rhetoric, lasting late into the Fifth Republic, made it easier to work with State representatives who embodied the general interest and served to stifle local opposition.[13] One noteworthy exception was the communes conquered by the Communist Party in the Paris suburbs, which were transformed into local strongholds and showcases for communist policies.

Thus the construction of a modern centralised State occurred with the participation of local authorities actively promoting a polity in which they could gain and preserve high levels of autonomy. All the complexity of centre-periphery relations during most

---

[10] Le Lidec, *Les maires dans la République*.

[11] G. Marrel, 'L'élu et son double. Cumul des mandats et construction de l'Etat républicain en France du milieu du XIXème au milieu du XXème siècle' (Unpublished PhD, IEP de Grenoble, 2003).

[12] G. Marrel and R. Payre, 'Le temps des maires : l'allongement du mandat en 1929: une redéfinition de l'espace politique municipal', *Politix*, n. 53 (2001), pp. 59–86.

[13] M. Kesselman, *The Ambiguous Consensus; a study of local government in France* (New York, Knopf 1967).

of the twentieth century originates from this period. The result was the strong position acquired by mayors, both locally and within the political system as a whole.

The mayor between centre and periphery

The processes whereby mayors emerged as key political figures, both locally and within the State, are closely linked. Too often, they have been seen as self-evident, based on the mayor's formal position and status. We suggest that, notwithstanding these formal rules, the processes resulted from the sum of mayoral strategies in response to the necessities of local politics (bringing together winning coalitions) and the need to defend mayoral interests and those of local government). Through their capacity to build political support, mayors could wield influence and obtain from the State decisions and aid for their communes reinforcing their political base.

It is during this first period that the mayoralty acquired its resources and symbolism. Many town halls were built at the turn of the last century: by their size and style, they were designed to demonstrate municipal power. Inside, a bust of Marianne, symbol of the Republic, conveyed the municipality's attachment to the Republican State. Mayors themselves wore tricolour sashes to distinguish them from other local elected officials and personify the Republic. More generally, all the apparel, particularly during national holidays, sought to show local officials' attachment to the Republic and mobilise the population in a show of unity. Mayors played important roles in drawing their constituencies into adherence to the Republic and acceptance of State authority. In exchange for their participation, they were enabled to uphold their position and status.

The Consecration of the Mayor (1945–1992)

During the Fourth (1945–1958) and Fifth Republics, mayors achieved clear recognition of their power. Not only did they play active parts in writing two constitutions, negotiating their support for the new regimes in return for a defence of their interests; they also resisted central government attempts in the 1960s to reduce their influence and contributed to de Gaulle's defeat in 1969. Thirteen years later, the Decentralisation Acts officially granted them the autonomy within a presidential system they had been seeking since 1958.

From strongholds to fiefdoms

To build and maintain political support during the second half of the twentieth century, mayors sought to bureaucratise their administrations, diversify their representation of local interests, and establish networks and clienteles within urban society. Their success on all three counts contributed to their survival for several terms in office.

Firstly, professional status was granted to municipal personnel (via fixed conditions of recruitment and career) in 1952 – many years after State personnel. This officially ended recruitment practices more often based on personal rather than professional criteria. But it implied that mayors find new ways of establishing their authority over administrative personnel. Not only was this necessary if they wished to effectively manage their commune, but municipalities were often one of the most important employers in town. Until the 1970s, mayors encouraged internal promotion in order to establish staff loyalty and continued, when possible, to recruit locally for less qualified jobs. From the 1970s, they began recruiting more qualified personnel and, after left-wing parties conquered many cities in 1977, they favoured personnel with political affiliations.[14] This practice rapidly ceased because of the many conflicts it raised. But mayors have since retained the habit of choosing their closest collaborators, if not on a political basis, at least on a combination of professionalism and personal sympathy. Thus, when political majorities change, new mayors normally recruit new staff and dismiss the previous team, even though civil servants are protected by professional status.[15] Since the 1980s, mayors and chief executive officers (CEOs) have adopted managerial techniques designed to obtain better results from their personnel, simultaneously privatising a whole range of utilities.[16]

Mayors secondly sought to strengthen political support by composing a municipal council with representatives of urban society in its diversity. Among these councillors, deputy-mayors play a special role, long unnoticed behind the mayor's central figure.[17] They act as spokespersons or mediators between the mayor and different groups and interests, thereby building legitimacy for the mayor and municipal government. They also have specific responsibilities within local government, acting on the mayor's behalf to promote policies and answer requests, thereby working with a variety of professionals and local groups. In this way, deputy-mayors are the centres of largely informal systems of functional representation reflecting local policy networks. This is perfectly compatible with a strong personalisation of power and the fact that mayors have always enjoyed high visibility and remain the most popular political figures. Mayoral leadership is actually the more powerful since, behind the positive image of authority mayors personify, that leadership rests on a collective logic of representation through the municipal council and deputy-mayor.[18]

The third means of extending political support was through local social and political networks. Mayors adopted two strategies here. The first concerned the interests they represented, particularly when their political orientation corresponded to clearly identifiable social groups. Thus, left-wing officials worked closely with party federations, trade unions and voluntary associations,[19] while their right-wing counterparts relied more often on employers' associations, social clubs, notability

---

[14] S. Dion, *La politisation des mairies* (Paris, Economica 1986).

[15] O. Roubieu, 'Des cadres gouvernants' (Unpublished PhD, Université de Paris 1, Panthéon-Sorbonne, 1998).

[16] D. Lorrain, 'De l'administration républicaine au gouvernement urbain', *Sociologie du Travail*, n. 4 (1991), pp. 461–84.

[17] O. Borraz, *Gouverner une ville. Besançon 1959–1989* (Rennes, Presses Universitaires de Rennes 1998).

[18] E. Négrier, 'Leadership, territoire et société. Georges Frêche et Montpellier', *Sciences de la Société* n. 53 (2001), pp. 63–87.

[19] D. Lacorne, *Les notables rouges: la construction municipale de l'Union de la Gauche* (Paris, Presses de la FNSP, 1980).

networks, the Catholic Church, and chambers of commerce and industry.[20] These two modes of representation illustrated a certain type of social and political aggregation: the 'stronghold'.[21] The second strategy concerned interest groups that were not at the core of traditional mayoral electorates, but which mayors needed to neutralise or enrol if they wished to gain advantage over opponents. This strategy blurred the usual correspondence between political affiliation and social structure, resulting in the emergence of a second model: the 'fief'.[22] From the 1970s, this last model tended to dominate the more traditional logic of strongholds.

These three modes of acquiring and enlarging political support all tended to de-politicise local government in order to achieve greater effectiveness, extend mayoral power bases and incorporate as many groups as possible in a common project. This de-politicisation, contrasting with how political support was built during the first period of local government, was compensated for by re-politicising local government in its relation with the State.

Reintroducing politics

Following the first period, during which mayors 'colonised' central government to promote regulation favourable to their position and local government interests, the Fourth Republic brought little change. As a parliamentary system, it still provided mayors with resources necessary to uphold their interests and influence the production of laws and decrees. Only with the advent of the Fifth Republic has change occurred, particularly after the 1962 referendum making Presidents directly elected. Within a semi-presidential system, mayors lost their influence since Parliamentary access was no longer sufficient.[23] This signalled a period of conflict, which can be observed on two accounts.

First, a political hiatus between national and local politics: while the Gaullist and Communist parties dominated national politics, most local governments were headed by a coalition of centre-right and centre-left parties. It was only in the 1970s that local politics were nationalised, i.e. reflected the confrontation between national political parties. However, this in turn produced a clash between left-wing municipal and right-wing national governments.

Second, under de Gaulle's presidency (1958–1969), a series of reforms were launched clearly aimed at transforming local government against mayoral interests. The idea was to modernise the political system and give more voice to dynamic social

---

[20] J. Lagroye, *Société et politique. Chaban-Delmas à Bordeaux* (Paris, Pédone 1973).

[21] E. Négrier, 'Les nouveaux fiefs. Les élections municipales de 2001', *Pôle Sud* n. 15 (2001), pp. 109–18.

[22] A stronghold is a mode of political aggregation that operates locally but refers to objectives that are defined nationally. The stronghold has contributed to the politicisation of local government, notably in the communist cities surrounding Paris. The fief is, by comparison, strictly local in its definitions of issues and objectives. This implies that the mayor as political leader must mobilise different interest groups, sometimes opposed to one another, within a territory and around projects which are distinct from one city to another.

[23] Le Lidec, *Les maires dans la République*.

groups in French society against the conservative forces embodied by local elected officials. These reforms largely failed and resulted in the defeat in 1969 of de Gaulle's attempt to reform the Senate (the parliamentary chamber most representative of local government interests). These failures had two consequences. First, they revealed a system of close cooperation between local officials (the *notables*) and local State representatives (Prefects and the field services of central ministries), on which their respective legitimacy and autonomy were based.[24] This cooperation served not only to adapt national regulation to specific local settings, but also to promote the interest of local government. Notables and Prefects shared common interests in preserving a system of relations offering opportunities to defend the interests of a commune or department within a centralised State. The second consequence was a clear understanding by central authorities that any voluntary reform of local government would fail if it went against the interests of local officials.

This understanding, along with the problems resulting from ill-managed urban growth, encouraged central government to adopt more negotiated procedures.[25] From the 1970s, the use of contracts – both with other levels of government and with private actors – became a common policy-instrument for cooperation. Contractual policies rapidly spread to different domains and helped modify the symbolic hierarchy between State and local officials – even though the State retained important power resources when negotiating with mayors.

Another distinct feature during this period is the capacity shown by local government in tackling different issues. Starting just after the Second World War, mayors and deputy-mayors displayed capacities for innovation: i.e. inventing solutions to collective problems, often anticipating State intervention on issues related to housing, elderly persons and poverty. This in turn underscores a key municipal characteristic: a system which adjusts to the emergence of new issues by differentiating itself: i.e. by adding new elements to the existing structure.[26] Deputy-mayors play important roles in this strategy: their number grows after every election, and mayors can entrust them with responsibility in different policy domains. The result is a system whose effectiveness in solving different problems rests upon redundancy and overlap, given the high number of deputy-mayors and services in charge of distinct issues and the low degree of coordination between them. Mayors rarely have interests in arbitrating between their deputies or seeking to introduce more coherence between them: not only would they risk losing allies, but it would imply choosing between divergent interest groups and defining priorities, all of which would weaken the mayoral power base. On the contrary, by maintaining a highly differentiated and weakly integrated system, mayors can preserve their institution's legitimacy and protect their own positions.

---

[24]   P. Grémion, *Le pouvoir périphérique. Bureaucrates et notables dans le système politique français*, (Paris, Seuil 1976).

[25]   Lorrain, 'De l'administration républicaine au gouvernement urbain'; J-P. Gaudin, *Gouverner par contrat. L'action publique en question* (Paris, Presses de Sciences Po, 1999).

[26]   Borraz, *Gouverner une ville.*

From around 1970, this capacity to tackle different issues took a radical turn. The growth of a large urban middle class produced new political elites.[27] Unlike their predecessors, these elites strongly mistrusted State officials and traditional political parties. Active in trade unions, voluntary associations, smaller left-wing movements (and later the new Socialist Party), these *militants* gained control of many cities in 1977.[28] Their program was clearly political: to change society from the bottom up. They set out to politicise their activity in a whole series of domains, including fields of State responsibility like the economy and planning: this triggered conflicts with State representatives and clearly indicated limitations on local political autonomy. As these conflicts increased, they fostered disputes over centralisation. With the 1981 Socialist victory at the national level, substantially due to the above-mentioned changes at local level, mayors seized the opportunity to push decentralisation reform giving them more autonomy and reducing State influence.

Alongside the State, mayors now had to find other partners among political, social and economic agents to undertake policy initiatives. They began establishing partnerships across a wide range of areas. Simultaneously, they started contracting-out a number of public utilities.[29] Furthermore, cities were now competing both with each other and other levels of local government (departments and regions) to attract investors, infrastructures, middle-class households, tourists and so on.[30] This necessitated marketing strategies wherein mayors played important roles in personifying their city.[31] Finally, they reverted to more de-politicised rhetoric and styles.

The mayor as entrepreneur

Throughout this second period, the mayor acquired visibility, authority and legitimacy as an entrepreneur. This can be observed in the building of cities as the population swelled after the Second World War, the production of services and amenities during the 1960s and 1970s and later the design of policies addressed at specific parts of the population. The rhetoric that mayors employed, either as city-builders, urban-developers or later as managers of their city, assisted with this role – as did their capacity to find the necessary resources, partners and capital to achieve their objectives (often through multiple-office holding).

It is during this period that political scientists have underscored the resemblance between the mayor and the French head of State. Yet, this image does not aid understanding of the mayoral situation. This position is both weak and strong: weak, since mayors are always dependent upon the different components of their coalition for their (re)election – they still owe their election to the municipal council since it

---

[27] P. Garraud, *Profession: homme politique. La carrière politique des maires urbains* (Paris, L'Harmattan, 1989).

[28] A. Mabileau and C. Sorbets, *Gouverner les villes moyennes* (Paris, Pédone 1989).

[29] D. Lorrain, 'Après la décentralisation. L'action publique flexible', *Sociologie du Travail*, n. 3 (1993), pp. 285–307.

[30] P. Le Galès, *European Cities. Social Conflicts and Governance* (Oxford University Press, 2002).

[31] C. Le Bart, *Les Maires. Sociologie d'un rôle* (Paris, Septentrion 2003).

is the latter which formally designates them. It is strong, given mayoral capacities to build majorities, speak on behalf of their city and forge partnerships with other actors. A governance approach to urban government helps understand this contradictory situation:[32] it stresses mayoral capacity to aggregate local interest and social groups, along with actors outside the city, into a common project promoting the city on a wider stage (regional, national, European, international) and in return provide resources for local development. This capacity rests on mayoral negotiating powers but also on their mastery of symbolic action, such as ambitious cultural policies, urban projects or sporting events. To build political support and wield influence, mayors must develop collective action and long-term political goals for the urban area.[33] In cooperation with other local elites (business, unions, university), they must try to organise their cities as collective actors with a system of governance emerging across Europe.[34] This implies promoting large urban projects which help give the city visibility on a wider scale, in order to attract investors, international firms and middle-class households. These leadership capacities, or social skills, are what most clearly distinguish urban mayors in France at the turn of the millennium.

Turning Mayors into Presidents

Since the 2001 municipal elections, the decline in mayoral power has become an issue for debate. This may seem surprising, given what we have just suggested, but can be understood by returning to the dimensions of political support and influence we used to describe the mayor's status and position. On both of these, changes have occurred entailing new forms of leadership.

Managing political uncertainty

As municipal governments have become fiefdoms, the conditions under which political support is achieved have changed. The competing coalitions all strive to enrol the different social and interest groups composing the city. In a way, these groups are much more available than heretofore, when they were clearly associated with the left or right. Thus, left-wing parties undertake to work with employers' associations, or build alliances with local business, to achieve greater credibility in their effort to attract investment and modernise their city's image. Meanwhile, right-wing parties have captured some of the more working-class cities by reaching out to second or third generation immigrants abandoned by the left,[35] and campaigning in the social-housing districts with pledges to provide a better environment. If it is too early to conclude that traditional political cleavages are blurring, this situation has

---

[32]   O. Borraz and P. John, 'The Transformation of Urban Political Leadership in Western Europe', *International Journal of Urban and Regional Research*, vol. 28.1 (2004), pp. 107–20.

[33]   G. Pinson, 'Les projets urbains et la recomposition de l'action publique à Venise, Turin, Nantes et Marseille' (unpublished PhD, Université de Rennes, 2002).

[34]   Le Galès, *European Cities*.

[35]   O. Masclet, *La gauche et les cités. Enquête sur un rendez-vous manqué* (Paris, La Dispute 2003).

nonetheless important consequences – increasing the uncertainties candidates face when running for election. And neither mayoral efforts to increase their visibility nor their deputies' capacity to reach out and represent the population's different components can reduce this fragmentation of the electorate.

Furthermore, the system is currently under pressure in terms of both electoral representation (due to declining voter turnout) and functional representation (due to multiple and fragmented local interests). French municipal elections have traditionally been characterised by high turnouts, but these have been dropping steadily to an all-time low of 61 per cent in 2001. Electoral participation among some groups (defined by social class, ethnicity and place of living) is particularly low. This implies potential problems of representation: the needs and demands of such groups, individuals and areas may receive less attention and understanding from political officials. Another difficulty arises from the increasing variety of political parties competing during elections, from an average of two to three in the 1970s to four and sometimes five in the last elections.[36] And among these, the rise of marginal or non-governmental parties is most noteworthy: the National Front on the far right from the mid-1980s, a series of far-left parties more recently. These have tended to draw many voters away from traditional parties, sometimes contributing to right-wing strongholds falling to the left – or vice versa.[37] Added to increasing electoral volatility, this makes it hard for mayors to consolidate their electoral base.

Hence, the plurality of urban political and social interests has become a problem for mayors. They can always return to the usual techniques, like subsidising groups or voluntary associations, to gain their allegiance.[38] They can also adopt more participatory procedures, like various types of consultation, referenda and procedures designed to promote dialogue on highly controversial issues. But mayors must acquire new skills to operate successfully in these areas and their outcomes often remain highly uncertain. Overall, mayors cannot count anymore on the stability their predecessors enjoyed and must constantly reaffirm their hold on their city and its government.

Rescaling local government

The 1992 and more recent 1999 laws on inter-municipal cooperation have had great impact on local government's form and content. According to the size of an urban area, three forms of cooperation can be adopted: *communautés urbaines* (CU) in the largest urban areas (over 500,000), *communautés d'agglomération* (CA) in the large and medium-sized cities (area over 50,000) and *communautés de commune* (CC) for the smaller communes. Over time the new co-operative bodies must achieve

---

[36]   V. Hoffmann-Martinot, 'Les grandes villes françaises: une démocratie en souffrance', in O.W. Gabriel and V. Hoffmann-Martinot (eds), *Démocraties urbaines* (Paris, L'Harmattan 1999), pp. 77–121.

[37]   P. Martin, *Les élections municipales en France depuis 1945* (Paris, La Documentation Française 2001).

[38]   C. Mattina, 'Mutations des ressources clientélaires et construction des notabilités politiques à Marseille (1970-1990)', *Politix* n. 67 (2004), pp. 129–55.

a uniform business tax (instead of permitting taxes to vary between neighbouring towns). Each entity finds itself with a set of compulsory competencies and the obligation to choose other optional competencies.

France now has 2,525 inter-municipal bodies (14 CU, 162 CA and 2343 CC), with specific and distinct tax bases. These institutions encompass 32,311 communes and over 84 per cent of France's population.[39] Their missions are often politically sensitive: urban planning, housing, economic development, environmental protection. They have begun assembling professional administrations and work closely with privately-run utilities. Although community councils are elected by municipal councils, and not directly by citizens, in a few years these structures have acquired a decisive influence on several policy areas.

This transformation has impacted on the position of mayors. While they continue to gather political support for their actions at the communal level, their influence is limited and they must work within ever more integrated inter-municipal institutions. Furthermore, they can only partially use the political support obtained within their commune to influence decisions at the inter-municipal level, since decisions are taken on a consensual basis. This in turn calls for a change in mayoral repertoires: while mayors in their own cities can easily impose decisions upon their councils, as soon as they move to the next level, they must find other skills. This is particularly evident amongst mayors of central cities who are simultaneously presidents of the wider *communauté*.[40] They must learn to take decisions that achieve unanimous agreement, and this calls for skills radically different from those of a mayor. Furthermore, presidents must learn to work with mayors of the other communes without having any hold over them, since each remains accountable to their own electorate.

While this might lead us to conclude that mayors are slowly losing ground to *communauté* presidents, and that they will shortly be left with secondary tasks with the most important decisions taken elsewhere, we must remain careful for two reasons.[41] The first relates to strong disparities between inter-municipal institutions. The *communauté urbaine* in Brest is only composed of seven communes while Lille Métropole has 87. Sometimes the new structure remains virtual, and power remains within the communes (Marseille). In other cases, it can capture a large array of services and extend its influence further than the law provided for (Amiens). The dynamics of inter-municipal cooperation are diverse, and this makes it difficult to observe a convergence – and thus a generalised fading of the mayoralty.

The second reason is that mayors, notably suburban ones, can actually exert influence within the executive council (formed by all the mayors), since decisions are always taken on a consensual basis. This gives them effective veto power, all mayors standing on equal terms whatever the population size of their commune. In other words, if mayors have lost some influence on key issues at the communal level,

[39]   E. Négrier, *La question métropolitaine. Les politiques à l'épreuve du changement d'échelle territoriale* (Presses Universitaires de Grenoble 2005).

[40]   R. Le Saout, *Le pouvoir intercommunal. Sociologie des présidents des établissements intercommunaux* (Presses Universitaires d'Orléans 2000).

[41]   E. Négrier, 'A French urban powershift? The political construction of metropolitization', *French Politics*, n. 1, (2003), pp. 175–98.

they have also gained influence elsewhere and can affect collective decisions. This amounts to a trade-off rather than a simple decline.

Nonetheless, change is inevitable given that, with the growing importance of inter-municipal institutions, a separation is appearing between garnering political support, on the one hand, and wielding influence, on the other.

A decoupling of power?

The preceding changes result in a form of decoupling: while partisan politics and political support-building remain communal activities, decision-making and the exercise of influence move to the inter-municipal level. This creates tensions at both levels.

Within the commune, gaining and maintaining political support will become harder as fragmentation grows and mayors lose their capacity to uphold their positions by exercising their authority in decisions and partnerships. At the *communauté* level, the absence of political support can weaken the potential impact and legitimacy of decisions, while the consensual style of decision-making can create tensions within political parties. It is difficult for the mayor or president to manage these different tensions and requires social skills, defining new objectives and inventing symbols (either architectural, cultural or rhetorical). At the communal level, mayors will be predominantly concerned with preserving local identity, a sense of belonging to a community and fostering cooperation between the different components of their cities on closely knit relationships. A law on 'democracy and proximity' passed in 2002 supports such a change, by promoting new forms of participation and stimulating political debate in what formally remains a representative system of government.[42] Meanwhile, on a *communauté* level, the president will try to create a sense of identity within an urban region through large-scale economic policies, infrastructures, marketing strategies, sporting and cultural events. The 2004 Decentralisation Act has given him/her some supplementary resources in order to facilitate cooperation between different institutional players locally. Nonetheless, questions remain about how to coordinate the communal and inter-municipal levels, and particularly how to deal with the inevitable conflicts arising between them.

Conclusion

Although French mayors are enjoying more autonomy, they must evolve within a system of constraints now defined by the EU, a restructured state and regions. This calls for the invention of new leadership styles, new processes of policy-making (notably through citizen participation) and new institutionalised procedures for collective action.

Mayors have always had the edge over other political and administrative actors when it comes to protecting their interests. And they have always been rather successful in turning new rules and procedures to their advantage, manipulating

---

[42]   B. Jouve and P. Booth (eds), *Démocraties métropolitaines* (Presses de l'Université du Québec 2004).

them to eliminate political rivals and strengthen their political control of the territory without too much concern for democracy.

Yet, the inter-municipal revolution is gradually reorganising French local government into a system wherein a few thousand inter-municipal governments play increasingly important parts within a more diverse and differentiated system. Furthermore, access to central government no longer provides the resources mayors need to uphold their position. Finally, social and political fragmentation accentuates the uncertainty they face in managing urban affairs.

These elements may not collectively indicate a general decline in the mayoral role, but they indubitably call for a transformation in their position and status. As some aspire to become *communauté* presidents with similar attributes to the strong mayors of the past, others will have to adapt to a complex institutional framework wherein the commune may retain only symbolic attributes. Quite possibly in future years, a highly differentiated pattern will emerge with very different roles for the mayors according to their local situation.

Figure 1.   Blackburn's Mayor lays the foundation stone of the Cotton Exchange in March 1863. The town's male elite take the opportunity to put themselves on display, their faces obligingly highlighted and rendered into portrait clarity by the painter Vladimir Ossipovich. The local volunteers enhance the splendour and visibility of the occasion. Image provided by the copyright holder for use in the Cotton Town digitisation project.

Figure 2.   By the end of the nineteenth century, mayors and their ceremonies had become particularly magnificent, all the more so when national and local urban rituals were combined together, as during the local celebrations of Queen Victoria's Diamond Jubilee. Alexander Carus, Mayor of the small Lancashire industrial town of Darwen 1899. Image provided by BwD for use in the Cotton Town digitisation project.

Figure 3. The same circumstances had similarly dramatic effects upon mayoresses, the pain of corsets notwithstanding: Mrs Alexander Carus, Darwen 1899. Image provided by BwD for use in the Cotton Town digitisation project.

Figure 4.   Many towns and cities had special coaches for mayoral ceremony. Liverpool's vehicle, with its two dedicated carthorses, was and remains a particularly fine example. Image reproduced by kind permission of the Liverpool Record Office, Liverpool Libraries.

Figure 5.   Mayoral receptions could involve their incumbents in some strange activity. Mayoral reception in Blackburn circa 1911. Image provided by BwD for use in the Cotton Town digitisation project.

Figure 6.   A ceremonial meeting between the head of the local state and his national counterpart at the start of a royal visit to Blackburn in 1913. Image provided by BwD for use in the Cotton Town digitisation project.

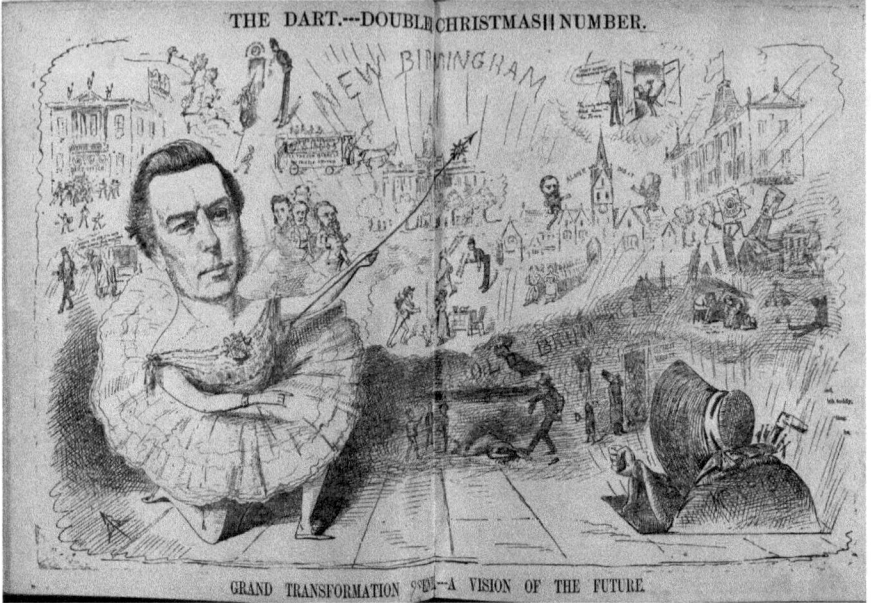

THE DART.---DOUBLE CHRISTMAS NUMBER.

NEW BIRMINGHAM

GRAND TRANSFORMATION SCENE---A VISION OF THE FUTURE.

Figure 7.   The executive mayoralty: a cartoon depicting Joseph Chamberlain's plans for the transformation of central Birmingham from *The Dart*, 23 December 1876. Image reproduced by Birmingham Library Services.

Figure 8.   The Mayor and Mayoress of Blackburn (both women) stop to greet John, a Great Dane, during the Parkwatch Community Festival nd. Image provided by LET for use in the Cotton Town digitisation project.

Figure 9.   Blackburn's Asian community gets some of the mayoral action: Lord
             Adam Patel and the Mayor of Blackburn at the Friends of Pakistan
             Forum at Bangor Street Community Centre, Blackburn nd. Image
             provided by LET for use in the Cotton Town digitisation Project.

© Aberdeen City Council · Library & Information Services

Figure 10.   Sir David Stewart, Lord Provost of Aberdeen 1889–95, in full
              regalia. Interestingly, pictures of early nineteenth century holders
              of the office in the city do not show the robes, though they do wear
              the chain. Perhaps, as with mayors south of the border, provosts
              and their ceremonies became more ornate as the century advanced.
              Reproduced by kind permission of Aberdeen Central Library.

Charles Parker Esq: Provost.   1861.-67.

Figure 11.   Charles Parker, Provost of Dundee 1861–7, again in full regalia. Later provosts added a magnificent chain and medallion. Reproduced by kind permission of Dundee Central Library.

Figure 12. Nan Hughes, one of the early women provosts and Scotland's first Labour incumbent (for Cumnock in Ayrshire). She's not wearing the traditional robes, perhaps because, being a socialist and daughter of Keir Hardy, she disapproved of such fripperies. Reproduced by kind permission of the Baird Institute in Cumnock and the Ayrshire Archive Centre.

Figure 13.   An 'honorary provost' being installed at the Selkirk Common Ridings during the 1980s. Reproduced by kind permission of the Ayrshire Archive Centre.

Figure 14. Mayoral problems in a divided community. The cartoon captures the mayhem generated by the election of Sinn Féin to Belfast City Council with the Lord Mayor trying to 'hold the ring' in the bear-pit of sectarian division – note Sinn Féin's mantra 'sráid tiocfaidh ár lá' ('our day will come') and the Orange Order's lambeg drums. Image reproduced by kind permission of the editors and proprietors of *Fortnight* and of Ian Knox (Blotski).

Figure 15. The Metropolitan Council of Montpellier at work: Communauté d'Agglomération de Montpellier, 2005. The session is chaired by the ex-mayor – he having been forced to choose between the role of mayor and that of chair of the metropolitan council. In fact, he managed to get his mayoral position filled by a trusted female associate. The Mayor and his officials seated at the desk at the front. Note the presence of the tricolour on the left hand side of the picture. Photograph by author.

Figure 16. The Mayor of Lavalette (44 inhabitants) welcoming the local Diane (local Hunters Committee) in the front of the town hall. Note again the national flags and the tricolour sash that the mayor is wearing, symbolising his role as an agent of the state. Note also the regional flag of Languedoc. Photograph by Claude Dennis.

Figure 17.   The official installation was an essential symbol of Dutch mayoralty. During the Occupation, NSB mayors tried to gain legitimacy by using this symbolic event. The picture shows the installation of NSB Mayor H. Froonhof (sitting behind the table) in March 1942 in the small town of Baarn. The mayor is being inaugurated by the Provincial Commissioner of Noord Holland, A. Backer (standing), also a member of the collaborating NSB Party. Image from the collection of the NIOD in Amsterdam.

Figure 18.   Mayors from the Valtaro area of Northern Italy at a gathering for the official visit of Prince Albert of Monaco on 9 July 2003 – the heads of relevant local states assembled to greet the visiting head of a foreign state. While, like the municipalities that they represent, Italian mayors are far more autonomous of the national state than their British or even their French counterparts, the wearing of sashes in the national colours indicates their role as agents of their state within their local areas. Reproduced by kind permission of the Valtaro web site.

Figure 19. Mayor William Donald Schaefer, left, cuts the ribbon signifying the formal opening of Baltimore's Harborplace, 2 July 1980. Maryland State Archives.

Figure 20.   Mayor Kurt L. Schmoke meets actor James L. Jones in Baltimore City Hall, 13 July 1993. Courtesy of the Mayor's office, Baltimore.

Figure 21. Mayor Martin O'Malley addresses Baltimore Veterans at the opening of the new War Memorial across from City Hall, 10 November 2005. Again note the symbolic intermixing of national and city flags. Courtesy of the Mayor's Office, Baltimore.

CHAPTER SIX

The Impact of the German Occupation (1940–1944) on the Belgian and Dutch Mayoralty

Nico Wouters

Historians often treat Belgium and the Netherlands homogeneously – as 'the low countries'. This is not wholly unreasonable, since these neighbours share a considerable pre-modern history, partially share a language (Dutch) and are comparable in size and population. However, the schism that ruptured the United Kingdom of the Low Countries in 1830 created two independent nation-states that subsequently followed distinct political-administrative paths. This separate development was reinforced in 1914, by contrasting experiences of war and occupation – Belgium being mostly occupied, the Netherlands remaining neutral. The difference also becomes very clear when we examine municipal administration, particularly the mayoralty.

This chapter compares the Belgian and Dutch mayoralties during the German occupation in World War II,[1] and focuses on interactions between municipal political-administrative culture and the impact of occupation. I will show firstly how the different Belgian-Dutch municipal political cultures influenced the experience of occupation and secondly how different occupation experiences in turn influenced the mayoralty's own longer-term development.

Two Countries, Two Mayoralties: The 1930s

Belgium's 1831 liberal constitution created the basis for the highly decentralised, autonomous Belgian municipal administration that developed later. The municipal and provincial laws of 1836 confirmed this trend. While the provincial level was rendered rather weak, municipalities were given substantial autonomy. This was largely based on the mayor's position. He was head of both the municipal council and the executive council of aldermen. As such, he had extensive administrative powers and headed the municipal police. Both mayor and provincial governor were crown-appointees but, while provincial governors were non-elected civil servants

---

[1] This chapter draws on my doctorate thesis, comparing local government during World War II in Belgium, the Netherlands and Nord-Pas-de-Calais (France): *Oorlogsburgemeesters (1940–1945). Lokaal bestuur en Nieuwe Orde in België, Nederland and Noord-Frankrijk* (Ghent, 2004). I published a book about the Belgian case: *Oorlogsburgemeesters 40/44. Lokaal bestuur en collaboratie in België* (Lannoo, Tielt, 2004). Both contain extended bibliographies on themes touched on by this chapter.

and central government representatives, mayors had to be elected members of municipal councils. This automatically meant that mayors were inhabitants and voters in their communities. After municipal elections, councils proposed candidates to the provincial governor, who advised the Minister of the Interior so that the Crown could appoint. Interwar municipal elections occurred every six years. The Belgian mayoralty was not a full-time salaried post, but rather a position that local dignitaries filled alongside their full-time jobs. Mayoral social profiles thus varied immensely, depending on local power relations. The mayor's democratic legitimacy was high: he was first and foremost a representative of local power groups.

The 1836 municipal laws strongly resembled France's law of 1884; the main difference was at intermediate level. Prefect-led French departments had much greater control over municipalities than governor-led Belgian provinces. Put simply, the basic legal principles of the Belgian and French municipal laws were similar, but the political-administrative cultures emerging from their practical application by central and intermediate authorities were different.

Belgium's strong political-administrative culture of municipal autonomy became the cornerstone of the country's administration. This almost sacrosanct principle derives partly from Belgian political *mentalité* – strongly negative attitudes towards state authority, based on a long history of foreign regimes or occupations. Germany's occupation of Belgium during World War I probably further reinforced such localism. This in turn strengthened post-war mayoral legitimacy and power.

Certainly, localism greatly helps explain why Belgium failed to follow its French, German and particularly Dutch neighbours in reforming municipal administration from the late-nineteenth century. When European cities encountered the manifold problems of industrialisation, debates began about fusing large core-cities with their conurbations, continuing well into the 1920s. For rural areas, municipal reform and amalgamation were considered important to combat municipal fragmentation and improve local government. While Belgium had 2,492 independent municipalities in 1830 and 2,676 in 1928, the Netherlands had only 1,072 during the 1930s (in May 1940: just over 1,000 municipalities with 925 mayors), even though similar in size and possessing a larger population.[2] More generally, critics considered Belgian mayors too political and the municipal police too amateurish. During the 1930s, this debate merged with the larger one about the workings of the parliamentary system in face of socio-economic and political crisis. The Study Centre for the Reform of the State (1936) proposed fundamental municipal reform. One proposal, inspired by contemplating the Dutch mayoralty, was to replace the (indirectly) elected mayor with a centrally appointed civil-servant mayor. However, political and legal obstacles prevented any change during the interwar years.

The Dutch provincial and municipal laws of 1850 and 1851 had also instituted decentralised government, giving elected municipal councils substantial powers. The Dutch head of the provincial executive had powers similar to his Belgian counterpart, but greater police and administrative power due to presiding over the provincial council. However, Dutch local autonomy was severely limited by the

---

[2]   Alain Colignon, 'Le nouvel ordre communal', in Francis Balace (ed.), *Jours de guerre. Jours mêlés 11–13*, (Bruxelles, 1998), pp. 35–92.

mayor's political-administrative position.[3] Article 143 of the 1848 constitution stated that the mayor was to be appointed by the Crown from *outside* elected municipal councillors. In office for six years, he was president of both municipal council (municipal law, article 72) and the city council of aldermen (the executive organ).[4] Unlike their Belgian counterparts, Dutch mayors were full-time civil servants, professionally educated and carefully selected by the state. Although most implicitly had a political colour, they were officially neutral. Unlike Belgian mayors, they did not generally originate from the village or city they governed. Indeed, a single Dutch mayor quite often headed several neighbouring municipalities. Mayors were first and foremost representatives of national authority at the local level. They were executives, had no vote in municipal councils and were basically there to control. They also had larger police powers than their Belgian counterparts, because Dutch municipal councils lacked control over mayoral police policy. Despite the formally decentralised administrative organisation, all this produced a dominant political-administrative culture of centralisation.

During the 1930s, Dutch mayors remained 'regents' or 'magistrates' and came from higher social levels than the local population and power groups. In 1930, 86 were sons of mayors and 86 of noble origin. In 1935, the Dutch government set a mandatory retirement age of 65 and many younger mayors were appointed. No such step was possible in Belgium's administrative context. The mayoral generation emerging from amongst councillors and aldermen after 1919 was mostly still there in 1940. Their high average age would prove important during the occupation.

After 1921, two fundamental electoral changes – the universal single vote system ('one man, one vote') and the proportional representation system – were introduced in Belgian local elections at the same time, fundamentally influencing the composition of municipal councils.[5] While absolute majorities (mostly Catholic in rural areas) were normal before 1914, coalitions to control the committee of mayor and aldermen were often necessary after 1921, gradually increasing party control over municipal administration. In contrast, the Dutch committees of mayor and aldermen during the 1930s often represented all local parties, not a specific political majority.

In Wallonia, the southern French-speaking part of Belgium, socialists gained the upper hand in most industrial urban areas, mostly choosing the smaller liberal party as coalition partners. Most large urban areas had socialist mayors, but catholic mayors dominated the countryside. Léon Degrelle's fascist party *Rex* remained weak (under 5 per cent of all votes in 1938), especially in urban areas and was rarely asked to join council coalitions. In Flanders, the catholic party remained dominant, but Socialist gains forced it into coalitions, normally after 1838 with Flemish Nationalists of the

---

3   W. Derksen and M.L. Van der Sande, *De burgemeester. Van magistraat tot modern bestuurder* (Deventer Kluwer, Leiden, 1984), p. 217.

4   H. Helsen, 'De burgemeesterfunctie in Nederland en België: een vergelijking van de rechtspositie, de taken en bevoegdheden', unpublished master thesis, Staats- en Bestuurswetenschappen, 1987; K. Canfyn, 'De provinciegouverneur in België en de commissaris van de koningin in Nederland', unpublished master thesis, Staats- en Bestuurswetenschappen, RUG, 1987.

5   Chantal Kesteloot, Ann Mares and Claudine Marissal, *Gemeenteraadsverkiezingen 1890–1970*. Databestand (Gemeentekrediet, Historische Uitgaven reeks in-8, nr. 95, Brussel, 1996).

fascistic *Vlaams Nationaal Verbond* (VNV). After the last pre-war local elections in 1938, the catholic party had 68 per cent of municipal councillors and about 80 per cent of mayors.[6] Socialist mayors were rare in Flanders.

In both Belgium and the Netherlands in the 1930s (like other surviving European liberal democracies), decentralised state organisation increasingly came under pressure. The Dutch problem was less sharp. Its level of decentralisation was much less strong from the outset, the country had introduced many municipal reforms and mayors had strong, uncontested status. Nevertheless, some additional reforms occurred in the 1930s, for instance transferring some police powers from mayors to the new police services under the Justice department.[7] These reforms further strengthened the centralist tendencies within Dutch municipal organisation. In Belgium, however, the debate about municipal organisation reached deadlock, only ending with German occupation.

It remains uncertain whether Belgian municipal administration was really defective, compared to its Dutch counterpart. What is important is that, during the 1930s, many Belgians believed this was so. The perception would play an important role during the occupation's first year.

The New Order and the Mayoralty, 1940–1941

Germany invaded Belgium and the Netherlands on 10 May 1940; both rapidly capitulated. The Germans installed a civilian occupation government in the Netherlands and a military one in Belgium. This meant that, in the Netherlands, purely political goals of nazification were more explicitly part of occupation policy and police and judicial reforms were led by a *Höhere SS-und Polizeiführer.* The difference in occupation regime itself, however, did not fundamentally influence municipal reform. The same is true of the very similar Belgian and Dutch indigenous regimes. Both countries found themselves without their governments and the highest-ranking public servant in each ministerial department, the secretary-general, became the highest central power. Although the administrative-judicial basis of their position differed fundamentally, the purely administrative character of their regimes and powers were very similar.

In 1940, both civilian and military occupation governments had only very general ideas about what to do with municipal administration. Aspirations existed to abolish local democracy, strengthen centralisation and diminish local autonomy, but neither occupation regime had a concrete programme. Initially, there was strong continuity. Both German and indigenous Belgian and Dutch elites sought administrative and

---

    6   Bruno De Wever and Petra Gunst, 'Van Kamerleden en burgemeesters', in Luc Huyse and Kris Hoflack (eds), *De Democratie heruitgevonden. Oud en nieuw in politiek België 1944–1945* (Van Halewyck, Leuven, 1995).

    7   Through the so-called 'Rijkspolitiebesluit' of 1935. Peter Romijn, 'Lokale Verwaltung, Aufrechterhaltung der öffentlichen Ordnung und Polizeiwesen in den besetzten Niederlanden 1940 bis 1941', in Johannes Houwink Ten Cate and Alfons Kenkmann (eds), *Deutsche und holländische Polizei in den besetzten niederländischen Gebieten* (Ville ten Hompel, Münster, 2002), pp. 9–29.

economic normality. The last thing the Germans wanted in 1940 was to disrupt local administration by initiating major changes in personnel or municipal machinery.

Personnel policy 1940

There were three main causes rooted in 1940 for the different subsequent developments concerning mayoral appointment in the two countries: 1) the different consequences of war in May 1940; 2) pre-war perceptions of a deficient Belgian mayoralty, and 3) the reaction of Belgium's German occupier towards municipal administrative legality.

In both countries, occupation caused a certain localisation of public life. The disappearance of central government ruptured the normal relationship between the local and central level. In the Netherlands, this localisation initially remained limited. The war terminated in four days and public administrative life was largely preserved. Most mayors, provincial Royal Commissioners and civil servants remained in post. Administrative continuity was almost absolute. Municipal administration could cope with the relatively modest consequences of a four-day war.

By contrast, during Belgium's 18-day war, many civil servants – among them municipal and provincial political administrators – deserted their posts and fled, alongside around two million citizens. Hundreds of mayors did not return until August or September 1940. Official sanctions were implemented against over a third. This left many in judicial limbo for months, severely weakening Belgian municipal administration and giving the Germans an immediate opening. Utilising a special *Verordnung* of 18 July 1940, the Germans immediately removed eight of the nine provincial governors, the mayors' immediate superiors. They were mostly replaced by newcomers – three from collaborationist New Order parties. Combined with the initial timidity of the Belgian Interior Secretary-general compared to his Dutch counterpart, this effectively decapitated Belgian municipal administration. Localisation of municipal administration was thus much stronger. While Dutch mayors fell back on the pre-war leadership from provincial Royal Commissioners, Belgian (acting) mayors and municipal administrators were thrown back on themselves.

This produced no fundamental administrative problems. In both countries, the priority was to resolve the many practical difficulties caused by war and occupation. At local and regional levels, shared interests in dealing with the consequences of war and occupation produced strong cooperation between mayoral/municipal and German administrations. There was a strong local convergence between German and indigenous material interests. Belgian municipalities could thus become independent administrative cells within a decapitated administration. However, this lack of central guidance and localisation encouraged a culture of municipal administrative resistance against central (German) power, and great improvisation and variety in local reactions towards central orders. Administrative desertions and decapitation in May 1940 therefore immediately reinforced the pre-war administrative culture of local autonomy.

A second factor was collaborationist party exploitation of pre-war perceptions of a deficient Belgian mayoralty. As noted, the Germans preferred pacts with existing pre-war administrative elites to wholesale changes of personnel. Appointing indigenous collaborators, lacking administrative experience and legitimacy, was highly illogical. The Germans gave the main collaborationist parties (the VNV in Flanders, Rex in Wallonia and the *Nationaal Socialistische Beweging* (NSB) in the Netherlands) formal political recognition, but no real power. This was especially clear with Rex and the NSB. The Flemish VNV, though no mass party, had stronger social bases through the broad 'Flemish Movement'. It was also (unlike Rex) well organised, with reliable local political cadres. When the VNV realised it would not be granted power in 1940, its local cadres started campaigning against municipal administrations, particularly the mayors. Significantly, this campaign mostly rested on neutral (a-political) and administrative arguments.[8] The VNV sensed that pre-war perceptions of fundamental deficiencies in the municipal apparatus had been greatly reinforced during summer 1940. During the summer of 1940, leading political circles shared widespread convictions that now was the time to carry out long-overdue municipal reforms. They particularly wanted to introduce centrally appointed civil-servant mayors. Even Interior Secretary-general, Jean Vossen, initially enthusiastically supported this project. Though he withdrew his support after August 1940, widespread convictions remained that Belgian mayors were too old, too political and too amateurish for the 'new times'.

The Germans also believed this. Many administrative technicians within the military occupation government, seem to have had preconceived ideas about Belgian municipal shortcomings based on previous occupation experience between 1914 and 1918.

The VNV's campaign keyed into these broader German and Belgian perceptions, and echoed arguments widely canvassed during the 1930s. Growing breakdowns in food provisioning after September 1940 reinforced this strategy. German convictions that this was caused by municipal, especially mayoral, deficiencies were strengthened by evidence of alleged mismanagement carefully supplied by local VNV divisions. By December 1940, the Germans had apparently changed their minds and began systematically supporting appointments of VNV mayors.

A third factor was German reactions towards specific problems of Belgian municipal administrative law. Unlike the Netherlands (and France), the Belgian central/provincial level could not legally dismiss or replace mayors.[9] When they were dismissed by German decision (*Amtsverbot*), Belgian law still considered them legally in place but temporarily prevented from executing their mandate. From October 1940, the Germans demanded the Belgian authorities produce permanent replacements. This became an escalating conflict, eventually leading in March 1941 to the dismissal of three secretary-generals and the replacement of the Interior Secretary-general by Gerard Romsée, a prominent VNV member.

The Germans used shock treatment to breach the administrative stalemate. They issued a decree on 7 March 1941, forcing all Belgian public servants to retire at 60. This caused a personnel revolution. Because of their high average age, 1,250 mayors

---

[8]   Nico Wouters, 'New Order and Good Government: Municipal Administration in Belgium 1938–1946', *Contemporary European History*, 13 (4), 2004, pp. 389–409.

[9]   The state's only legal means of dismissing Belgian mayors was article 56 of the municipal law, allowing the Crown temporarily to suspend or dismiss them for 'apparent misconduct or severe negligence'. This however, was rare.

were eventually dismissed through this measure alone. Romsée fundamentally adapted Belgian municipal law, preserving the formal legal framework but undermining its content. Centrally appointed civil-servant mayors, often drawn from outside municipal councils, even municipal areas, and financially 'rewarded' by the state, now became the norm. As a result, nearly 70 per cent of the Flemish mayoralty eventually became infiltrated by the VNV. In Wallonia, Rex did significantly less well. Its wave of mayoral appointments only properly began after the winter of 1942–1943. Even then, only around 13 per cent were Rex appointees, though admittedly these were concentrated in the large urban areas, governing more than 60 per cent of the population. The underlying reason was that Rex lacked German support.

In contrast, Dutch municipal and intermediate administration had coped well with the transition in May 1940. Consequently, the Germans had no immediate reason for far-reaching, disruptive reform. Personnel and structural municipal continuity was maintained, much stronger and longer than in Belgium. The Netherlands basically lacked the two main factors encouraging Belgian municipal reform. First, there was no credible alternative to the highly professional Dutch municipal apparatus (certainly not the marginalised NSB) and no legacy of pre-war municipal criticism to help legitimise reform in 1940. Second, the German occupier did not need extreme measures because no administrative stalemate emerged. Existing Dutch administrative legislation provided all the necessary instruments.

Only after the end of 1940, when relationships between occupier and occupied country deteriorated, did the Germans intervene more strongly in appointments to the Dutch mayoralty. Indeed, they started fully supporting NSB nominees as mayors only after the winter of 1942–1943. At its peak, the NSB occupied more than one third of Dutch mayoralties, governing about 55 per cent of the population, outside Amsterdam.[10]

Structural reforms

Both occupation governments implemented the so-called *Führerprinzip* (leader principle) in 1941. This was the long-term German ambition from the start. *Verwaltungschef* Eggert Reeder abolished Belgian municipal councils on 11 April 1941. On 28 May, Romsée transferred their powers to mayors and aldermen. The Netherlands situation was more complex. In March 1941, the Germans abolished municipal and city councils in large cities (Amsterdam, Hilversum, Zaandam, Haarlem, Rotterdam, Den Haag, Maassluis), replacing mayors with centrally nominated 'governmental commissioners' (*regeringscommissarissen*). The *Führerprinzip* was implemented more generally on 12 August, abolishing provincial and municipal councils and transferring their powers to the executive, particularly provincial commissioners and the remaining mayors. The essential difference between city commissioners and surviving mayors was that the latter were controlled by provincial commissioners, while city commissioners were responsible directly to the Department of the Interior. The Germans further

---

[10]   Peter Romijn, 'Ambitions and dilemmas of local authorities in the German-occupied Netherlands', 1940–1945, in Bruno De Wever, Herman van Goethem and Nico Wouters (eds), *Local government in occupied Europe, 1939–1945* (Academia Press, Ghent, 2005).

reinforced the *Führerprinzip* by abolishing decentralised government and enlarging control and tutelage from the central levels.

At the central level, Dutch and Belgian occupation administrations became reverse mirror images of each other after March 1941. Belgium's military government avoided conflict with the Judiciary by appointing a VNV-member (Gerard Romsée) as Interior Secretary-general but a 'neutral' civil servant as Secretary-general of Justice. At that same moment of rupture in the Netherlands, an NSB-member (Schrieke) became Secretary-general of Justice while Karel Johannes Frederiks, the pre-war Interior Secretary-general, remained in post until September 1944.

These changes reinforced Belgian administrative 'decapitation' after March 1941. By then, the country's mayors (certainly the Flemish ones) were led by an administrative hierarchy composed of political collaborators. The department of the Interior (Romsée and his personal cabinet), all Flemish provincial governors, the majority in the provincial *députations permanents* and about two third of all district commissionners (*commissaires d'arrondissements*) were members of the VNV. After 1942, this situation also emerged in Wallonia. These VNV (and later also Rex) governors, and especially Interior Secretary-general Romsée, clearly followed a political line and possessed little legitimacy in the minds of pre-war mayors. Also, in crucial policy-fields like mandatory labour, these governors and the Department of the Interior often refused to give clear guidance. Belgian mayors were thus left to their own devices, since their administrative hierarchy seemed neither legal nor legitimate. In the Netherlands, the old pre-war administrative hierarchy could play a much larger role for much longer. Secretary-general Frederiks and some provincial commissioners retained control over the pre-war non-NSB mayors, often giving clear instructions in difficult issues.

One other reform in each country needs mentioning: the creation of Belgium's great urban agglomerations and the police/judicial reforms in the Netherlands. The basic reasons for creating the great urban agglomerations have already been explored. City-suburban relationships had been central to Belgian municipal debate since the late-nineteenth century. Large-city problems were again pivotal to debates about municipal deficiencies during the summer of 1940. From the beginning, the German occupiers explicitly supported some form of 'unification' there. In the three largest cities (Brussels, Antwerp and Liege), they quickly initiated informal unification of administrative and police policies. Initially, they were met halfway by obliging city and provincial governments. After 1940, however, the Germans stimulated far-reaching unifications of several cities. Secretary-general Romsée created Greater Antwerp, Ghent, La Louvière, Charleroi, Brussels, Bruge and Liège between September 1941 and October 1942. He thereby abolished many suburban municipalities, creating large new entities, each under the political and administrative control of a city council, a mayor and aldermen, who were always members or affiliates of collaborating parties. Romsée's cabinet strongly relied on pre-war studies of Belgian urban problems and he explicitly legitimised the new agglomerations with pre-war arguments about efficiency and good government. However, these constructions were clearly illegal in terms of both the Belgian constitution and municipal legislation. After a long legal battle with the Belgian judiciary, the creation of new urban agglomerations was halted in 1943. By then, the largest Belgian cities had been unified and brought under collaborating-party control.

These agglomerations were essentially compensations for New Order failures in police and judicial reform. Unlike the Netherlands, centralised state police were never created, although 'localised state police' forces did emerge in these Belgian agglomerations, especially in Greater Brussels. The central consequence thus was not administrative, but the unification of police and political control.

In the Netherlands, the most important reforms influencing and severely limiting mayoral power related to the judicial and police apparatus. As in Belgium, these were stimulated and legitimised by the resurfacing of discussions originating in the 1930s.[11] The powerful Hans Albinn Rauter, who combined the functions of *Generalkommissar für das Sicherheitswesen* and *Höhere SS-und Polizeiführer*, used the willingness of several Dutch secretary-generals and high-ranking police dignitaries in 1940 to initiate far-reaching reforms. He unified and centralised existing police structures under the Justice Department, and appointed NSB members to leading posts. This culminated in the *Polizeiorganisationsverordnung* of March 1943, which – amongst other things – transferred most control over the police to the 'directorate-general of the police', while most powers of police tutelage were transferred to provincial and city 'police presidents'. This basically meant a centralised state police. After March 1943, municipal police remained operational in only 130 medium-large cities; even here, mayoral police powers were limited. Although they had already begun eroding in the 1930s, the radicalism of these reforms presented an entirely new situation.

This was a major difference from Belgium. Belgian mayors maintained, even enlarged, their administrative and police powers during the occupation, but Dutch mayors lost most of theirs to more central authorities.

Consequences 1942–1944

Some comparative points need stressing. In Belgium, the rupture in administrative legality was greater, mayoralty's politicisation started earlier and was more intense, mayoral powers broadened while they diminished in the Netherlands and Belgian provincial and national authority was far weaker. This 'weakness' rested on several factors: early administrative 'decapitation' in August 1940; the weak legitimacy of collaborating party members in leading administrative posts, and Interior Secretary-general Romsée's deliberate lack of leadership. It also rested upon much longer-term local administrative traditions.

To summarise the general consequences of the 1940–1942 municipal reforms, I would like to use the concept of 'focal points'. In Belgium the focal points for collaboration with state organisation were local and municipal and primarily lay with the mayoralty. In the Netherlands they lay above and beyond municipal administrations – with the police and security services and the Justice department. In Belgium, the Germans became increasingly reliant on the municipal level, often bypassing central and intermediate levels, while in the Netherlands a centralised and

---

[11]   The 'Rijkspolitiebesluit' (1935) had transferred many police tutelage powers from the Interior to the Justice department and provoked debate about the division of power that was still ongoing in 1940.

politicised police and security apparatus quickly became the main indigenous pillar for the occupation regime.

Generally speaking, Belgian local autonomy strongly increased after municipal reform. However, reform and autonomy were causally inter-related. The Germans had no clear municipal programme, rather a stumbling series of *ad hoc* responses to the specific Belgian situation. In 1940, they encountered great difficulties in handling, even understanding, Belgian municipal legality. So Belgium's deep-rooted municipal culture of local autonomy was as much cause as consequence. The Netherlands were different. Dutch municipal administration was already much closer to the German model. On the other hand, due to the character of the civilian occupation government, the main focus of German reforms was initially and successfully on the police and judicial apparatus. In consequence, a better-developed programme emerged.

Generally speaking, these New Order changes had similar basic long-term consequences. First of all, the quality of local administration diminished, initially mostly in Belgium. The New Order was deficiently organised, while the collaborating parties that took over local government had no administrative programme to deal with problems like food-provisioning, or socio-economic issues. Secondly, the gradual politisation of local government caused many administrative problems since it eroded mayoral legitimacy to implement unpopular measures. Thirdly, in the age of total war (1943–1944), the central power imposed its own specific set of short-term goals on local government (labour deportation, political repression, Jewish persecution) making local government a mere instrument of Nazification and subsequently stimulating global local administrative resistance.

Determining the more detailed practical consequences of these changes is difficult, partly because other factors, like different policy-perceptions caused by different occupation and pre-occupation histories, were also in play. I will concentrate on general relationships between mayors and their professional and social environments.

Firstly, we will examine the 'new mayors', drawn from New Order parties. Major tensions arose when their mayoral authority was questioned. This took many forms: administrative, where citizens chose to ignore particular mayoral orders; legal, where experienced municipal secretaries ignored newly-appointed mayors' orders on legal grounds; symbolic, with municipal personnel ostentatiously refusing to attend meetings organised by the mayor; or outright political opposition involving resistance activities. Given what we have said so far, one might expect greater tensions between these mayors and their environment in Belgium than in Holland, given Belgium's far greater rupture in administrative legality. However, this was not the case. Rather, although Dutch NSB mayors operated amidst greater legal-administrative continuity, it was much easier for collaborating VNV and even Rex mayors to reach 'consensus' with their municipal personnel and local populations. One main reason lay with specific political-administrative municipal cultures.

In the Netherlands, NSB mayors were appointed in a municipal context and culture provoking tensions and conflict. First, there were strong perceptions about Dutch mayors as 'neutral' and professionally trained civil servants. While in Belgium, the VNV could use widespread negative perceptions about municipal government against the system itself, the NSB could not do this in the Netherlands.

Unlike Belgian collaborating parties, the NSB even organised administrative courses with fully-fledged exams to 'professionalise' their candidate-mayors. Ironically, this resulted in NSB mayors being ridiculed as incompetent.

Dutch mayors were, above all, Crown and state representatives. Consequently, they were traditionally embedded in political symbolism that became even more important during the occupation. The mayoralty was one of the last remaining symbols of 'Dutchness'. NSB contamination of this Dutch bastion provoked extreme hostility in most Dutchmen. Typical were mayoral ceremonies, where the ceremonial chain of office was bestowed and inaugural speeches given. NSB candidates, seeking legitimacy, highly valued this ceremony. However, many of the traditional elite, particularly municipal personnel, often boycotted it. Such symbolic ceremonies did not play important roles in Belgium.[12] Remarkably, NSB mayors often provoked largely symbolic conflicts over issues of principle with their immediate administrative environment. Typical was the demand to support certain New Order social associations like *Winterhulp-Nederland* or the *Nederlandse Volksdienst*. While *Winterhulp-Nederland* became a central conflict-point between NSB mayors and municipal personnel, in Belgium (particularly Flanders) recognition of equivalent organisations often raised few problems between pre-war local catholic elites and VNV-mayors and aldermen. In Flanders, matters were often pragmatically resolved through personal relations on the local level. This was further helped by the fact that, although after Romsée's reforms, mayoral appointments from outside the municipality were possible, most Rex and VNV mayors still came from within the community.

Particularly after 1919, Belgian mayors normally had strong party affiliations. Thus traditional municipal culture was still apparently respected. Dutch traditions produced very different consequences. In Dutch municipal culture, most mayors were strangers to the community they governed. During the occupation, the consequences for NSB mayors were particularly problematic, making pragmatic understandings with the local environment doubly difficult. Furthermore, NSB mayors' very explicitly political behaviour was anathema to traditional Dutch municipal culture.

These conflicts obviously say much about the political attitudes of collaborating parties and their positions in their respective societies. As noted, VNV members were often quite well integrated into Flemish society, while local Rex organisations and/ or Rex-mayors in Francophone Belgium mostly had the good sense to avoid over-political mayoral ceremonies (and even other similar public meetings). Dutch NSB-mayors meanwhile showed a fanatical and somewhat clumsy stubbornness when dealing with their non-NSB environments. We have already referred to the conflicts over issues of principle with their administrative environment. There were many other practical examples, ranging from showing up in NSB-uniform at the wrong occasion to overzealously defending the Germans in public speeches and provoking direct conflicts with local patriotic opponents over purely symbolic issues. Contrary

---

[12]   There was no 'official', centrally guided appointment-ceremony for Belgian mayors, although they obviously were held in the larger cities. But they were more informal and not invested with as much national symbolism as was the case in the Netherlands.

to Rexists, many NSB-mayors seemed to have genuinely wanted to convince or convert their inhabitants, with counterproductive results.

The essential conclusion again is that the politics of collaboration and longer-term traditional municipal cultures mutually interacted. In the Netherlands, strong legal continuity proved a disadvantage: NSB mayors had to cope with a strong tradition of symbols and patterns of expectation connected with mayoralty. In Belgium, the dominant autonomous character of municipal administration and mayoralty possessed few intrinsic characteristics that would easily provoke conflict. Indeed, its culture left much room for conflict-avoidance. In Belgium, many VNV and even Rex appointees could reach 'marriages of reason' with their environments, because their mayoral positions gave them space to do so.[13] Belgian municipal reforms did not diminish the culture of localism when it came to how mayors executed their day-to-day duties. Local autonomy even grew once collaborating party members infiltrated the mayoralty. Given their political affiliations, these mayors were in stronger positions than traditional ones when dealing with higher authority. Under the formal smokescreen of radical legal rupture, the strong Belgian culture of localism could prevail during the occupation.

Similar conclusions apply to 'traditional', pre-war mayors who stayed in office in Belgium. Although a majority of mayors were sacked fairly quickly, the survivors could often preserve legitimacy through their everyday administration and the advantages it provided for their population. Again, the rupture in municipal legality did not fundamentally affect mayoralty's actual workings. Local consensus had to be preserved in much the same way as during the 1930s. Continuing local autonomy and weak central control over how mayors actually operated was often advantageous. Belgian mayors had to operate in a context of a collaborating administrative hierarchy, which lent many of their administrative actions an air of 'resistance'. This was especially so when they put local above central interests (over food provisioning for example).

In the Netherlands, traditional pre-war mayors were strongly guided by a traditional administrative hierarchy in a context of legal continuity. Secretary-general Frederiks' priority was to avoid an NSB takeover of power, and he was prepared to compromise extensively with German demands. Most Dutch pre-war mayors were formed in a professional culture of obedience to central authority. This could be exploited to the full. Consciously disobeying or resisting apparently legal administrative authority was mostly alien to them. This was far less evident in Belgium. There, administrative resistance, even early on, was stimulated by mayors' lack of inhibition about ignoring collaborating authority. Furthermore, Belgian mayors automatically fell back on active memories of World War I.

Dutch administrative continuity therefore was again disadvantageous. Mayors were caught in a culture of obedience. Whereas, until the winter of 1942–1943, staying in office was still generally perceived as responsible and even patriotic, this perception changed after the May 1943 general strike. Many traditionally obedient mayors came into conflict with their often-younger municipal personnel, who

---

13   Tension-avoidance was important because small incidents often escalated. Collaborating mayors in both countries strong tended to fall back on German power when their authority was questioned or threatened.

wanted more active resistance. The idea that conscious 'administrative resistance' could be legitimate only very gradually gained a stronger foothold with traditional Dutch mayors.

In the last phase of occupation, the localisation of public authority became general in both Belgium and the Netherlands. Central power lost its grip on local events, while mayors had to make individual decisions in a context of illegitimate higher authorities, uncertain legitimacies and conflicting local-central interests. In some regions or localities, this localisation even turned into a disintegration of public authority. Informal, clandestine local leaders and groups largely replaced the 'official' municipal government which by then had lost all control and authority. These informal local groups were often tied to the pre-war local elite, but sometimes also involved new local leaders from the resistance. Also, many collaborating mayors began to mitigate their collaboration, searching for a new local consensus. This disintegration of local government was especially widespread during the hunger-winter of 1944–1945 in the Netherlands. The pre-war local elite that re-emerged in 1944 played an important role in the period of transition after the liberation.

In conclusion, it is therefore remarkable to see that while in both countries a highly centralised municipal system was established and implemented, this produced an extreme localisation in which local government in the end even 'withdrew' itself from central authority.

Transition

The transition from occupation and *Neuordnung* (the process of New Order reform) to democracy was delicate, involving purging collaborators and re-installing the authority of severely de-legitimised democratic states. Municipal administration in both countries had been strongly affected by New Order reforms. Both governments took immediate measures to resume pre-war political and administrative normality. In very general terms, the pre-war legal situation returned, especially in Belgium, where occupation reforms were all annulled, producing an immediate return to the pre-May 1940 personnel and institutional situation. A central problem in both countries was the intertwining of administrative purges with the political restoration of power. However, each dealt with this in different ways. I will only concentrate on the key differences.

Occupation had severely affected the Belgian, especially the Flemish, mayoralty. Because Belgian mayors were elected, they immediately and frequently became targets for local political hostility. To cope with this, the government opted for a long transition to the first post-war municipal elections (November 1946) in order to create a 'normal', stable electoral climate. Because all occupation legal reforms and appointments were annulled, extra-municipal mayoral appointments were considered null and void. Most Rex mayors therefore were not even given *post hoc* sanction during the purges since, according to Belgian law, they were never legally in office. By contrast, Flemish VNV councillors had often been elected in 1938, and could therefore legally become mayors. This helped make the Flemish situation much more complicated than that in Francophone Belgium: the conflicting needs of administrative purge and political restoration were much stronger in Flanders.

The first post-war municipal elections generally produced strong continuity. Seventy per cent of Flemish municipal councillors and about 75 per cent of Flemish mayors survived. In Wallonia, the Communists profited somewhat from their resistance record, although socialists remained the leading party in most urban-industrialised regions. The Communists were considerably weakened in the following 1952 elections. Occupation seems to have had no effect on the municipal political division of power. Nevertheless, both in Flanders and Wallonia, a new generation of mayors and aldermen clearly emerged. However, these had often been 'coming men' during the 1930s.

Most dominant issues of municipal debate from the 1930s were immediately laid aside. Belgium would only carry out large-scale municipal amalgamation at the end of the 1970s, while debates about centrally-appointed, civil-servant mayors were closed for good, wholly discredited by the Occupation. The integration of the municipal police into a newly created state-police would only be implemented after the infamous Dutroux scandal of the late-1990s. There is insufficient evidence about Occupation's effect upon post-war debate on municipal reform, direct reference to it being scarce. Nevertheless, it certainly silenced the debates of the 1930s, and confirmed the political and legal status quo existing since 1919.

The Netherlands situation was different in many respects, none of which were as important as the fact that the post-war Dutch mayoralty could not be legitimised through municipal elections. The Dutch state itself had to judge its civil servants. Unlike Belgium, the mandates of NSB mayors appointed during the occupation were considered legal. Purging these collaborating mayors, first by administrative and then judicial means, proved fairly easy. Judging traditional, pre-war mayors was much more difficult. The main problem was that mayors, selected by the Dutch state for characteristics like administrative obedience, would now be responsible for mistakes often made on the basis of those characteristics. Mayors, with sometimes decades of loyal civil service, faced being dishonourably sacked without compensation.

To a large extent in so doing, the Dutch state was looking critically in the mirror. Briefly, authorities dealt with this problem by showing substantial understanding for specific 'administrative mistakes' (such as providing help in the Jewish persecution or handing over an allied pilot to the Germans) made by patriotic mayors, but much less forgiveness for 'political mistakes' (having shown support for the NSB or other New-Order institutions) by mayors whose patriotism could be questioned. In the first post-war decades, this predominantly patriotic paradigm formed the basic framework for interpreting and judging mayoral occupation behaviour. Their wartime difficulties even became the basis of a well-known Dutch aphorism: feeling like 'a mayor in wartime'. Thus, the particular difficulties and outcome of mayoral purges was pre-eminently determined by the specific legal-administrative position of Dutch mayors.

As in Belgium, occupation experience did not produce any fundamental structural or legal reform: the only visible rupture was in personnel. Many old mayors were replaced after the war, although this occurred gradually over some years and mostly could not directly be connected with occupation. In both Belgium and the Netherlands, a new post-war generation of young and dynamic mayors could benefit from a prosperous economic situation. The Dutch term *bouwburgemeesters* ('building-mayors') refers to the energy and technocratic attitude of this generation.[14] Their reign was based on strong post-war legitimacy and came to an end by the second half of the 1960s.

Conclusion

I have argued that the different national pre-war political cultures of municipal government in general and mayoralty in particular were dominant in determining firstly the outcome of municipal reforms during the occupation, and secondly the actual workings of the two mayoralties. This traditional municipal culture – autonomous in Belgium, strongly hierarchical in the Netherlands – fundamentally determined the conduct both of new occupation appointees and pre-war mayors remaining in office. That this culture also determined the post-war purges and transition was clearest in the Netherlands, where both government and society showed substantial understanding for the errors and dilemmas of patriotic mayors.

The second part of my initial question remains, namely occupation's influence on longer-term municipal and mayoral development. As noted, initial findings suggest this impact of occupation was negligible in both countries. Occupation's aftermath showed not rupture but strong continuity in both personnel and legal-structural terms.

This is only a part of broader issues about the impact of occupation in Belgium, Holland and elsewhere in Western Europe. Although some argue that its broad political and other impact was not seriously disruptive of developments between the 1930s and the 1950s (and beyond), others like myself disagree. My final conclusion must remain tentative since much basic empirical research remains to be done. During the 1930s, the international European context was in favour of centralisation and diminishing local autonomy. The occupation disrupted the normal relationship between state and local government. Even though it was a revolution implemented by a foreign occupant, the experiment of the New Order clearly showed the disastrous results of extreme authoritarian centralisation attempts and of central power trying to impose its own logic on local government. In the end, local government and informal local leaders withdrew themselves from central authority and its goals, directly and solely catering for local interests. Local government entered the post-war period strengthened. The quick re-establishment of state authority was in no small part built on a local foundation. The occupation and transition period – I believe – strengthened the post-war position of local government *vis-à-vis* centralist tendencies and enhanced the culture of local self-government and autonomy for decades to come. In this rehabilitation of local autonomy, I believe the occupation caused a clear rupture with the 1930s.

Also, occupation experience had fundamental influence on political *mentalités*, and certainly affected popular attitudes towards (and against) state authority. During the occupation, 'normal' relationships between official dignitaries and large parts of the

---

[14]   Peter Romijn, *Ambitions and dilemmas.*

local population often changed dramatically. State administration was often infiltrated by political collaborators and frequently unable to provide decent government and protection. Disobedience or even resistance against supposedly local officials like mayors, policemen and inspectors became widely normative. Then pre-war 'normality' was suddenly restored. Nevertheless, it seems highly improbable that these experiences left no permanent marks on the way especially younger people responded to local authority. A change in political *mentalité* against local authority figures like mayors might not have become manifest in the early post-war years, but might help explain some longer-term changes during the 1950s and especially 1960s.

However, empirical historical and sociological research to support or undermine this is still lacking. It would be interesting to explore occupation's long-term impact on popular attitudes and behaviour towards local authority in general and mayors in particular; also on mayoral attituds towards their populations, in Belgium, the Netherlands and occupied Western-Europe.

CHAPTER SEVEN

Servants of the State, Agents of the Party, Representatives of the People: The German Mayoralty in the Twentieth Century

Anthony McElligott

For most of the twentieth century, German mayors found themselves facing at least three ways. As public officials and administrators their first duty was to the state. But increasingly their loyalties were also to political parties as German society found itself organised around political systems. Finally, the creation of a modern public sphere wherein 'the masses' became a key agency meant that mayors had to respond to collective aspirations and interests, acting as popular representatives *vis-à-vis* state and party. This triple role is the more interesting given Germany's chequered twentieth-century history, stumbling from autocracy to democracy in 1918, dictatorship in 1933, then democracy and dictatorship from 1945. Because the mayoralty was the fulcrum wherein state, party and people came together, as Wolfgang Hofmann seminally reminded us many years ago,[1] mayors have played central parts in this history.

It is surprising, therefore, that the twentieth-century German mayoralty still lacks a dedicated history. There are seminal works on municipal self-government,[2] and numerous studies of individual mayors, mostly under Weimar, but few attempts at general synthesis – leaving aside Hofmann's study of Weimar mayors or Schwabe's useful edited essay collection, examining the mayoralty in terms of its rich social history.[3] This is still more surprising given that, for much of the period, Germany's

---

[1] Wolfgang Hofmann, *Zwischen Rathaus und Reichskanzlei. Die Oberbürgermeister in der Kommunal- und Staatspolitik des Deutschen Reiches von 1890–1933* (Stuttgart, Kohlhammer, 1974), pp. 51–6.

[2] Arnold Köttgen, *Die Krise der kommunalen Selbstverwaltung* (Tübingen, Möhr, 1931). Heinrich Heffter, *Die deutsche Selbstverwaltung im 19. Jahrhundert* (Stuttgart, Kohlhammer, 1950); Hans Herzfeld, *Demokratie und Selbstverwaltung in der Weimarer Epoche* (Stuttgart, Kohlhammer, 1957); Horst Matzerath, *Nationalsozialismus und kommunale Selbstverwaltung* (Stuttgart, Kohlhammer, 1970); Günter Püttner (ed.), *Handbuch der kommunalen Wissenschaft und Praxis* I (Berlin, Springer 1981).

[3] Klaus Schwabe (ed.), *Oberbürgermeister. Büdinger Forschungen zur Sozialgeschichte* (Boppard am Rhein, Harald Boldt, 1981). Emplary studies include: Christian Engeli, *Gustav Boß Oberbürgermeister von Berlin 1921–1930* (Stuttgart, Kohlhammer, 1971); Dieter Rebentisch, *Ludwig Landmann: Frankfurter Oberbürgermeister der Weimarer Republik* (Wiesbaden, Frankfurter historische Abhandlungen vol. 10, 1975); also useful is Ines Reich, *Carl Goerdeler. Ein Oberbürgermeister gegen den NS-Staat* (Cologne, Böhlau, 1997).

mayoralty was a contested site with mayors either invested with power derived from state, party and people, or reduced to powerlessness as any or all of these agencies withdrew their approval.[4]

Here I will discuss the fluctuating fortunes of the German twentieth-century mayoralty. First, I will briefly sketch its institutional and constitutional evolution since around 1800, then provide a generic picture of mayoral social backgrounds. The third section focuses on the difficult Weimar and Third-Reich years when the office was politicised in very different ways. This section challenges some scholarly assumptions about mayoral decline under the Republic, while supporting perceptions of its nadir under the Third Reich. The Nazi governmental system's collapse revitalised the mayoralty. In the context of defeat and potential upheaval, there was conscious re-connection with the interwar period. This is the focus of the chapter's fourth and fifth parts. I argue that earlier institutional structures, personnel and ideas relating to the mayoralty under Weimar and Nazism were revived. A break – if there was one – only occurred from the late-1960s and early-1970s. I will not discuss the post-re-unification period, though scholars mostly agree that, as with earlier so-called 'breaks' in recent German history, resilience and continuity were mayoralty's dominant characteristics.

The Mayoralty

Germany's modern mayoralty originated in the 1808 civic reform, initiated by Karl vom Stein in Prussia as part of the overhaul of government and administration following defeat by Napoleonic France in 1806. The new municipal statute revamped Prussian self-government, undergoing revision in the nineteenth century's middle decades. After the failed 1848 revolutions, other German states also reformed their local statutes. These civic reforms redefined the local community's relationship to the state and instituted the local government structure that remained largely unchanged until the mid-twentieth century.[5]

Until 1935, mayoral powers varied according to whether the *Bürgermeisterverfassung* or the *Magistratsverfassung*, the two systems mostly

---

[4]   For contrasting historical receptions of mayoralty and mayors, see Horst Matzerath and Jeremy Noakes in Gerhard Hirschfeld and Lothar Kettenacker (eds), *Der 'Führerstaat': Mythos und Realität. Studien zur Struktur und Politik des Dritten Reiches* (Stuttgart, Klett-Cotta, 1981).

[5]   Ernst Rudolf Huber, *Deutsche Verfassungsgeschichte seit 1789: Band I Reform und Restauration 1789 bis 1830* (Stuttgart, Kohlhammer, 1957), pp. 122–5, 172–8; idem, *Deutsche Verfassungsgeschichte seit 1789: Band III Bismarck und das Reich* (Stuttgart, Kohlhammer, 1963), pp. 126–8; idem, *Deutsche Verfassungsgeschichte seit 1789: Band IV Struktur und Krisen des Kaiserreichs* (Stuttgart, Kohlhammer, 1969), pp. 385–436, passim. Georg-Christoph von Unruh, 'Ursprung und Entwicklung der kommunalen Selbstverwaltung im frühkonstitutionellen Zeitalter', in Püttner (ed.), *Handbuch*, pp. 57–70; Bernhard Kirchgässner and Jorg Schadt (eds), *Kommunale Selbstverwaltung: Idee und Wirklichkeit* (Sigmaringen, Thorbecke, 1983); Thomas Ellwein and Joachim Jens Hesse, *Das Regierungssystem der Bundesrepublik Deutschland* (Opladen, Westdeutscher Verlag, 1987), chapter 2.

governing German local representation and administration outside Bavaria and Württemberg, held sway. Under the former unicameral system usually found in the Rhineland, mayors governed in executive roles, with their chief officers acting as advisors. This was quite different from the bicameral *Magistratsverfassung*, common in most parts of Prussia and some other German states. As under the *Bürgermeisterverfassung*, councils elected the mayor for a 12 year period (in Bavaria he was elected for ten), but as *primus inter pares* he worked in tandem with the lower chamber rather than as its chief executive.[6]

Following universal suffrage in 1918, there was vigorous debate among mayors and municipal experts about the appropriate balance between a professional administration chaired by the mayor and the public's participation in city government. Some feared the *Bürgermeisterverfassung* would alienate the public from civic life, since mayors were not subject to daily democratic controls. Others worried the *Magistratsverfassung*, with its greater emphasis on the lower chamber, would reduce local administration to a 'horse trade' as political parties jostled for key offices in the executive, further politicising the mayoralty. Conservatives viewed the *Bürgermeisterverfassung* as a bulwark against incursion by the mob into town-hall debating chambers after 1918. Halle's lord mayor, Richard Rive, clearly favoured the *Bürgermeisterverfassung* as a corrective to the crowd in light of 'recent experiences'. Rive was an old-fashioned conservative in 'permanent struggle' with the SPD in the city council and had difficulty coming to terms with universal suffrage. Under the new conditions, he believed the *Magistratsverfassung* would hold the mayoralty hostage to partisan interests, a view shared by several counterparts, including Georg Voigt of Frankfurt, Hans Luther of Essen and Konrad Adenauer in Cologne.[7] But while there was much debate, there was little effective action to curb political democracy in the town halls. Nor was the state any better at redefining mayoralty

---

[6]   *Wörterbuch des deutchen Staats- und Verwaltungsrechts. Zweiter, völlig neu gearbeitete und erweiterte, Auflage*, ed., Max Fleischmann, Vol. 2 (Tübingen, Möhr, 1913), pp. 39–156 and Vol. 3 (Tübingen, Möhr, 1914), pp. 419–24. *Statistisches Jahrbuch Deutscher Städte*, Vol. XXIII (Jena, Fischer, 1928), pp. 263–5; Hofmann, *Zwischen Rathaus und Reichskanzlei*, pp. 62–92 passim; Wolfgang R. Krabbe, 'Der Bürgermeister in der Preußischen Magistratsverfassung', *Die alte Stadt* 11 (1984), pp. 41–7; Christian Engeli, Wolfgang Haus, *Quellen zum modernen Gemeindeverfassungsrecht in Deutschland* (Stuttgart, Kohlhammer, 1974). Roger H. Wells, *German Cities: A study of contemporary municipal politics and administration* (Princeton University Press, 1932), chapter 3: 'Structures of City Government'. In Bavaria and Württemberg the South German Council Statute (*Stadtratsverfassung*) allowed for a directly-elected mayor who acted as chairman of a single chamber council but who was not as powerful as under the *Bürgermeisterverfassung*. For the later period in the former West Germany, see Ellwein and Hesse, *Das Regierungssystem*, p. 519.

[7]   Landesarchiv Berlin (hereafter LAB) 142/1 StB 2934. See also LAB 142/1 StB 1181. Richard Robert Rive, *Lebenserinnerung eines deutschen Oberbürgermeisters* (Stuttgart, Kohlhammer, 1960), pp. 295f., 306–10, 317, 320–22; Wolfgang Haus, 'Biographien deutscher Oberbürgermeister', *Archiv für Kommunalwissenschaft* 4 Jg (1965), p. 133. Everhard Holtmann, 'Die Krise des Föderalismus und der kommunalen Selbstverwaltung', in idem et al., *Die Weimarer Republik. Vol. 3: Das Ende der Demokratie 1929–1933* (Munich, Bayerische Landeszentrale für Politische Bildungsarbeit, 1995), p. 195.

into its field administration.[8] By the late-1920s, a conservative shift was underway in Germany. In Prussia, and those states where the *Magistratsverfassung* prevailed, the shift culminated during the depression, with a standoff between city administrations and intransigent councils over budgets.

As Weimar's economy began teetering, municipal cut-backs were demanded. Numerous mayoral attempts to balance the books foundered on factional hostility within councils, cities often being left without operational budgets. Sometimes opponents called for 'no confidence' votes in the mayor – as happened to Ludwig Landmann in Frankfurt. Demands for such votes were not unusual under Weimar and, although they had no legal basis, they publicised the growing 'crisis of confidence' in town halls noted the previous year by Oskar Mulert, the chairman of the Deutsche Städtetag.[9] To break the gridlock, special state commissioners were appointed in around 600 towns and cities (mostly in Prussia) to set budgets and rehabilitate municipal finances. What is sometimes overlooked is that many state commissioners were themselves mayors, equipped with special powers to by-pass councils. Thus Max Brauer in Altona could eventually reassert his mayoral authority over a particularly fractious council, as could Solingen's mayor.[10] In Berlin, Heinrich Sahm (who succeeded the disgraced Gustav Boß) was given executive powers over his council after the local statute was amended to resolve the city's acute financial crisis.[11] The measure, therefore, was not just a financial one. In *Magistratsverfassung* areas the crisis produced far-reaching political change, signalling power-shifts from councils to mayor as chief executives.[12]

The German Municipal Statute (*Deutsche Gemeindeordnung*, DGO) of January 1935 provided the first unitary and centralised framework for local governance

---

[8]   Hofmann, *Zwischen Rathaus und Reichskanzlei*, p. 69.

[9]   LAB, StA 6031, Bl Städtetag,.17, Deutsche Städtetag, Annual General Meeting, 27 Sept. 1929; cf., LAB 142/1 StB 435, Preussischer Städtetag Nr 250, 21 Oct. 1930. Oberregierungsrat Romig, Kiel, 'Sind Mißtrauensvoten von Stadtverordnetenversammlungen rechtswirksam?', *Frankfurter Zeitung*, Nr. 966–968, 30 Dec. 1930. LAB 142/1 StB955, Stadt Darmstadt, Der Oberbürgermeister (Wilhelm Glässing) to Oberbürgermeister Dr Mitzlaff, Deutsche Städtetag, 8 Nov. 1925.

[10]   Anthony McElligott, *Contested City: Municipal Politics and the Rise of Nazism in Altona 1917–1937* (Ann Arbor, University of Michigan Press, 1998), pp. 141–4; Volker Wünderich, *Arbeiterbewegung und Selbstverwaltung. KPD und Kommunalpolitik in der Weimarer Republik mit dem Beispiel Solingen* (Wuppertal, Peter Hammer, 1980), p. 98.

[11]   Otto Ziebill, *Bürger – Städte – Staat* (Stuttgart, Cologne, Kohlhammer, 1963), p. 50. Martina Sönnichsen, 'Heinrich Sahm', in Wolfgang Ribbe (ed.), *Stadtoberhäupter: Biographien Berliner Bürgermeister im 19. und 20. Jahrhundert* (Berlin, Stapp, 1992), pp. 230–231, 248. On Boß see Engeli, *Gustav Boß* op cit.; Hans J. Reichhardt, *Berlin in der Weimarer Republik: die Stadtverwaltung unter Oberbürgermeister Gustav Boß* (Berlin, Presse- und Informationsdienst, 1975).

[12]   *Kommunales Jahrbuch* (Jena, Fischer, 1931), p. 47; Holtmann, 'Die Krise des Föderalismus und der kommunalen Selbstverwaltung', p. 196. Wolfgang Hofmann, 'Konrad Adenauer und die Krise der kommunalen Selbstverwaltung in der Weimarer Republik', in *Konrad Adenauer: Oberbürgermeister von Köln. Festgabe der Stadt Köln zum 100. Geburtstag ihres Ehrenbürgers am 5. Januar 1976* (Cologne, Rheinland Verlag, 1976), pp. 329–54.

(Berlin had received its own statute in 1934).[13] It also completed the process the budgetary crisis began by privileging the *Bürgermeisterverfassung* system over the *Magistratsverfassung*. It reduced councils to advisory bodies whilst giving mayors power of (albeit limited) decision-making. Consequently, a more executive style of government was instituted emphasising mayoral functions as state agents within a chain of command led by the higher echelons of bureaucracy in the interior ministry. Historians now acknowledge the DGO actually strengthened the mayoralty *vis-à-vis* the Nazi Party's regional and local offices rather than the reverse. But mayors were also subjected to greater scrutiny and interference from state bodies.[14] This was nothing new. Nearly a century earlier, Prussia's mayoralty had been severely circumscribed after the municipal statute was amended in 1853 and 1856, thus reducing mayors to the monarch's local agents.[15]

The DGO disappeared in 1945 along with the Nazi state, but soon re-emerged in variously revised forms in all four occupation zones. For example, Württemberg's post-war municipal statute of December 1945 was based almost entirely on the DGO (with only the 'Nazi' clauses removed). This was not uncommon. In the British Zone (covering largely what had been Prussian territory in north Germany), an attempt was made to radically break with German traditions by introducing a revised statute in April 1946, partly based on the English model of 'depoliticised' mayors representing the people and town clerks responsible for overseeing administration.[16] But as both Otto Ziebill and Wolfgang Rudzio have shown, this effort was incomplete.[17] Instead, a mixture of the British model and *Magistratsverfassung* emerged in much of north Germany, with councils as sole and decisive organs and mayors merely their representative agents.[18]

If in the British zone German mayors were modelled on their English counterparts, in the French zone they were to resemble *prefects* in a chain of command. This version held sway particularly in the Rhineland and Saarland. Here, mayors had greater powers and served longer terms. In Bavaria, Hesse and Baden-Württemberg, where American influence was strongest, mayors derived their legitimacy as chief

[13]   Roger H. Wells, 'Municipal Government in National Socialist Germany', *The American Political Science Review*, 29, 4 (Aug., 1935), pp. 652–8. The fullest discussion of the DGO remains Matzerath's, *Nationalsozialismus und kommunale Selbstverwaltung*.

[14]   Jeremy Noakes, 'Oberbürgermeister and Gauleiter City Government between Party and State', in Hirschfeld and Kettenacker (eds), *Der 'Führerstaat'*, p. 205. LAB Rep. 142/1 StB 2934, and Rep. 142/1 StB 2376.

[15]   *Wörterbuch des deutchen Staats- und Verwaltungsrechts*. Vol. 3, p. 424. Rolf Richard Grauhan, 'Zur politischen Theorie der Stadt', *Archiv für Kommunalwissenschaft* 4 Jg. (1965), p. 88.

[16]   Wolfgang Rudzio, *Die Neuordnung des Kommunalwesens in der Britischen Zone. Zur Demokratisierung und Dezentralisierung der politischen Struktur: eine britische Reform und ihre Ausgang* (Stuttgart, Deutsche Verlags-Anstalt, 1968), p. 49; Rainer Frey, 'Kommunale Selbstverwaltung im Verfassungsstaat', in idem (ed.), *Kommunale Demokratie. Beiträge für die Praxis der kommunalen Selbstverwaltung* (Bonn-Bad Godesberg, Verlag Neue Gesellschaft, 1976), pp. 18, 21. Wolfgang Haller und Karl-Heinz Naßmacher, 'Rat und Verwaltung im Prozeß kommunalpolitische Willensbildung', in Frey, op cit., p. 160.

[17]   Ziebill, *Bürger – Städte – Staat*, p. 63; Rudzio, *Die Neuordnung*, pp. 58ff.

[18]   Wolfgang Rudzio, *Das politische System der Bundesrepublik Deutschland* (Opladen, Leske und Budrich, 2003), pp. 404ff.

executives of city administrations and councils from the electorate. The Americans, like the British, were careful both to avoid investing too much power in the mayor's office without appropriate checks and to ensure that mayoralty was protected from the arbitrary interferences characteristic of the DGO. Thus:

> In order to encourage local responsibility, we [the American military authorities] are forbidding provisions which would allow an official of one unit to pass upon or remove the officials selected by the councils or popular election, or to have a general veto power over their decisions.

General Clay's directive also ensured that 'In addition, no chief executive will have power to veto the actions of the elective council'.[19] Meanwhile, after the 1946 reform in the Russian zone, mayors were largely reduced to party/state functionaries, roles even more accentuated under the SED-led German Democratic Republic. Thus, in the four zones, mayors could be either representatives of the people, servants of the state or its substitute (i.e. the military authorities until 1949), or agents of a political party, or any combination of these.[20]

With the Basic Law of 1949, some autonomy was restored to West Germany's municipalities (Art. 28); at the same time, their place within the overall structure of government and administration was clarified by restating the mayor's ultimate responsibility to the state. This aspect of local government was underscored with amendments to local statutes in 1953 and 1956 apparently reinforcing the executive *vis-à-vis* councils, while simultaneously identifying mayors as the agents responsible for translating into practice Bundestag-approved policies.[21] These measures appeared to emphasise more the mayoralty as state agent, mirroring, superficially at least, developments in East Germany. Moreover, the term of office was shortened to between five and eight years, notwithstanding possible re-election.[22] But the picture was complicated by the fact that from the 1950s mayors were increasingly answerable either to their party machines or competing council factions. Less certain is how far this trend towards mayoralty becoming an arm of government or a party office was

---

[19]   *The Papers of General Lucius D. Clay, Germany 1945–1949*, Jean Edward Smith (ed.) (Bloomington, Indiana University Press, 1974), p. 76.

[20]   Frey, 'Kommunale Selbstverwaltung', p. 18; Jürgen Bertram, *Staatspolitik und Kommunalpolitik. Notwendigkeit und Grenzen ihrer Koordinierung* (Stuttgart, Kohlhammer, 1967), pp. 148–55; Dorothee Führe, *Die französische Besatzungspolitik in Berlin von 1945 bis 1949: Déprussianisation und Décentralisation* (Berlin, Weissensee-Verlag, 2001); Martin Broszat and Hermann Weber (eds), *SBZ-Handbuch. Staatliche Verwaltungen, Parteien, gesellschaftliche Organisation und ihre Führungskräfte in der Sowjetischen Besatzungszone Deutschlands 1945–1949* (Munich, R. Oldenbourg, 1993), pp. 89, 300–303.

[21]   Hubert Fink, 'Der Ulmer Gemeinderat in Spannungsfeld zwischen Representation und Verwaltung', in Hans Eugen Specker (ed.), *Tradition und Wagnis: Ulm 1945–1972. Theodor Pfizer, 1948, Oberbürgermeister der Stadt Ulm als Festschrift gewidmet* (Ulm, Forschungen zur Geschichte der Stadt Ulm vol. 12, 1974), pp. 151–2.

[22]   Rudzio, *Das politische System*, pp. 407–9. Gerd Schmidt-Eichstaedt, Wolfgang Haus and Isabell Janner-Stade, *Die Gemeindeordnungen in der Bundesrepublik Deutschland* (Stuttgart, Kohlhammer, 1975).

challenged by the 1968 student protest movement, with its message of 'bottom up' and 'direct' politics that increasingly fed into local and street-based initiatives.[23]

The Mayors

Traditionally, mayors were drawn from urban elites with legal training, as required for entry into the civil service or judiciary. Commonly in their early 40s, they usually acquired administrative experience, either as privy counsellors in regional government offices, city treasurers or deputy mayors, before becoming mayoral candidates. By 1900, social exclusivity was being challenged by a new breed of upwardly mobile administrators from lower middle-class backgrounds, reflecting the great industrial and urban transformation of late-nineteenth-century Germany. With a grandfather who had been a bank clerk and a father a clerk in a court of appeal, Cologne's lord mayor, Konrad Adenauer, for example, was clearly *petit bourgeois* (although he quickly foresook his humble origins). But the main corps of imperial Germany's mayors, especially those in larger towns and cities, like Richard Rive in Halle, Alois Wermuth in Berlin, Theodor Spitta in Bremen and Franz Adickes in Frankfurt, hailed from a patrician administrative elite.[24]

In spite of the attempt under Weimar to open the administration to non-traditional groups, the mayoralty continued to be filled largely by career administrators. As Wolfgang Hofmann has shown in his study of big-city lord mayors, the 1918 revolution had only limited impact upon the mayoralty. While in some localities mayors or their deputies took permanent leave, or were occasionally hounded from office by revolutionary workers and soldiers' councils, most mayors survived and indeed sought to regain the political initiative.[25] Where change occurred, it was mainly through local elections (1920/1921, 1924 and 1929). But even universal suffrage did little to transform mayoral social profiles. Social Democrats like Robert Leinert in Hanover, Philip Scheidemann (the republic's first minister president) in Kassel, Max Brauer in Altona[26] and Heinrich Beims in Magdeburg, all of whom were 'outsiders'

---

[23]   Rainer Frey, 'Verwaltungsreformen in Deutschland: Voraussetzung zur Verwirklichung lokaler Demokratie?', in idem, *Kommunale Demokratie*, pp. 97, 103–129. Haller and Naßmacher, 'Rat und Verwaltung', p. 142.

[24]   Hofmann, *Zwischen Rathaus und Reichskanzlei*, p. 33*ff*; idem, 'Oberbürgermeister als politische Elite im wilhelminischen Reich und in der Weimarer Republik', Schwabe (ed.), *Oberbürgermeister*, p. 22. Theodor Spitta, *Aus meinem Leben. Bürger und Bürgermeister in Brmen* (Munich, Paul List, 1969), p. 25. Heinrich Bleicher, 'Franz Adickes als Kommunalpolitker', *Franz Adickes, Sein Leben und Sein Werk. Frankfurter Lebensbilder XI*, (Frankfurt, Englert und Schlosser, 1929).

[25]   Hofmann, *Zwischen Rathaus und Reichskanzlei*, pp. 59–68; Wilhelm Ribhegge, 'Die Systemfunktion der Gemeinden. Zur deutschen Kommunalgeschichte seit 1918', *Aus Politik und Zeitgeschichte. Beilage zur Wochenzeitung Das Parlament* B47 (Nov. 1973), p. 9; Bogdan Dopierala, 'Die Rolle des Oberbürgermeisters und des Berufsbeamtentums in der Entwicklung der deutschen Stadt', in Wilhelm Rausch (ed.), *Die Städte Mitteleuropas im 20. Jahrhundert* (Linz and Donau, Österreichischer Arbeitskreis für Stadtgeschichtsforschung, 1984), pp. 119–20.

[26]   Erich Lüth, *Max Brauer, Glasbläser, Bürgermeister, Staatsmann* (Hamburg, Lichtwark Stiftung 1972).

rather than legally-trained career administrators, were the exception.[27] The Third Reich produced little change, for all the apparent rupture in 1933 as parvenu Nazi activists laid claim to the mayoralty.[28] With the introduction of the DGO in 1935, professional administrators returned to mayoral office. Honorary, layman mayors could be found only in smaller rural communities.

Until 1933, mayors were powerful, independent figures whose influence extended beyond the municipality to that of region and nation. Under the imperial system, mayors not infrequently sat in the upper chamber of the Prussian parliament (*Herrenhaus*) or in the Council of State (*Staatsrat*); very often they took seats in the regional parliament, the Landtag. This tradition survived (albeit in transformed conditions) under the republic.[29] Several mayors became ministers in various Weimar cabinets, while Essen's lord mayor, Hans Luther, became chancellor in the mid-1920s. During the 1920s, some mayors enjoyed the status, power and influence usually associated with ministers. After the dismissal of the Prussian administration in summer 1932, chancellor Franz von Papen appointed Franz Bracht, Luther's successor as lord mayor of Essen, plenipotentiary of Prussia; meanwhile Leipzig's mayor, Carl Goerdeler, was co-opted to the cabinet charged with formulating proposals for rehabilitating municipal finances, and continued in this role under Hitler (until the mid-1930s).[30]

Collectively, mayors had a voice through their organisation, the *Deutsche Städtetag*, comprising nearly 300 lord mayors of large towns and cities. The *Städtetag* participated vigorously in the *Reichsreform* debates on restructuring the Reich's administrative framework.[31] Finally, until the mid-twentieth century, mayors were usually confirmed in office for periods of ten or 12 years, and often remained in office for much longer, thereby providing significant stability at local level (Rive, for instance, led Halle from 1906 until retiring in 1933 at 68). We should remember this when considering the general political instability of Reich cabinets under the republic. Indeed, Weimar should be seen more as a 'golden age' for the

---

[27]   Ernst Rudolf Huber, *Deutsche Verfassungsgeschichte seit 1789: Band VI Die Weimarer Reichsverfassung* (Stuttgart, Kohlhammer, 1981), pp. 776–7; Suzanne Miller, 'Sozialdemokratische Oberbürgermeister in der Weimarer Republik', in Schwabe (ed.), *Oberbürgermeister*, pp. 109–24. Herbert Jacob, *German Administration since Bismarck: Central Authority versus Local Autonomy* (New Haven, Princeton, 1963), p. 97.

[28]   For some good examples, seem Barbara Fait, 'Die Kreisleiter der NSDAP – nach 1945', in Martin Broszat, Klaus-Dietmar Henke and Hans Woller (eds), *Von Stalingrad zur Währungsreform. Zur Sozialgeschichte des Umbruchs in Deutschland* (Munich, R. Oldenbourg, 1990).

[29]   Bertram, *Staatspolitik und Kommunalpolitik*, pp. 150–51; Dieter Rebentisch, 'Die Selbstverwaltung der Weimarer Zeit', in Püttner (ed.), *Handbuch*, pp. 93–4; Rive, *Lebenserinnerung*, chapters 7 and 8.

[30]   Bracht was appointed Reich interior minister without portfolio in October, continuing until 20 January 1933. From the later 1930s Goerdeler found himself at odds with the regime, becoming involved with the resistance and plot to kill Hitler. He was tried and executed in 1944, Reich, *Carl Goerdeler*, op cit.

[31]   Wolfgang Hofmann, *Städtetag und Verfassungsordnung: Position und Politik der Hauptgeschäftsführer eines kommunalen Sptizenverbandes* (Stuttgart, Kohlhammer, 1966).

mayoralty than a period of decline, as sometimes portrayed. It was the Nazi seizure of power in 1933 that inaugurated an era of mayoral instability.

Mayoralty's importance and influence waned during the Third Reich. Karl Fiehler, mayor of Munich, in spite of being *Reichsstatthalter* (Reich governor) responsible for communal affairs, was ultimately a lightweight figure increasingly with little influence over Reich policy (ironically, least of all over communal matters!).[32] The Third Reich's collapse saw mayoral status revive, especially during reconstruction in the Federal Republic (though less is known about mayors in the Democratic Republic). Thus in West Germany many lord mayors sought and attained roles taking them beyond their parochial boundaries. Konrad Adenauer's and Willy Brandt's careers show how after 1945 mayors might still make the journey from *Rathaus* to chancellor's office (Brandt spoke of his period as Berlin's mayor as a 'testing ground' for the chancellorship).[33] Indeed, any mayor of divided Berlin would perforce be thrust to national and international prominence, as the examples of Ernst Reuter during the Berlin Blockade, Richard von Weizsäcker (later president of the Federal Republic) in the early 1980s, or Walter Momper as the Berlin Wall was breached in 1989, demonstrate.

Difficult Times

Baron vom Stein envisaged local self-government as a protection against an impersonal and over-weaning bureaucracy. Whether governing under the *Bürgermeisterverfassung* or the *Magistratverfassung*, mayors were often viewed as 'men of the people'. If they did not come from the towns or cities they presided over, they quickly integrated into the leading social circles. Mayors quite often made a career in their hometown. There are many striking examples of this. Adenauer, for example, after studying law in Munich and Bonn, returned to Cologne to a legal post, before becoming a privy counsellor (*Beigeordneter*) to the city council in 1906. His success as an able administrator, and not least his political acumen, eventually led a small clique of city fathers to invite him to apply for the mayoralty in 1917, the post he held until the Nazis removed him in 1933.[34] His example is not atypical, as the careers of several contemporaries like Theodor Spitta (Bremen) or, indeed, many Nazi mayors show. Nor was this just an early-twentieth-century phenomenon, as we shall see with Arnulf Klett and Theodor Pfizer, discussed below, and more broadly in Rolf-Richard Grauhan's study of 20 large cities.[35] Such mayors were rightfully billed

---

[32]   Matzerath, *Nationalsozialismus und kommunale Selbstverwaltung*, pp. 204, 245; Helmut M. Hanko, 'Kommunalpolitik in der "Hauptstadt der Bewegung"', 1933–1935. Zwischen 'Revolutionärer' Umgestaltung und Verwaltungskontinuität', in Martin Broszat, Elke Fröhlich and Anton Grossmann (eds), *Bayern in der NS-Zeit*, Vol. III (Munich, R. Oldenbourg, 1977), pp. 410, 440.

[33]   Willy Brandt, *My Life in Politics* (Harmondsworth, Penguin, 1993) p. 22.

[34]   Hans-Peter Schwarz, *Adenauer. Band 1: Der Aufstieg . 1876–1952* (Munich 1994, orig. Stuttgart, Deutsche Verlags-Anstalt, 1986), pp. 133–73.

[35]   Rolf-Richard Grauhan, 'Die Wahl ansässiger und auswärtiger Bewerber zu Oberbürgermeistern. Auswirkungen von Urwahl und indirektor Wahl', *Archiv für*

'sons of the city' – a designation providing an interesting discourse of mayoralty in twentieth-century Germany that emphasised locality over nation, and populism over administration.

We should remember that before 1918 mayors might purport to act in their communities' interests, but this did not necessarily imply they were truly 'representatives of the people'.[36] Until universal suffrage in November 1918, active and passive citizenship was restricted to a privileged and monied few. The vom Stein reforms envisaged a threshold of 150 thaler and as much as 200 thaler in cities to determine a citizen's right to choose his council and mayor. In Prussia's capital, Berlin, only 11,000 from 156,000 residents – a mere 7 per cent – qualified to vote in the first post-reform municipal elections in April 1809. In 1849 a three-class franchise was introduced that divided the electorate into three equally-weighted classes according to aggregate tax paid, a system skewed in favour of the wealthy. A notorious example of the resultant inequality can be found in Essen where, between 1886 and 1894, Alfred Krupp was the only voter in Class I. In Cologne in 1909/1910 there were just 875 voters in Class I, but over 11,000 in Class II and a staggering 78,682 in Class III. This system was not confined to Prussia: the liberal state of Baden, for instance, had also introduced a similar tax threshold in 1837 designed to maintain bourgeois municipal hegemony. The proportion of the population entitled to vote varied from state to state and within Prussia, even between provinces, also from town to town as local by-laws were introduced around 1900 aimed at preventing working-class entry into local politics. Thus until 1918 Germany's mayors were not only faithful servants of the crown, but also governed as representatives of local elites, and acted as conservative bulwarks against Social Democracy.[37]

One allegation commonly levelled by the political right under Weimar was that political parties, notably the Social Democrats, had hijacked the mayoralty and municipal administrations. Mayoralty may indeed have become politicised after 1918, but only in the sense that the office was now subjected to the democratic process. In fact, no single party dominated. For example, of the 36 lord mayors who at some point governed the 20

Kommunalwissenschaft 1Jg. (1962), pp. 93–105, and p. 95 for reference to 'sons of the city'. For Brauer see, Lüth, *Max Brauer*. Notwithstanding the pioneering work of Matzerath and Noakes, there is still no comprehensive history of Third-Reich mayors.

[36] Herzfeld, *Demokratie und Selbstverwaltung*, p. 31; Frey, 'Kommunale Selbstverwaltung', pp. 15–16.

[37] Joachim Streisand, *Deutschland von 1789 bis 1815. Von der Französischen Revolution bis zu den Befreiungskriegen und dem Wiener Kongress* (East Berlin, VEB Deutscher Verlag der Wissenschaften 1977), p. 165; Wolfgang R. Krabbe, *Die deutsche Stadt im 19. und 20. Jahrhundert* (Göttingen, Vandenhoeck und Ruprecht, 1989), pp. 48–67; Heffter, *Selbstverwaltung*, p. 615; James J. Sheehan, *German Liberalism in the Nineteenth Century* (Chicago, London, University of Chicago Press, 1982, orig. 1978), p. 245; Wolfgang Hofmann, 'Preußische Stadtverordnetenversammlungen als Repräsentativ-Organe', in Jürgen Reulecke (ed.), *Die deutsche Stadt im Industriezeitalter. Beiträge zur Modernen deutschen Stadtgeschichte* (Wuppertal, Peter Hammer, 1978), p. 49. Helmuth Croon, 'Das Vordringen der Parteien im Bereich der kommunalen Selbstverwaltung', in idem, Wolfgang Hofmann and Georg Christoph von Unruh, *Kommunale Selbstverwaltung im Zeitalter der Industrialisierung* (Stuttgart, Kohlhammer, 1971), pp. 15–58.

largest Prussian cities under the republic, six were Social Democrats, five were Liberals, four from the Catholic Centre Party, five from the *Deutsche Volkspartei* (DVP), two from the *Deutsche Nationale Volkspartei* (DNVP), while 13 belonged to no party and only one represented a regional party. Even though these mayors, mostly, had strong party ties and their political philosophies informed their economic and social policies, there is little to suggest they privileged any particular party. Nor would this have been easy. Under Weimar nearly all major cities and towns were governed by coalitions, often with mayor and deputy-mayor drawn from the majority party and coalition partner. Inevitably, this meant municipal policy was often based on compromise.[38] Even where mayors were politically non-aligned, they still had to work closely with coalitions of parties. The lord mayor of Breslau, Otto Wagner, a career administrator with no immediate party affiliation, had to contend with a fractious council dominated by the SPD and the DNVP. Because Breslau had the *Magistratsverfassung*, Wagner would have needed all his skills of diplomacy and persuasive powers to manoeuvre his policies through.[39] His colleague Franz Bracht in Essen also faced a fractious council, but because Essen had the *Bürgermeisterverfassung*, Bracht was not hampered by the obstructions of the communist party (who held a quarter of council seats); he also could rely on a coalition made up of his own party, the Zentrum, and the minority SPD.

From 1933 to 1945, mayors, regardless of any allegiance to Nazism, were torn between their positions as state servants, their roles as the party's agent on the ground, and the rhetoric of people's representative.[40] For in spite of mayoralty's politicisation under the republic, the political claims upon the office only became acute after the Nazis came to power.[41] By late-summer 1932, many lord mayors already had been politically isolated after von Papen's 'constitutional putsch' against Prussia produced the removal of many political appointees from the Prussian administration.[42] After Hitler became chancellor in January 1933, mayors themselves became targets as local Nazi bosses moved against them. Between the end of January and mid-March most lord mayors were removed from office. While some were removed for political reasons, others, like Robert Lehr in Düsseldorf, were victims of personal vendettas.[43]

---

[38]   Ribhegge, 'Systemfunktion', pp. 8–9.

[39]   Krabbe, *Die deutsche Stadt*, p. 141.

[40]   Bruno Jung, *Der Bürgermeister als Diener des Volkes* (Stuttgart, Kohlhammer, 1937). Jung was a career administrator and lord mayor of Göttingen. Rudolf Suthoff-Gross, *Die Rechtsstellung des Bürgermeisters in seinem Verhältnis zum Staat und zu den übrigen Beamten der Gemeinde* (Berlin, C. Heymann, 1941).

[41]   Matzerath, *Nationalsozialismus und kommunale Selbstverwaltung*, pp. 229ff.; Krabbe, *Die deutsche Stadt*, pp. 141–2.

[42]   *Akten der Reichskanzle Weimarer Republiki: Das Kabinett von Papen I and II* (Boppard am Rhein, Harald Boldt, 1989), Doc. 73, pp. 267–72, and Doc. 197, pp. 888–9; Harry Graf Kessler, *Tagebücher 1918–1937. Politik, Kunst und Gesellschaft der zwanziger Jahre* (Frankfurt a.M., 1961), entry 21 Sept. 1932, 691; Thomas Trumpp, 'Franz von Papen, der preußisch-deutschen Dualismus und die NSDAP in Preußen. Ein Beitrag zur Vorgeschichte des 20 Juli 1932' (D.phil. diss., University of Tübingen, 1963).

[43]   Peter Hüttenberger, *Düsseldorf. Geschichte von den Ursprüngen bis zur 20.Jahrhundert, Band 3: Die Industrie- und Verwaltungsstadt im 20.Jahrhundert* (Düsseldorf, Schwann, 1990), pp. 465, 469.

In Germany's largest 48 cities, only eight lord mayors were considered 'reliable' or indispensable by the new regime: these included Heinrich Sahm in Berlin (elected 1930 and dismissed 1935),[44] Arthur Menge in Hanover (elected 1925, dismissed 1937), Julius Friedrich in Wuppertal (elected 1931, also removed in 1937) and Walter Hartmann in Remscheid, who had survived the revolution of 1918 only to be removed from office in 1937. The mayoral purge also extended to smaller communities, albeit on a lesser and more uneven scale.[45] In some *Gaue*, particularly in rural Bavaria, Thuringia and eastern Prussia, several mayors remained (initially) unaffected by the 'seizure of power' due to local resistance to Nazi attempts to commandeer the mayoralty.[46]

The purges plunged the mayoralty and local government into crisis as qualified mayors virtually disappeared. In their place came a generation of younger incumbents with little preparation for office. The Gau leadership of Rhineland Pfalz reported in October, 'The experiences we have so far made show that the men we have appointed to communal organisations are in the majority unqualified newcomers, who have not yet fully grasped the nature of municipal policy'.[47] The reason was that local Nazi cells had 'seized' the mayoralty (and town halls) in March 1933. According to the NSDAP's internal survey of 1935, 47 per cent of Germany's 2,228 mayors had joined the Party before January 1933 (though this does not mean they were in office when they became members), 31 per cent had joined since March, while only 22 per cent were not members. In smaller communities, the corresponding figures were: 19.3, 40.6 and 40.1 per cent.[48] Franz Buchner, mayor of Starnberg who headed the NSDAP's municipal office in the Gau of Munich Upper Bavaria,[49] reported a dearth of suitably qualified party members leading him to rely on 'fellow travellers' (i.e., non-Nazis) to fill 10,000 mayoral and councillor posts (which he claimed to have achieved by the mid autumn).[50] How to strike a balance between suitable

[44] Described by Sönnichsen, as a 'willing instrument' of the Nazis, 'Heinrich Sahm', pp. 251, 256.

[45] See Noakes, 'Oberbürgermeister and Gauleiter', passim, and Horst Matzerath, 'Oberbürgermeister im Dritten Reich', in Hirschfeld and Kettenacker (eds), Der 'Führerstaat', p. 235.

[46] Bundesarchiv Berlin-Lichterfelde (hereafter Barch) NS25/123iii Bl.113–114, NSDAP Gauleitung Thüringen Amt für Kommunalpolitik to Oberste Leitung der P.O. der NSDAP Amt für Kommunalpolitik, 17 Jan. 1934. NS25/123iv Bl. 4–9, NSDAP Gau München-Oberbayern to Oberste Leitung der P.O. Kommunalpolitische Abteilung, Berlin, 17 Oct. 1933.

[47] Barch NS25/123i, Bl. 81, NSDAP Gauleitung Rheinpfalz to Oberste Leitung der P.O. der NSDAP, 10 Oct. 1933; Bl.65–6, Betr. Telefongespräch v. 18 Jan. 1934 mit Pg. Wahl, Gauamtsleiter für Kommunalpolitik des Gaues Pommern (re: activity report Dec. 1933). Albert Krebs, The Infancy of Nazism: The Memoirs of Ex-Gauleiter Albert Krebs 1923–1933, (ed. and trans.) William Sheridan Allen (New York, New Viewpoints, 1976), p. 270.

[48] Martin Broszat, Der Staat Hitlers Grundlegung und Entwicklung seiner inneren Verfassung (Munich, Deutscher Taschenbuch Verlag, 1969), pp. 303–304. Ribhegge, 'Systemfunktion', p. 15.

[49] Fait, 'Die Kreisleiter der NSDAP – nach 1945', pp. 263–72.

[50] Barch NS25/123i Bl.2 Gau-Amtsleitung für Kommunalpolitik des Gaues München-Oberbayern an die Oberste Leitung der P.O. der NSDAP Amt für Kommunalpolitik 16 Nov. 1933. See ibid Bl.22 for dismissals. NS25/123iv Bl.5–6, 8.

mayoral candidates who were either National Socialists or experts (or ideally both) continued to vex regional leaders throughout the 1930s and really entailed finding a compromise between Party, people and bureaucracy.[51]

The search for compromise and suitable mayors proved difficult. Indeed, in some *Gaue*, party activists appointed as commissarial mayors soon had to be dismissed because they lacked the requisite qualities or because of financial impropriety. Meanwhile several career administrators who replaced Nazi mayors after the introduction of the DGO, and remained reluctant to join the party after the ban on membership was lifted in 1937, attracted criticism from Martin Bormann, who threatened them with dismissal for their diffident attitudes or their 'lack of political understanding'.[52] This tension between the demand for professional administration and the primacy of politics dogged mayoralty throughout the Third Reich.

To complicate matters further, not all the regime's new lord mayors were appointed simply because they were fanatical Nazis like Emil Brix in Altona (removed in 1936 for malfeasance). In a few significant, if sometimes short-lived, cases they were selected either as part of empire-building by the local *Gauleiter*,[53] or to appease locally entrenched elites, like Carl Vincent Krogmann the scion of a Hamburg patrician family with close connections to the city's mercantile elite; Dr Edmund Stoeckle, as well as being eminently qualified, an academic who fitted well into Augsburg circles; 70 year old Thomas Reissmann-Grone with close connections to Essen's mining industry.[54] As mentioned earlier, the new regime had to draw on expertise where it could find it. Fourteen lord mayors of larger cities appointed during the Third Reich managed to keep their distance from the Nazi Party, though here a deputy who was a party member was commonly appointed.[55] Occasionally, the regime was fortunate in having candidates within its own ranks qualified to undertake the complex tasks of municipal administration: Dr Fritz Krebs in Frankfurt am Main, Dr Karl Strolin in Stuttgart, Bruno Schüler in Dortmund; Dr Hellmuth Will in Königsberg; and not least Karl Fiehler, who had joined Munich's administration in 1919 and became mayor in

---

[51]   Barch NS25/123iv Bl. 27–28 Der Untergauleitung to Oberste Leitung der P.O. in Berlin, 10 Oct. 1933.

[52]   Barch NS22/848, Der Stellv. Des Führers (Bormann) 8 May 1939, Anordnung Nr 101/39 'Betr. Anweisung an die Beauftragter der NSDAP in der Gemeinde'. Hanko, 'Kommunalpolitik', p. 416.

[53]   Jeremy Noakes, 'Viceroys of the Reich? Gauleiters 1925–1945', Anthony McElligott and Tim Kirk (eds), *Working Towards the Führer. Essays in Honour of Sir Ian Kershaw* (Manchester University Press, 2003), pp. 133–4.

[54]   See Carl Vincent Krogmann's questionnable self-apologia, *Es ging um Deutschlands Zukunft 1932–1939. Erlebtes täglich diktiert von dem früheren regierenden Bürgermeister von Hamburg* (Leoni am Starnberger. See, Druffel, 1976); Helmut M. Hanko, 'München 1933–1935. Das Rathaus unterm Hakenkreuz', Rausch (ed.), *Die Städte Mitteleuropas*, pp. 290ff; Gerhard Hetzer, 'Die Industriestadt Augsburg. Eine Sozialgeschichte der Arbeiteropposition', in Martin Broszat, Elke Fröhlich and Anton Grossmann (eds), *Bayern in der NS-Zeit*, Vol. III (Munich, R. Oldenbourg, 1977), pp. 80–81, fn. 180, for Stoeckle. Edward Petersen, *The Limits of Hitler's Power* (Princeton University Press, 1969), p. 355.

[55]   Noakes, 'Oberbürgermeister and Gauleiter', op cit. Conversely, a non-party deputy with administrative expertise was often appointed to assist Nazis who lacked municipal experience.

1933 shortly before his 38th birthday, had municipal experience. Close scrutiny of Third-Reich mayors shows that the shortage of quality was located mostly in smaller communities, where mayors frequently possessed only limited education and lacked the training to comprehend the almost constant flow of decrees and laws.[56]

Whatever the mayor's background, he was expected to fit the 'leadership' role favoured by the regime. Buchner believed 'mayors should not be administrators but leaders of their communities, shapers of the small and smallest cells of the new state … Not just knowledge qualifies for leadership but above all character and personality and faithfulness to the movement'.[57] Unlike ostensibly weak Weimar mayors, buffeted between parties, Nazi mayors were to be men of action, decisive and independent of vested interests. Buchner's colleague in the Main Office for Municipal Policy (HafK), Dr Schön, described (in rather rosy terms) the difference between conditions before and after 1933:

Today an action of the communal leadership is not based on the decision of many men, who perhaps arrived at this decision after excruciating squabbling under unacceptable conditions. Instead, today's communal leadership lies in the hand of a single man supported by a number of men who advise, but who do not decide.[58]

Schön warned mayors not to get lost in the minutiae of office work but delegate this to others, concentrating on the important job of explaining and enacting the regime's broader vision.

This was fine in theory, but the reality was very different outside towns and cities with large administrations and well-paid mayors.[59] Most mayors neither had armies of competent officials to support them nor high salaries. After the DGO's introduction, the mayoralty in communities with less than 10,000 inhabitants became an honorary office, unless otherwise stipulated by the chief regional administrator (*Regierungspräsident*), remunerated on an expenses-only basis. Several mayors in Schleswig-Holstein soon complained the scale of allowances was set too low, especially in those communities that were virtually dormitory towns to Kiel or the Greater Hamburg conurbation. Here mayoral workloads were fairly demanding, requiring high levels of competence, much time and energy, often at the expense of one's own livelihood. The mayor of Quickborn to the north of Hamburg, who was also a farmer, complained that as mayor he had to bear a monthly shortfall of 15 Reichsmark. He told the Gauleiter's office that he was no longer willing to jeopardise

[56] Barch NS22/848 Reischleitung Hauptamt für Kommunalpolitik (Schön), 'Rundschreiben G 34/37', 2 June 1937, pp. 1–2.
[57] Barch NS25/123iv Bl. 7, NSDAP Gau München-Oberbayern to Oberste Leitung der P.O. Kommunalpolitische Abteilung, 17 Oct. 1933.
[58] Barch NS25/568ii Bl. 123, Amtsleiter Dr Schön, 'Nationalsozialismus und Gemeindepolitik', p. 5.
[59] Mayoral and lord mayoral salaries ranged from 12,000 Reichsmark to 18,000 Reichsmark. Barch NS25/123iv Bl. 8, NSDAP Gau München-Oberbayern to Oberste Leitung der P.O. Kommunalpolitische Abteilung, 17 Oct. 1933. NS 25/346 Bl. 196, NSDAP Gauleitung Schleswig-Holstein Amt für Kommunalpolitik to Reichsleitung für Kommunalpolitik (Munich), 2 Sept. 1936.

his business. There were many like him. Sievers, the municipal policy chief for the Gau and mayor of Flensburg, feared he would be unable to find replacements should these mayors actually resign, producing a crisis in local administration.[60]

These small community mayors were mayoralty's soft under-belly during the Third Reich and propaganda efforts were made to bolster morale and cast them in a positive light. In Willi Harms' novel *Der neue Bürgermeister* (1942), the adventurer Hartwig Klockmann becomes mayor and breathes new life into the small community over which he presides. He is presented as an optimistic and worldly figure and an agent of modernisation.[61] In the same year the novel was serialised in *Der Angriff*, several documentaries were mooted that also would present local administration and mayors in a positive light, and as the bulwark of the national community (*Volksgemeinschaft*).[62] The director of Saxony's Gau Office for municipal policy, Dr Heberer, argued that especially under wartime conditions, mayors had to ensure their community 'is also at the same time a collection point for the flowing energies that in turn are made useful by the generality [nation] ...'.[63] In reality these mayors were caught between several forces over which they had little control.

The contradiction facing mayors during the Third Reich – whether to be servants of the state, agents of the party and representatives of the people – became particularly acute during the war years, when they had to be all three. In themselves, these roles were not necessarily polarities. But the Third Reich's internal dynamics, fed by the demands of 'total war', produced chaotic conditions in local administrations, with many mayors, especially in smaller communities, at their wits end as competing agencies and popular expectations pulled them in different directions.[64] Some committed suicide, while those deemed to have failed the regime were summarily executed in the Third Reich's final days. Yet, as in 1918, the mayoralty did not disintegrate upon defeat. Indeed, for all the difficulties, it proved remarkably sturdy, once more becoming the vehicle for orderly transition from war to peace.

[60]   Barch NS25/346 Bl. 136–7, NSDAP Gauleitung Schleswig-Holstein Amt für Kommunalpolitik to Reichsleitung für Kommunalpolitik, 2 Sept. 1935.

[61]   Willi Harms, *Der neue Bürgermeister* (Munich, Eher, 1942), pp. 185, 189.

[62]   Barch NS25/1267, correspondence between several mayors, HafK and Wien-Film Abteilung Kulturfilm, in May 1942. Barch NS25/1050 Bl. 12.

[63]   Barch NS25/3, Bl. 29–59, 'Die sächsische Gemeinden im Kriegseinsatz. Kommunalpolitische Arbeit der Heimatfront im Kriegsjahr 1942', Bl. 30.

[64]   Barch NS25/654 Bl. 29, 31, 36–7, Hauptamt für Kommunalpolitik (Dr Patutschnick) to SS-Sturmbannführer Dr Gengenbach, reports Oberdonau April 1941, Südetenland Feb. 1941, Halle-Merseburg March–May 1941. Anthony McElligott, 'The German Local Government Statute, 1935–1945 and the crisis of self-government and local administration' in Hermann van Goethem, Bruno Wevers, Nico Wouters (eds), *Local government in occupied Europe (1939–1945). Acts of the international conference University of Antwerp, 15–16 November 2002* (Gent, Academia Press, 2005).

New Beginnings?

Mayoralty's resilience made the transition to peacetime easier than it might have been. As in November 1918, in spring 1945 there was continuity of administrative personnel and experience. Indeed, in some areas, the war's end produced some odd scenes. In Stuttgart the French military commander, General Schwartz, reconfirmed the Nazi mayor Karl Strölin in office and ordered him to nominate his successor. Strölin, mayor since 1933, even participated in the swearing-in of Arnulf Klett on 22 April, and only then was he arrested by American military authorities.[65] Such incidents of smooth handover ensured Germany's military defeat did not produce a collapse of civilian administration and thus order.

With Nazi defeat a brief interregnum began during which mayors became *de facto* agents of the occupying powers, although they may not have seen themselves as such.[66] Many first-wave mayors had a foot in the past. When military commanders sought mayoral candidates, they ideally wanted someone unblemished by Nazism and with administrative skills, either in public service or private enterprise. In Wiesbaden, the French military authorities re-appointed the city's former mayor under Weimar, Dr Georg Krücke. Konrad Adenauer, now seventy, was invited by the Americans to return as mayor of Cologne (later dismissed by the British).[67] In Hamburg Rudolph Petersen, a scion of one of Hamburg's liberal patrician families who for generations had dominated the *Rathaus*, took over the reins of the city (to be electorally usurped by the sexagenarian Brauer the following year). In Berlin the Soviets appointed as mayor Dr Arthur Werner, the pre-war senator for buildings (Stadtbaurat) in Frankfurt an der Oder. Another Weimar mayor, 66 year old Otto Ostrowski, who had led Prenzlauer Berg during the 1920s, replaced Werner after a council vote in 1946.[68]

The pressing need to rapidly establish German civilian administration meant very often there was little time for thorough checks on candidates. Moreover, the military officers presiding over occupied towns were often young men with little experience of municipal administration let alone the country. This did not deter the British in

---

[65]   Paul Sauer, *Arnulf Klett: Ein Leben für Stuttgart* (Gerlingen, Bleicher, 2001), pp. 65–7; Hermann G. Haufler, 'Impressionen eines Zeitgenossen', in *Oberbürgermeister Dr. Arnulf Klett zum 25. Jährigen Dienstjubiläum gewidmet vom Gemeinderat der Stadt Stuttgart* (Stuttgart, Ernst Klett, 1971), p. 46; Kurt Leipner (ed.), *Fünfundzwanzig Jahre Oberbürgermeister: Festschrift für Dr. Klett* (Stuttgart, Klett Cotta, 1971), p. 44. Kurt Leipner (ed.), *Chronik der Stadt Stuttgart 1933–1945* (Stuttgart, Klett Cotta, 1982), p. 1024.

[66]   Leipner (ed.), *Fünfundzwanzig Jahre Oberbürgermeister*, pp. 41, 44, 47; Kurt Wernecke, 'Arthur Werner', in Ribbe (ed.), *Stadtoberhäupter*, p. 347.

[67]   Wolf-Arno Kropat, *Hessen in der Stunde Null 1945/47. Politik, Wirtschaft, Bildungswesen in Dokumenten* (Wiesbaden, Historische Kommission für Hessen, 1979), p. 46. Schwarz, *Adenauer*, pp. 428ff. Konrad Adenauer, *Memoirs 1945–1953*, transl. Beate Ruhm von Oppen (London, Weidenfeld and Nicolson, 1966), pp. 20–35.

[68]   Wernecke, 'Arthur Werner', op cit.; Wolfgang Ribbe, 'Otto Ostrowski', in idem (ed.), *Stadtoberhäupter*, pp. 360–66.

particular, who in 'colonial style' relied on local dignitaries to act as their agents.[69] In Oldenburg, the officer in charge of operations on the ground, Major Norris, who before the war had worked in insurance, appointed a lawyer, Fritz Koch, as mayor. Without impugning his character, there was a question mark over Koch. He had had long involvement in local administration and politics, joining the Free Corps as a student during the revolutionary period before travelling the political spectrum from the conservative German People's Party in the 1920s, to the ultra-nationalist German National People's Party in 1930, before finally joining the Nazi Party in May 1933. Koch remained in the city's administration until the end of the war. While briefly mayor, Koch faced some awkward questions about his activities during the Third Reich, before being cleared by a de-nazification tribunal. The military appointed former Oldenburg Provincial Bank director, Heinrich Krahnstöver, a more venerable local dignitary with a long history in regional and local administration as temporary lord mayor but retained Koch as his deputy. Even after the first municipal elections in 1946, Koch – who was apparently an indispensable administrator – embarked upon a new career as town clerk (*Stadtoberdirektor*).[70] Although Koch's Nazi membership was probably nominal, his appointment illustrates the military's difficulties in finding suitable mayoral candidates in the occupation's early days.

In the city-state of Bremen, the British military authorities appointed Erich Vagts, former German People's Party council-leader under the Republic. But Vagts too had had an ambivalent relationship with Nazism. He had been Bremen's special envoy in Berlin during the Third Reich, but his links to freemasonry had precluded Nazi Party membership. He thus appeared to fulfil two key criteria for candidacy: administrative experience and no taint of Nazism (for all his proximity to the regime). Vagts later recalled the circumstances of his appointment:

> I was again summoned to him [Major General Hakewell-Smith] on the 2 May and he told me in no uncertain terms 'you are now the governing mayor of Bremen'. I was not given permission to say anything, instead I was told I could either accept or decline. I accepted after a moment's thought, influenced by the conviction that possibly a communist could get the job.[71]

However, the Americans who shortly took over as military authority in Bremen, found Vagts 'totally unfit' for the job. Acting less colonially than their British counterparts, the Americans, after consulting local groups, removed Vagts in August,

---

[69] Rudzio, *Die Neuordnung*, p. 38. Ullrich Schneider, 'Nach dem Sieg: Besatzungspolitik und Militärrregierung 1945', Josef Foschepoth, Rolf Steininger (eds), *Britische Deutschland- und Besatzungspolitik 1945–1949* (Paderborn, Ferdinand Schöningh, 1985), pp. 57–62. See James Pollock, *Besatzung und Staatsaufbau nach 1945. Occupation Diary und Private Correspondence 1945–1948*, edited Ingrid Klüger-Bulcke (Munich, R. Oldenbourg, 1994), p. 166, for references to the British tendency to behave as 'colonial masters'.

[70] Fritz Koch, *Oldenburg 1945. Erinnerungen eines Bürgermeisters*, with a postscript by Albrecht Eckhardt (Oldenburg, H. Holzberg, 1984), pp. 31–5, 37, 39, 41, 51, 77ff., 138–45, passim.

[71] Hans Jansen and Renate Meyer-Braun, *Bremen in der Nachkriegszeit 1945–1949. Politik, Wirtschaft, Gesellschaft* (Bremen, Steintor, 1990), p. 20. Rudzio, *Die Neuordnung*, p. 37, for a similar account of the appointment of Bochum's mayor.

appointing instead 58 year old Wilhelm Kaisen, a respected Social Democrat leader under Weimar whose mandate was confirmed by the November 1946 election.[72]

Meanwhile, Soviet commanders usually satisfied themselves with candidates who had been either 'anti-fascists', concentration camp inmates or communists. Wolfgang Leonhard, reared as a young functionary in Soviet Russia during the 1930s and returning to Germany with Walter Ulbricht and other German Communist leaders in 1945, described the process in Berlin:

> After the order had been given to establish borough mayoralties, a [Soviet] commander simply went out onto the street and tugged at the sleeve of a man who happened to be passing by, and who appeared ..., for whatever reason, to be sympathetic-looking, telling him: 'Come here, you are now mayor'. He had inadvertently made a good choice for this man turned out to have ability.[73]

Leonhard also had to find a mayor for Berlin's Wilmersdorf district. He eventually did, but again purely through chance meeting. Within minutes, the Russian commandant for Wilmersdorf had 'sworn in' and toasted with vodka Dr Willenbücher, a former government counsellor and DVP member arrested by the Nazis after the failed plot to assassinate Hitler.[74] With Willenbücher, the Soviets and German communist leadership again struck lucky. But as Leonhard recalled:

> unfortunately, this was not always the case. Sometimes it came to light after a few days that the so-called 'anti-fascist', KZ-inmate, or 'old communist', were in fact opportunists, incompetent people, dubious characters, and in a few cases, even formerly active Nazis.[75]

But Ulbricht had not just to create an effective (and unsullied) municipal administration but also to mould it. The first Berlin council (elected for two years under the city's transitional constitution), led by Arthur Werner, who Leonhard described as 'feisty', had the huge task of organising food and fuel for the capital's population, and clearing rubble. But although Ulbricht tried to influence the council through Werner's appointment as mayor, neither he nor its members were 'men of straw, rather they were to a great degree their own persons with exceptional expertise who presented themselves with confidence and acted independently'.[76] Notwithstanding the acute difficulties facing it, this first council could thus respond effectively to the exhortations of Berlin's Soviet commandant, General Bersarin, for rapid restoration of normal life.

Mayors' everyday concerns in the weeks and months following defeat strikingly resembled those faced by their immediate predecessors. The task of reconstruction remained a project for the future notwithstanding the fairly short time it took to establish local government structures. There was little sense of a 'new beginning',

---

[72]   Kaisen remained in post until 1965, ibid., pp. 21–2, 269.

[73]   Wolfgang Leonhard, *Die Revolution entlässt ihre Kinder* (Cologne, Kiepenheuer und Witsch, 2003, orig. 1955), p. 438.

[74]   ibid, pp. 440–43.

[75]   ibid, pp. 438.

[76]   ibid, pp. 466, 468, 467; Wernecke, 'Arthur Werner', p. 343.

with mayors driven less by idealism than pragmatism. The war had killed nearly 10 per cent of Germany's population (pre-1938 borders); large swathes of most cities had been destroyed creating sanitary problems and acute housing shortages compounded by a large refugee population; moreover stark reductions in cereal yields and livestock further weakened an already hungry and sick population; to cap it all, Germany, as most of Europe, was hit by ferocious winters, exacerbated by acute fuel shortages. Unsurprisingly, Harold Zink, chief historian to the American High Commissioner, concluded: 'It was not ... for many months or even several years that local governments in anything like the normal sense existed in Germany.'[77] If somewhat exaggerated, Zink's observation caught the contemporary mood.

As during the war, it was the mayor often working alone if in a smaller community, who had to cope with these post-war contingencies. He had to provision the population with food and basic necessities, manage shortages, regulate the market, ensure order and sometimes was responsible for denazification. In smaller communities especially, this could render the mayor isolated. One of Germany's celebrated authors from the Weimar era, Hans Fallada, appointed mayor of the small community of Feldberg in Mecklenburg from June to October 1945, described things graphically in his semi-autobiographical novel *Der Alpdruck* (1947). Fallada's alter ego in the novel, Dr Doll, faces mountainous tasks, countless orders and endless quotas (but was spared the ritual humiliations of some real-life mayors by hostile Soviet officers[78]). The resulting petty conflicts alienate neighbours (a skin-deep friendliness anyway). Mirroring Fallada's real life, Doll the fictional mayor eventually suffers from self-doubt, nervous disorder and turns to alcohol and morphine to alleviate the depression produced by disillusion.[79]

But we should differentiate between appointed or even 'accidental' mayors, like Fallada or Dr Willensbücher, and those chosen for their previous experience. When Pollock travelled to Bremen in September 1945 to investigate various administrative difficulties besetting the enclave, he 'sat with the Oberbürgermeister (Kaisen) and received a wonderful illustration of a restrained official who didn't suggest what we should do, but expressed the hope that we should let the German officials know our decision at once'.[80] And Otto Engler who became Gießen's lord mayor from 1948 to

---

[77]   Harold Zink, *The United States in Germany, 1944–1955* (Princeton N.J. Van Nostrand, 1957), p. 173. John Gimbel, *The American Occupation of Germany. Politics and the Military, 1945–1949* (Stanford, Calif., Stanford University Press, 1968), pp. 46–51.

[78]   Norman M. Naimark, *The Russians in Germany. A History of the Soviet Zone of Occupation, 1945–1949* (Cambridge Mass., London, Belknap Press of Harvard University Press, 1995), pp. 60ff.

[79]   Hans Fallada, *Der Alpdruck* (Berlin, Aufbau Taschenbuch Verlag, 1998, orig. 1947), pp. 60–83. Jürgen Manthey, *Hans Fallada in Selbstzeugnissen und Bilddokumenten* (Reinbek, Rowohlt,1963), pp. 143–52, 158–9; H.J. Schueler, *Hans Fallada. Humanist and Social Critic* (The Hague and Paris, Mouton, 1970), pp. 88, 101. Benjamin Robinson, 'Hans Fallada Fixes at Zero Hour: A Bad Example for Rethinking the Postwar Canon', *German Studies Review* 27/1 (2004), pp. 63–82.

[80]   *Occupation Diary*, entry 21 Sept. 1945, p. 92.

1954, was described by Darmstadt's regional administrator as a man who 'spoke well and made an excellent impression' as both administrator and city representative.[81]

Rebuilding civilian life was a priority throughout occupied Germany. This meant restoring some political – and thus – democratic responsibility, starting with local elections in rural areas, followed by larger urban communities after new codes were introduced in 1946, as noted above. The Potsdam Agreement had called for the speedy restoration of democratic forms of government in Germany. The American authorities, particularly, were keen to rapidly establish an autonomous German administration. The British wanted to re-invigorate local representation, but in their own image as noted above. The Soviet authorities also sought to quickly re-establish the principle of local self-administration by introducing a new municipal code in September 1946. But they reserved the right (like the other military powers) to remove mayors and other municipal personnel.[82] The deterioration in allied political relations boded ill for municipal life in the Soviet Zone. The 1946 elections had been a success for the newly founded Socialist Unity Party: it gained over three-quarters of the vote in all five Soviet-Zone states, but also faced intractable problems from coalitions of the Christian Democratic Union (CDU) and Liberal Democratic Party (LDP) in several cities. Thus in Dresden, Dessau and Postdam, communist mayors had to relinquish their posts to LDP and CDU candidates. In fact the SED only managed to retain the mayoralty in areas where former-Social Democrats (now SED) had a strong showing, as in Leipzig and Magdeburg.[83] And the most stinging result for the SED came in Berlin, where it was pushed into third place behind the Social Democrats and Christian Democrats, in spite of Ulbricht's efforts to manipulate the outcome (this election led to Ostrowski becoming mayor).[84] The SED's problem was that it was viewed as the 'Russenpartei' – agent of the resented and much-feared Soviet authorities.[85]

The 1946 elections were to be the only occasion in the Soviet controlled zone when voters were given a choice. Within two years the situation altered drastically as the Cold War's onset triggered tightening totalitarian controls over free political expression. Party placemen either 'shadowed or replaced popular local leaders and mayors'. The mayoralty was thus progressively stymied as an autonomous expression of popular choice, while simultaneously becoming a contested site as the Communist leadership sought to transform the mayor into an agent of party and state (not unlike under the Third Reich).[86] With the hardening of the Cold War from the late-1940s, mayors who demonstrated too much independence fell foul of the SED and an increasingly paranoid Moscow. Potsdam's mayor, Erwin Köhler, a

[81]   Walter Mühlhausen (ed.), *Ludwig Bergsträsser. Befreiung, Besatzung, Neubeginn. Tagebuch des Darmstädter Regierungspräsidenten 1945–1948* (Munich, R. Oldenbourg, 1987), pp. 317–18.
[82]   Institut für Zeitgeschichte Munich (hereafter IfZM), 7/28–2/24–30 ufd, 'Confidential: OMG BS. VA PAB 42, Mag. Session, 24 September 1947, Dr Friedenburg O[ber]B[ürgermeister] to District Bürgermeister'. Broszat and Weber (eds), *SBZ-Handbuch*, p. 313; Ellwein and Hesse, *Das Regierungssystem*, p. 59.
[83]   Broszat and Weber (eds), *SBZ-Handbuch*, p. 306.
[84]   Leonhard, *Die Revolution*, pp. 440, 463, 466–7.
[85]   ibid., p. 558.
[86]   Broszat and Weber (eds), *SBZ-Handbuch*, pp. 307–13.

leading figure in the East German CDU, for example, was accused of espionage and executed.[87] Trusted party men replaced them. In Berlin, Friedrich Ebert, the son of the Weimar Republic's first president, was appointed mayor (in the Soviet Zone) in December 1948, and remained autocratically in office for the next two decades. Thus winter 1948–1949 marked a turning point for the mayoralty in what was soon to become the German Democratic Republic (GDR).

Meanwhile the 1948 elections, held in the other zones of Germany administered by the western allies, saw many existing mayors (appointed in 1945 or elected in 1946) confirmed in office. American observers noted that most incumbent mayors in small towns in Hesse and Bavaria were re-elected in the spring of 1948.[88] These elections showed a rightward shift, especially in rural areas. But in some areas they also appeared to negate the efforts of those charged with Germany's political rehabilitation, by electing former Nazis to the town halls, provoking Stuttgart's American consul to write of the 'renazification [sic] of German public life' in his report to Washington.[89] A notorious example occurred in the small town of Schwäbisch-Gmünd in the Pfalz region where the former Nazi mayor and party district leader, Franz Konrad, received three-quarters of the 16,695 votes (representing an 85 per cent turnout), and so ousted the incumbent mayor and founder of the Christian Democrat Party in the town, Franz Czisch. Ugly scenes reminiscent of late-Weimar political conflicts had surrounded the election campaign, with supporters singing 'the S.A. is on the march and Konrad is with us' to the melody of the Horst Wessel Song – recalling the fact that Konrad also had been the leader of the town's Storm Troopers. Czisch's shop windows were smashed, and the Star of David daubed on his property (Czisch was a converted half-Jew). Konrad's level of support showed he was clearly the 'people's choice' – leading the town and its local dignitaries into direct confrontation with the American military authorities who sought to remove him.[90]

---

[87] This occurred in 1951 when a Soviet Military Tribunal tried over 400 Christian Democrats and handed down 45 death penalties, Hubertus Knabe, *Tag der Befreiung? Das Kriegsende in Ostdeutschland* (Berlin, Propyläen, 2005), p. 270f. Leonhard, *Die Revolution*, pp. 652, 654f.

[88] IfZM, OMGUS DMG CAD 26 April 1948 (report of Richard M. Scammon, Chief Political Activities Branch). Ibid, 27 April 1947 (report of H. Philip Hatton, deputy Director Civil Administration Division.

[89] IfZM, MA-430/1–8, Polad 798/32–33 1948: American Consulate Stuttgart to Secretary of State, Washington, 28 July 1948, p. 12. Pollock, *Occupation Diary*, 19 May 1948, p. 307.

[90] IfZM, MA-430/1–8, Polad 798/32–33 1948, Military Governor Charles La Follete, 'Delinquency and Error Report'. Ernst Lämmle, 'Schwäbisch Gmünd vom Kaiserreich über die Zeit der Weltkriege bis zur demokratischen Republik', in Stadtarchiv Schwäbisch Gmünd (ed.), *Geschichte der Stadt Schwäbisch Gmünd* (Stuttgart, Konrad Theiss, 1984), pp. 483–4. Lämmle's apologia of Konrad's role as mayor during the Third Reich and of this episode is lamentable, given he was the city archivist at the time of writing. See Ortrud Seidel, *Mut zur Erinnerung. Geschichte der Gmünder Juden. Eine persönliche Spurensuche* (Schwäbisch Gmünd, Einhorn-Verlag Eduard Dietenberger GmbH, 1991), p. 153, for a brief account of the attacks against Czisch and Gmünd as a 'brown town'.

It is an open question if Konrad's election was symptomatic of a general pattern anticipating the restorative trend associated with Adenauer's chancellorship. But the consul's fear of a 'renazification' of the mayoralty has some corroboration in many examples that could be cited – mostly of small towns and rural communities like Schwäbisch-Gmund or Pfaffenhofen in Bavaria, where the local population doggedly re-elected a mayor with an active Nazi past.[91] In *Landkreis* Celle, Hanover province's largest county and at that time the Federal Republic's second largest county, at least two post-war mayors had Nazi pasts. August Lammers, a farmer from Bannetze, had served as mayor from 1924 until 1938, before becoming County Leader of Farmers (*Kreisbauernführer*). After internment, he was re-elected mayor (as a member of the Free Democrat Party, FDP), remaining in office for 20 years until 1972, retiring at the age of 74. We do not know how deeply involved Lammers had been with the Nazi Party, whether or not he was a so-called *Märzgefallene* (i.e. joining in March 1933), like Wilhelm Heinichen, a former government counsellor in the Prussian administration, who was appointed county manager (Landrat) in 1919, a post he held until 1945, and Celle's lord mayor from 1952 to 1964, before becoming an 'honorary citizen' at 81.[92]

The fact Heinichen had joined the NSDAP in March 1933, and thus could be viewed as a *Mitläufer* or 'fellow traveller' rather than a fanatical Nazi, meant that after the introduction of new electoral laws mentored by the allies, he was eligible for public office (after formal scrutiny from a de-nazification committee before confirmation by the interior ministry of the respective Land). None of these examples were isolated, as the 1,520 requests for confirmation for public office in the small state of Hesse show.[93] The Soviet military authorities in their zone adopted similar measures in June 1946.[94] But, even before the relaxation of the criteria for office, the Soviet military authorities had proven themselves as flexible as their American and British counterparts. In Berlin, this had given Arthur Werner the opportunity to become mayor, in spite of a brief flirtation with Nazism in 1932.[95]

A Mayor for all Seasons

From the later-1940s, as the contours of political life returned to Germany's town halls, so too did some old debates concerning the nature and role of the mayoralty. Was the mayor a servant of the state, or an agent of the party, or representative of the people? This did not exactly create a crisis of identity, but it unsettled some mayors leaving them facing stark choices. One of Germany's most popular post-war mayors, Walter Kolb, summed up the dilemma facing mayors when asked in an interview why he had decided to leave Düsseldorf for Frankfurt: 'look, two spirits also reside in my

---

91   http://www.rspaf.pfaffenhofen.de/Bürgermeister.htm.

92   Rainer Schulze (ed.), *Unruhige Zeiten Erlebnisberichte aus dem Landkreis Celle 1945–1949* (Munich, R. Oldenbourg , 1991), pp. 340–43, for biographical notes on both men.

93   Mühlhausen (ed.), *Ludwig Bergsträsser*, p. 317, n. 121.

94   Christoph Kleβmann, *Die doppelte Staatsgründung. Deutsche Geschichte 1945–1955* (Göttingen, Vandenhoeck und Ruprecht, 1991), pp. 83–4.

95   Wernecke, 'Arthur Werner', op cit.

heart ... the professional administrator backed by a methodical training and ... the politician ...'[96] Kolb was uncomfortable with the British concept of the mayoralty as a mere figurehead while administration was left to the newly-established office of town clerk. In Frankfurt (in the American Zone) the mayoralty still offered opportunities to combine administration, populism and politics. Yet his idea of mayoralty as part of a popular administration both serving the state and representing the people came dangerously close to the ideas of Buchner or Schön in the mid-1930s.

> I reject the pallid career civil service: it conceals mostly a deficit in principles. We need in the people's state a new type of civil servant ... one who is honest, highly qualified and ... rooted in the people as a citizen among citizens.[97]

Kolb, a career public servant and active Social Democrat, clearly believed mayors should not just be figureheads, as envisaged in the new British-mentored municipal statute. For him both personality and political agency should combine as effective civic management emphasising independence from state administration. In many respects this understanding echoed Weimar's 'politicised' mayoralty. Neither Ernst Reuter nor his protégé Willy Brandt would have attained the mayoralty without previously garnering the support of the Berlin SPD party machine (and in Reuter's case, the support of intriguers like Franz Neumann who engineered Ostrowski's downfall).[98] But none would deny either man was a charismatic mayor who served well both city and West German state. This 'type' of mayor dominated town halls until the early-1970s. Kolb died prematurely in 1956, but several contemporaries presided over their respective town halls for long periods, becoming powerful independent figures in the early Bonn Republic.

Thus, when appointed Stuttgart's mayor, Arnulf Klett was just 42, an ambitious man entering his prime. James Pollock, who met Klett in 1945, was impressed by 'one of the most promising of the younger municipal administrators in Germany'.[99] Klett's appointment was confirmed by council in 1946 and he was re-elected in 1948, now by popular vote (though on a relatively small turnout), and in face of a whispering campaign regarding his private life.[100] As a 'son of the city' Klett portrayed himself as a man 'above politics', tirelessly reconstructing Stuttgart after wartime ravages, even proposing the city become capital of the newly-established republic. Yet he was also a

---

[96]   Thomas Bauer, *'Seid einig für unsere Stadt': Walter Kolb, Frankfurter Oberbürgermeister 1946–1956* (Frankfurt am Main, Waldemar Kramer, 1996), p. 21; Helli Knoll, *Walter Kolb. Ein grosser Oberbürgermeister* (Frankfurt am Main, 1956). For Kolb's period in office in Düsseldorf, see Peter Hüttenberger, *Düsseldorf*, pp. 679–95.

[97]   *Frankfurter Rundschau*, 22 June 1948, quoted by Bauer, '*Seid einig für unser Stadt'*, p. 106. The original is difficult to translate: 'Ich lehne das farblose Berufsbeamtentum ab; hinter ihm verbirgt sich meist Charakterlosigkeit. Wir brauchen einen neuen Typ des Beamten, nämlich den sauberen, fachlich hochqualifizierten und im Volk als Bürger zu Bürger stehenden Menschen.'

[98]   Ribbe, 'Otto Ostrowski', op cit. Führe, *Die franzöische Besatzungspolitik*, pp. 148–50, 158, 162.

[99]   *Occupation Diary*, p. 314.

[100]   IfZ OMGUS Polad 798/32–33 1948, Copy of Enclosure American Consul Friedrich J. Mann to Secretary of State, Subject: re-election of Dr Klett as Lord Mayor of Stuttgart, 15 March 1948.

highly political animal (close to local industrial circles and the CDU), often in conflict with local unions and left-wing councillors. But his larger-than-life personality coupled with pragmatic instincts enabled him to ride out political controversy, continuing as mayor for a quarter century. Klett sought to combine the role of public servant with that of people's representative, eschewing political partisanship for 'common sense' apoliticism.[101] Klett's style of mayor was reminiscent of the conservative tradition that had typified the mayoralty of the Rhineland, but also evident in Bavaria, and even in the ostensibly more 'liberal' north.[102]

Theodor Pfizer, former head of the German Railways (1932–1945) and elected mayor of the southern German town of Ulm in April 1948, would have been comfortable alongside Rive, Luther and Adenauer. For Pfizer personalities not political parties should be the chief determinants of civic life. Pfizer's understanding of the mayoralty echoed the *Bürgermeisterverfassung* under which councils advised and mayors governed. As his biographer noted, Pfizer 'never made a secret of the fact that party ideologies and group interests in the council, indeed, their very party political formations, were a thorn in his side'.[103] Unsurprisingly, there was much friction between Pfizer's vision of the mayoralty and council expectations. Like Klett (but unlike Kolb), Pfizer saw the mayoralty as 'above politics', as leadership with a populist 'touch', eschewing political majorities in favour of decisive leadership (resonating with Buchner's ideal mayor and the DGO): the mayor served the state while representing the people. The South German Municipal Statute stipulated that the mayor be popularly elected. This strengthened his position *vis-à-vis* the council and was moreover, underwritten by Baden-Württemberg's new constitution (11 November 1953) allocating municipal self-government broad scope and the new 1956 statutes.[104] Against this background of a legally-enshrined dominant mayoralty, Pfizer dominated Ulm town hall for the next quarter century.

The emphasis upon personality among traditionalists in the early decades after 1945 is partly explained by the all-too vivid memory of sharp political divisions before 1933 and the mayoralty's bastardisation after 1933. It also betrayed the period's deep conservatism, as well as mayoral social origins. Pfizer, for example, came from a long line of public service and was trained as a judge. His understanding of mayoralty – which so obviously ran counter to the idea of democratic politics – was not anomalous, but reflected the *Zeitgeist* of the era of reconstruction and 'Economic Miracle'. With the passing of this generation of mayors by the later-1960s and early-1970s, a change of guard in terms of age and outlook was evident in both halves of Germany as a new cohort of mayors emerged owing its position more to technocratic training and party machinery than populism. For mayors like Hans-Jochen Vogel, who became mayor of Munich at 34 in 1960, careers were forged

---

[101]   Sauer, *Arnulf Klett*, pp. 90–93.

[102]   Leipner (ed.), *Fünfundzwanzig Jahre Oberbürgermeister*, p. 28. Spitta, *Aus meinem Leben*, p. 269.

[103]   Fink, 'Der Ulmer Gemeinderat', pp. 156–8.

[104]   Hans Reske, 'Die städtische Selbstverwaltung', in Theodor Pfizer (ed.), *Baden-Württemberg. Staat, Wirtschaft, Kultur* (Stuttgart, Deutsche-Verlags-Anstalt, 1963), pp. 131–3, 139.

through political parties, with mayoralty figuring merely as a useful and sometimes necessary stepping-stone to national politics.[105] The larger-than-life independent mayor of Weimar and the post-war years thus faded into history. Already in a lecture series held in 1963, the eminent municipal historian Otto Ziebill lamented the passing of old-style mayors.[106] The shift took longer in East Berlin where Herbert Fechner, Ebert's mayoral successor in 1967 and, like Ebert, the son of a famous Weimar Social Democrat politician, presided until 1974. His successor, 44 year old Erhard Krack, whose formative years were shaped by the Ulbricht era, was an able technocrat and loyal SED functionary, remembered less for any populist appeal (which he had) than for being the last mayor of East Berlin, disappearing from view along with the Wall in 1989.

The role of the party machine – whether in former GDR or in the Bundesrepublik – in influencing the mayoralty can be over-emphasised, but while it clearly played an increasingly important role in post-war Germany, paradoxically, it also aided its de-politicisation.[107] This latter aspect, however, probably owes much more to mayoralty's transformation in the late-twentieth century into a state administrative organ and its closer confluence with politics and economy.[108] Nonetheless, the late-twentieth century mayor was not necessarily a faceless professional administrator or party apparatchik. Sometimes, national and international events challenged mayors to show their mettle and propelled them to centre stage: Reuter during the Berlin Blockade; Brandt during the Berlin Crisis a decade later; Herbert Weichmann during Hamburg's calamitous flood in 1962; Hans-Jochen Vogel during the 1972 terrorist atrocity at the Summer Olympics in Munich; and Walter Momper at the fall of the Berlin Wall. Such dramatic examples of leadership should not distract from the fact that at lesser everyday-life level, the demands of administration, municipal ambitions, political rivalries and the need to elicit popular support, require individual mayors to demonstrate managerial skills, offer civic vision and possess skills of political brokerage in order to retain grip on the mayoralty.[109]

---

[105]   Although it should be noted that Vogel served as lord mayor for 12 years before becoming involved in national and party politics under Brandt and then Helmut Schmidt.

[106]   Ziebill, *Bürger – Städte – Staat*, p. 64.

[107]   Haller and Naßmacher, 'Rat und Verwaltung', op cit. Bertram, *Staatspolitik und Kommunalpolitik*, pp. 134ff., especially, p. 142 Frey, 'Kommunale Selbstverwaltung', p. 21. Generally, Martin Neuffer, *Entscheidungsfeld Stadt. Kommunalpolitik als Geselschaftspolitik – Standortüberprüfung der kommunalen Selbstverwaltung* (Stuttgart, Deutsche Verlags-Anstalt, 1973), pp. 165–81.

[108]   Frey, 'Kommunale Selbstverwaltung', pp. 22–3.

[109]   Alexander Stock, *Der Bürgermeister der Zukunft: Manager, Visionär, Politiker und Moderator* (Aachen, Shaker, 2000). Hans-Georg Wehling, 'Auswirkungen der Kommunalverfassung auf das lokalee politisch-administrative Handeln. Erfahrungen mit dem baden-württembergischen Modell', Dieter Schimanke (ed.), *Stadtdirektor oder Bürgermeister. Beiträge zu einer aktuellen Kontroverse* (Basel, Boston, Berlin, Birkhäuser, 1989), pp. 84–95.

*

A comprehensive history of Germany's mayoralty since the late-nineteenth century has still to be written. Nevertheless, what emerges from the little we know, is that for much of the twentieth century Germany's mayors were often caught in both a creative and sometimes destructive tension as they sought to balance their roles as servant of the state, agents of political parties (whether formally or informally acknowledged) and popular representatives.[110] But for all the personal travail of individual mayors, the mayoralty itself proved remarkably resilient in face of the turmoil besetting Germany at various times in the twentieth century, providing the nation with continuity and, ultimately, stability.

---

[110] Arnold Köttgen, *Kommunale Selbstverwaltung zwischen Krise und Reform. Ausgewählte Schriften* (Stuttgart, Kohlhammer, 1963), pp. 7–8; Ziebill, *Bürger – Städte – Staat*, p. 49. Wolfgang Gisevius, *Der neue Bürgermeister. Vermittler zwischen Bürgern und Verwaltung* (Bonn, Dietz, 1999).

CHAPTER EIGHT

The Mayoralty in Italy

James L. Newell

Introduction

This chapter's purpose is to consider how the characteristics of the Italian mayoralty have changed since 1945 – the underlying assumption being that such analysis requires examination of the formal and informal relations between mayoral incumbents and the 'bearers' of structures with which the office is linked. In light of this, my main focus is on changes in mayoral relations with political parties, their constituents and the state apparatus as a whole. I hope thereby to shed light on changes in:

- the mayoralty's legal and political functions *vis-à-vis* the local governmental and national political systems;
- how mayoral incumbents are recruited and what their voters expect of them;
- the social features of incumbents, and the reasons mayoral candidates aspire to office.

The topic's importance stems from at least three considerations. First, if local government can offer benefits of diversity by bringing political institutions close to citizens, then, amongst local office-holders, it is the heads of such institutions who can have greatest impact on how far potential is translated into reality. They can do this through their activities of processing demands from their localities, managing local bureaucracies and negotiating with central state bodies. Second, local political leadership has become much more challenging – and politically significant – due to broad changes which, in recent decades, have led local government to give way to local governance.[1] These include internationalisation of economies (with localities having to compete for investment from businesses much more mobile than before); the Europeanisation of policy-making (thereby involving local leaders in direct links with the supranational level); new policy challenges (like migration, environmental damage and aging populations). Third, partly reflecting these processes, 1993 saw the passage of some very important reform legislation in Italy, fundamentally altering the recruitment of Italian mayors and their powers *vis-à-vis* other significant local actors. The reform was hoped and expected significantly to improve the quality of Italian local governance.

Since this book seeks to analyse comparatively the past and present of mayors, we must first consider how far, and in what senses, the Italian mayoralty is equivalent to offices with the same and similar titles elsewhere. We must also justify our choice of time period.

---

[1] Peter John, *Local Governance in Western Europe* (London: Sage, 2001).

As far as the first question is concerned, all or most so-called 'advanced liberal democracies' have local government systems presided over by a single, recognised 'head'. Furthermore, the development of modern local government in these countries was bound up with the rise of the nation-state from the sixteenth century onwards. As monarchs fought to advance their power, so they sought to extend and consolidate their internal rule, the more effectively to extract the resources needed for war. And if this led to the standardising of local patterns of administration (i.e. state-building), then it led too to nation-building – the attempt to develop viable polities by breaking down local loyalties and developing symbols of unity to secure the allegiance of the territory's inhabitants to the state institutions claiming sovereignty over it. Developing a local government system – that is, a structure of local authorities, each with a denoted geographical area within which it had the power, authority and resources for the execution of public tasks given it by central government – responded to the needs of both state- and nation-building. By giving each authority equivalent allocations of tasks, central government could impose some uniformity in administration across the nation-state. By allowing local authorities themselves to decide the *manner* in which their centrally allocated tasks should be executed, central government enabled them to be responsive to local variation in citizens' demands.

If local authorities 'thus became basic elements in national systems of government',[2] then they were (and are) ambiguous entities, both agencies of the central state and representatives of the inhabitants within their areas of jurisdiction. This ambiguity meant their discretion was circumscribed by nationally determined bodies of law; but also that the spread of democratic principles at *national* level would equally affect authorities operating at *local* level. (In fact, in most countries, franchise extensions occurred at local level *before* being granted nationally.) In turn, the combination of these characteristics implied the need for a local authority head – someone both elected (directly or indirectly) by the community, and its representative within the broader national political structure of which it was part (as well as being the state's principal local representative).

If these features accurately define the mayor's role in Italy, they also constitute the common denominator underlying the offices focused on elsewhere in this volume. English mayors, for example, differ from Italian mayors in that they do not have formal executive powers,[3] but the remaining role characteristics all apply. That is, they are elected by their communities (indirectly in the English case); they see themselves, and are regarded by others, as their communities' representatives in the wider world and they are definitely representatives of the state as a whole (doubly so because of the operation of the *ultra vires* principle in British politics, according to which local councils, over whose deliberations mayors traditionally preside, may do nothing not explicitly authorised by Parliament). The same characteristics apply to French communal *maires*, German *bürgermeisters* and American city mayors.

---

[2]   Alan Norton, *International Handbook of Local and Regional Government: A Comparative Analysis of Advanced Democracies* (Cheltenham: Edward Elgar, 1994), p. 9.

[3]   See John Garrard's chapter for the argument that, until at least 1914, they often did in practice.

There are two reasons for our choice of time period. The first relates to the change of regime occurring at the end of the war and the promulgation of the republican constitution on 1 January 1948. Before this, local authority heads had been fundamentally different creatures, in terms of their recruitment and their relationship to the wider political system. Until 1896 (after which they were elected locally), mayors had been appointed from among the councillors by the government after recommendation from the provincial Prefect – a Rome appointee whose sweeping powers enabled him to ensure local government was carried on according to government wishes. The mayor's main roles, in conjunction with the Prefect, were to perpetuate municipal control by the dominant local elite and the return of government candidates at general elections. On the one hand, the Italian state's weakness meant that Prefects had to rely on local 'notables' in recommending mayoral appointments. On the other, in return for leaving municipalities (*comuni*) 'free' in this way, Prefects and governments could rely on mayors to use their powers (to draw up electoral rolls, issue passports, trading documents and so forth) in such a way as to ensure appropriate candidates were returned at general elections.[4] Under Fascism, central government tutelage of mayoral activities became virtually complete. Indeed, in 1926, all mayors were dismissed, along with their councils and replaced in each *comune* by a *podestà*. 'The *podestà* was appointed by the Prefect; he could be dismissed at any time by the Prefect; and he could be transferred to another *comune* by the Prefect.'[5] In looking for a reliable *podestà*, the Prefect usually chose elderly conservative gentlemen, finding that retired colonels were ideal as they had plenty of time and needed no pay.[6] The 1948 Constitution, then, represented a *caesura*. Until its promulgation, the liberal and Fascist regimes could intervene with impunity in mayoral functions since rights to local self-government had no constitutional recognition. This now changed: as constitutionally recognised elements in the national system of government, *comuni* could appeal to the courts if the centre took action corrosive of their constitutional status.[7] This, then, is a first reason for our temporal focus. A second is that this focus enables us to consider the effects of the above-mentioned 1993 reform by a 'before-and-after' comparison while holding constitutional and other variables, as it were, 'constant'.

The Mayoralty 1948–1993

Since the Republic emerged, the legal framework wherein Italian mayors have discharged their functions has been created by a combination of constitutional and ordinary law. Article 114 of the 1948 constitution states that 'The Republic is divided into Regions, Provinces and Municipalities', meaning that the legislature cannot abolish the *comuni* simply by passing ordinary legislation. And though article 128 leaves both the principles of their internal organisation and their functions to

---

[4]   Martin Clark, *Modern Italy 1871–1995*, 2nd edition (London: Longman, 1996), pp. 58–61.
[5]   ibid., p. 235.
[6]   ibid., p. 236.
[7]   Norton, *International Handbook of Local and Regional Government*, p. 9.

ordinary law to determine, the *comuni* have general competence within the law. Thus, in radical contrast to their British counterparts, they need not seek their powers from parliamentary legislation; rather the onus, in any given instance, is on Parliament to show *comuni* have acted unlawfully. In practice, of course, variations between smaller and more populous municipalities and awesome economic disparities across the country (especially the north-south divide) have created real differences in local authority abilities effectively to use their powers. In this respect small, rural, southern *comuni*, have always operated within completely different parameters to wealthy northern cities. In the latter, progressive administrations – especially ones dominated by the Communist Party, excluded from national power and therefore anxious publicly to display what efficient Communist government could achieve – were, in the initial post-war decades, instrumental in providing a generous range of services. Thereby, they lent enormous prestige and popularity to the mayors who led them – men like Giorgio La Pira of Florence and Guieseppe Dozza of Bologna.

Until 1990, the principles governing the internal organisation of the *comuni* were contained in various laws predating the Constitution. However, all essentially followed parliamentary models of government in having a directly elected council (*consiglio*) and an executive arm (the *giunta*) headed by a mayor (or *sindaco*), with both *giunta* and *sindaco* chosen by, and responsible to, the *consiglio*. From 1990, a single law (number 142) determined the internal organisation of the *comuni*. This also sought to increase governing stability in local authorities by stipulating that mayors and *giunta* should be chosen by open, not secret, voting; that this should occur within 60 days (on pain of council dissolution); that no-confidence votes in mayors and *giunta* were only valid if 'constructive'. That is, they had to be accompanied by the names of the persons replacing the mayor and members of the *giunta*.[8] Since, theoretically at least, the reform considerably strengthened the mayor's position within the municipal authority, it significantly loosened the bonds that, prior to the 1990s, held mayors hostage to party political machinations.

That nationally organised parties came to dominate municipalities and mayoralties when Italian democracy was restored after the war was of course nothing unusual. What *was* unusual was how this domination was exercised and its consequences. For it meant that the practical autonomy of mayors was – especially if they belonged to a governing party – very heavily circumscribed by their location in the power-hierarchies and clientele-chains operating through the parties. The reasons for this are inseparable from the specific political and economic circumstances in which democracy was restored.

The decisive political factor was the Cold War. From the first post-war parliamentary election in 1948, this ensured that the second largest party, the Italian Communist Party (PCI), was permanently excluded from national government through a *conventio ad excludendum* operated by the remaining parties in the legislature. Since the party furthest to the right, the neo-fascist Italian Social Movement, was similarly excluded, government remained permanently controlled by varying combinations of the centre-placed Christian Democrats (DC) along with

---

8   Luciano Vandelli, *Sindaci e miti: Sisifo, Tantalo e Damocle nell'amministrazione locale* (Bologna: il Mulino), pp. 12–13.

four other smaller parties (Socialists, Social Democrats, Republicans and Liberals). From the 1950s, these parties' permanence in office enabled them to consolidate a type of rule known as '*partitocrazia*' ('rule by parties') a term encapsulating their occupation of every conceivable state agency in order to exploit it for patronage purposes. There were several, interlinked reasons for this. In essence, excluding the far-left and far-right meant there could be no alternation in office. This in turn meant governments were under little pressure and had little power to enact coherent legislative programmes – for the absence of any possibility of alternation also removed pressure to construct governments with real cohesion and therefore power *vis-à-vis* the legislature. Meanwhile, each governing party was a 'veto player'[9] with power and incentive to block any substantial policy initiative that might leave any group of followers worse off. Consequently, whilst the main basis of support for governing parties in their competition with the main opposition party was ideological (i.e. anti-communism) small-scale distributive measures, allowing the parties to establish clientele relationships with their followers, became their preferred means of mobilising and retaining electoral support in competition amongst themselves. Thus negotiations leading to the formation of governments – there were over 50 between 1945 and 1992 – essentially concerned how ministries and under-secretarial positions would be distributed among parties anxious to control them for patronage purposes. This allowed parties – and party factions – to control access to, and decisions of, all manner of public institutions. By permitting considerable overlap between party personnel and administrative incumbents, *partitocrazia* misted the boundaries between these entities and made it difficult to know, in any given case, in what capacity individuals were acting.[10] Consequently, the real channels through which power flowed were less the formal ones created by state institutions than informal channels, within parties, with party leaders standing at the apex of the apparatus. Mayors, like other party-appointed public officials, had to take their place in, and to tailor their behaviour to, the demands of this apparatus.

What this meant for how mayors performed their legally prescribed duties we shall see shortly. For now, we should note that the economic circumstances responsible for mayoral subordination to the party-run power apparatus lay in the simple fact that, in the war's immediate aftermath, significant parts of Italy, especially the south, were poor. Unemployment was high. Traditionally, much private economic activity has been state-dependent for its implantation and development.[11] Suspicion and mistrust frequently made collective action difficult. Elected politicians thus found that they both controlled access to the principal source of wealth and were faced with a mass of isolated individuals (electors) each in search of a protector.[12] Taken

---

[9]   George Tsebelis, 'Veto Players and Law Production in Parliamentary Democracies: An Empirical Analysis', *American Political Science Review*, vol. 93, no. 3 (1999), pp. 591–608; George Tsebelis, *Veto Players: How Political Institutions Work* (Princeton University Press-Russell Sage Foundation, 2002).

[10]   Newell, James L., *Parties and Democracy in Italy* (Aldershot: Ashgate, 2000), p. 48.

[11]   Percy Allum, *Politics and Society in Post-war Naples* (Cambridge University Press), p. 166.

[12]   Newell, *Parties and Democracy in Italy*, p. 48.

together, these political and economic circumstances meant mayors found themselves working in contexts where it was impossible to regard sub-national or local levels of government as having any autonomy from clientelistic processes of power-broking working from the top downwards. This fact in turn gave distinctive colouring to how mayors came by their positions; how they acted on behalf of their constituents; how they represented, and sought to obtain resources for, their communities.

Whether driven by self-regarding, altruistic, national or merely local ambitions, aspiring mayors initially required an electoral following, or *clientela* – that is people who, in exchange for various favours, would reliably vote either for the aspirant himself, or another politician the aspirant was known to support. *Clientela*-building might start with one's relatives and work up from there. By placing one's packets of votes at the disposal of politicians further up the hierarchy – provincial and regional councillors, parliamentarians and so forth – one acquired the contacts necessary to provide the favours needed to maintain and expand one's electoral following, while also enhancing the likelihood of selection for those party positions that might one day allow one to launch a bid for the position of mayor. Of course, we should remember that models of clientelism like this are based predominantly on the south[13] and their nation-wide applicability was not necessarily unvarying. For example, it was probably less applicable in the so-called 'red belt' of central Italy where Communist-dominated councils 'displayed a dynamic innovativeness and managerial qualities in local government with a stress on the general interest'.[14] However, it is worth noting that Sidney Tarrow's well-known study of grassroots politicians in Italy and France led the author to conclude that the clientelistic system of distribution constrained even Communist mayors.[15] They inevitably found this system profoundly coloured their relationship with their constituents and the way they performed their duties on their constituents' behalf. For one thing, the mayor's legal duties were wide-ranging:

The *sindaco* calls meetings of the council and *giuntà*, [sic] issues agendas, watches over the performance of the *assessori*[16] in their spheres of delegation, carries responsibility for carrying out the decisions of the council and *giuntà*, [sic] signs documents on behalf of the commune, represents the commune in legal actions, supervises the administrative departments of the council and can suspend communal employees subject to confirmation by the *giuntà* [sic] and council. He is responsible for the direction of administrative bodies and institutions set up by the commune, and represents the commune in external relationships. Among his state responsibilities are registration, certification and health and public works matters, securing law and order and publishing state laws and other legal instruments. He or she is responsible for urgent action and co-ordination of public services in the event of emergencies.[17]

[13] Norton, *International Handbook of Local and Regional Government*, p. 9.
[14] ibid., p. 225.
[15] Sidney Tarrow, *Between Center and Periphery: Grassroots Politicians in Italy and France* (New Haven: Yale University Press, 1977), p. 174.
[16] Variously translated as 'deputy mayors' or 'aldermen', *assessori* is the term used to refer to the members of the *giunta*, each of whom has a defined area of executive responsibility.
[17] Norton, *International Handbook of Local and Regional Government*, p. 228.

Perhaps unsurprisingly given the sheer range of such responsibilities, a significant proportion of Tarrow's mayors complained their constituents tended to see the mayor as a paternalistic figure, perceiving him unrealistically 'as a magician of public life ... capable of solving all their problems'.[18] Mayors tended to view with distaste the constant demands for favours associated with the 'service-delivery' aspects of their roles: 'the job ... has some real disadvantages. For example having to face scores of supplicants ... looking for work, and even some who are looking for illegal help'.[19] But although far more mayors saw seeking support for the modernisation of their communities as the more important aspect of their job than saw personal services for their constituents in such terms, we cannot overlook the structural constraints conditioning mayoral relationships with constituents. Most important amongst these is the simple fact that the relationship is grounded in electoral competition and will cease if the mayor and his party fail to win that competition. Thus it is clear that in certain contexts not only mayors, but local politicians generally, could be counted upon to use the enormous scope for patronage inherent in Italian local government to maintain and enhance their power. In representative democracy, the presence of competitor politicians means electors are not totally dependent on single politicians in searching for advantage. Hence the latter can only retain power so long as they supply the kinds of resources voters seek. Numerous studies have pointed to the instrumental quality of partisanship in Italy's poorer regions in the decades following the war.

Rather similar structural constraints confronted mayors when searching for resources in their capacity as community representatives in the wider political context. Implementing national policies often required local initiatives to try capturing resources from the state, thus ensuring mayors became 'policy-brokers'.[20] For example, concern about local unemployment might get a mayor to try to attract industry by persuading the state to declare his community a 'depressed area', thus ensuring its qualification for special tax incentives and so forth. As mediators, then, between state bureaucracies and local associations, Italian mayors frequently found their demands upwards were blocked by bureaucratic inefficiency, forcing them instead to channel those demands through the party system. Since such channels were *in*formal, rather than the *formal* ones of bureaucratic procedure, demands had to be presented in particularistic and clientelistic, rather than universalistic, terms. In other words, mayors looked to their contacts further up the party hierarchy for help in getting projects funded and persuading the bureaucracy to act. Such requests had to be reciprocated: 'We often turn to the local deputies for help in speeding up applications at the ministries.' 'More than help us out, they take an active interest, promising help in the hope of getting paid back politically some day for the contributions they can make.'[21]

In short, in a context of *partitocrazia* whose mode of functioning was clientelistic exchange, mayors found themselves and their demands integral components of informal power hierarchies wherein constant negotiation was the norm. It meant

[18]   Quoted in Tarrow, *Between Center and Periphery*, p. 123.
[19]   Quoted ibid., p. 198.
[20]   ibid., p. 128.
[21]   Quoted in ibid., p. 177.

mayors easily fell victim to deals cut at the top of the apparatus – as the case of Achille Lauro testified. Lauro, born in 1887, was a wealthy ship owner who, as monarchist mayor of Naples from 1952, was given a free hand to commit all kinds of irregularities because the votes of monarchist parliamentarians were occasionally necessary to ensure the DC's survival in office at national level. Later, fearful that Lauro's movement might spread beyond its Neapolitan stronghold, DC general secretary Amintore Fanfani got Interior Minister Fernando Tambroni to dissolve the Neapolitan council for administrative irregularities. The importance of electoral patronage was revealed by the fact that, though the dissolution provided Lauro with a ready-made general election platform in 1958, his movement's vote failed to increase. Meanwhile, the DC set about dismantling his party by enticing councillors to abandon him, something made possible because they were businessmen whose need for credit facilities required them to turn to DC-controlled banks and thus seek the intervention of local DC leaders.[22] On the other hand, the clientelistic hierarchy did not necessarily mean local politics was rigidly controlled from the centre; on the contrary, since the main aim in national-level negotiations was always to manipulate as many contractual resources as possible, national-level politicians had always 'to be clever enough not to disclose a more global design'.

> Indeed, in the context of very articulate negotiations in which parties tend to use as a resource the very opposition of their own local groups to the party line and the vetoes of other political forces, it would be counter-productive to show too great a capacity for control of local tensions and conflicts.[23]

If one very salient consequence of this form of power-broking and of *partitocrazia* was thought to be policy ineffectiveness and governing instability at local as at national level, then it was widely hoped that law number 81 of 1993 would significantly improve matters by making mayors directly elected and freeing them in other ways from party influence. We now turn to the provisions of this law and the circumstances surrounding its introduction.

Law no. 81/1993

Because of the Italian political system's supposed policy ineffectiveness, law 81 was, when passed, widely hailed as a significant achievement. Introduced on 25 March 1993, it was a direct product of the party-system upheavals beginning with the Berlin Wall's collapse in 1989, and of the organisational disintegration of most traditional government parties because of anti-corruption investigations beginning in February 1992. This is not the place to analyse the party-system transformation or the resulting regime change (still incomplete), something I have done elsewhere.[24]

---

[22]   Allum, *Politics and Society in Post-war Naples*, pp. 274–89.

[23]   Luigi Graziano, Fiorenzo Girotti and Luciano Bonet, 'Coalition Politics at the Regional Level and Centre-Periphery Relationships', *International Political Science Review*, vol. 5, no. 4. (1984), p. 435.

[24]   Newell, *Parties and Democracy in Italy*.

Suffice it to say the change was driven by a popular, cross-party movement seeking institutional and, especially, electoral-system change through recourse to the Italian constitution's provision for popular referenda on legislation.[25] Law 81/1993 was introduced under direct pressure from this movement and the concern it expressed about party behaviour at local level. The law's appearance at this precise historical moment should not, perhaps, surprise. As Pitruzzella has argued:

> laws governing local-level competences are, in effect, the laws which govern the interface between society and state so that it is natural that, as soon as a new regime begins establishing itself, new legislation concerning local competences comes into force as a consequence of the relationship the regime intends to establish with the surrounding community.[26]

The new law changed the position of mayors in five very fundamental ways:

1. It transformed the municipal electoral system, making mayors directly elected. Until then, mayors, as we have seen, were chosen by the *consigli*. In turn, the latter were elected using the party-list system of proportional representation.[27] The new law provided that, in muncipalities above 15,000 inhabitants, mayors would be elected contemporaneously with councillors. That is, each mayoral candidate would be obliged, in announcing his or her candidature, to declare affiliation with one or more party lists containing the names of council candidates. Voters could vote for a party list and affiliated mayoral candidate simply by placing a cross against the relevant party symbol. Alternatively, voters could choose a mayoral candidate *un*affiliated to the chosen party list – i.e. they could cast split ballots. Mayoral candidates attracting an absolute majority would be declared elected. Mayoral candidates attracting relative majorities would face run-off ballots with second-placed candidates. Council seats would be distributed proportionally. But, where a mayor emerged at the first round, lists affiliated to him/her would, if achieving 50 per cent of the vote, be assigned 60 per cent of the seats.[28] Where a mayor emerged at the second voting round, the lists affiliated would, if no other list or group of

---

[25] Article 75 of the Italian constitution makes it possible, after presentation of a petition containing at least half-a-million signatures, to hold referenda asking the electorate to pronounce on proposals to strike down laws or parts of laws. Referenda cannot be used to force onto the statute book completely new laws (though obviously clever framing of proposals to strike down parts of existing laws will create new laws in all but name) and they are null and void if they fail to attract at least a 50 per cent turnout. Since 1974, when the first referendum was held, some 60 further referenda have been held.

[26] Giovanni Pitruzzella, 'I poteri locali', pp. 472–6 in: Paul Ginsborg (ed.), *Stato dell'Italia* (Milan: il Saggiatore, 1994), p. 473, my translation.

[27] Except in *comuni* below 5,000 inhabitants where a majoritarian system was mostly used.

[28] This meant winning mayors could find themselves without majorities – which subsequently happened in a few cases. Consequently, law 120 of 1999 altered the system such that from then on, where mayors emerged at the first voting round, their affiliated lists would, if they had achieved 40 per cent of the vote and no other list or group of lists achieved 50 per cent, be assigned 60 per cent of the seats.

lists achieved 50 per cent, be assigned 60 per cent of the seats. Remaining seats would be distributed proportionally. In municipalities below 15,000, the mechanism envisaged was simpler. Each party would present a list of council candidates and an affiliated mayoral candidate. The voter would place a cross against a mayoral candidate, each list being assigned as many votes as the votes received by its affiliated mayoral candidate. The candidate receiving most votes would be declared elected and his/her affiliated party list given two thirds of the available council seats. Remaining seats would be distributed proportionally.

2. It sharply separated *consiglio* and *giunta* by removing the choice of *giunta* members from the council and giving it to the mayor, who could also freely dismiss them. *Giunta* members could be chosen from within or outside the council. Members chosen from councillors, if accepting nomination, would have to resign council seats, vacancies being filled from best-placed non-elected candidates.

3. It eliminated an important conflict in the mayoral role, thereby making it easier for candidates, once elected, to act as heads of the entire community – this by establishing that mayors would no longer chair council meetings (a duty necessarily demanding impartiality – difficult for mayors given the partisan bases whereby they acquired and held office). Instead, meetings would be chaired by a president, chosen by the council from among its members.

4. If councils passed a no-confidence vote in the mayor, dissolution of the entire administration and new elections would automatically result. A mayoral resignation would have the same effect.

5. Mayors could not hold office for more than two consecutive terms (since 1999, a third consecutive term has been possible where one of the preceding terms has lasted less than two-and-a-half years for reasons other than voluntary resignation).

In formal terms, then, the law considerably strengthened the mayor *vis-à-vis* the council (particularly due to the first, the second and the fourth of the changes above). And it was introduced just at the time when the above-mentioned corruption scandals were loosening established governing parties' grip on power and causing them to implode. These two circumstances led observers to believe the outcome would considerably raise mayoral visibility and importance, rendering mayors spearheads of a local governmental renaissance in Italy. On the one hand, with absolute majorities to back them, freedom to appoint and dismiss members of the executive and opportunities to force through policies by threat of resignation, mayors were given powers anticipated to render local policy-making much more efficient and effective. Before this, mayors' achievement and continuation in office was entirely dependent on shifting distributions of power amongst council-based political parties. On the other hand, established parties' loosening grip on national government seemed to portend the collapse of *partitocrazia*, and thus the freeing of sub-national politicians from subordination to the demands of national-level intra- and inter-party power-broking. Together with enhanced opportunities for constructing power-bases independent of national-level party structures apparently afforded by direct election, this was expected greatly to raise both mayoral visibility and bargaining power in the political system as a whole.

Events in the immediate aftermath of the law's passage seemed to justify this optimistic scenario. For Bruno Dente, for example, the law's outcome was 'spectacular':

> Between 1992 and 1993, the class of municipal politicians was completely renewed through the election of mayors who were either new to politics (e.g. Castellani in Turin, Sansa in Genoa, Illy in Trieste and Di Cagno in Bari) or different from the usual politicians (e.g. Cacciari in Venice, Rutelli in Rome, Orlando in Palermo and Bianco in Catania). Furthermore, the composition of the executives ('personally selected' by the mayors) combined with the transfer of powers away from local authority legislatures, completely transformed local-authority policy-making by substantially depoliticising it.[29]

Since then, contrasting voices have begun being heard and, after 12 years, a more long-term, dispassionate, assessment of its impact is possible. We now turn to this task.

Consequences of 81/1993

Some insight into how far mayors have actually been freed from the pressures of inter- and intra-party power-broking are available from cases where mayors and their *giunte* fail – through no-confidence motions or mayoral resignations – to reach the end of their natural terms. Prior to 1993, party vetoes within municipal councils and the local consequences of national-level coalitional dynamics ensured that stability amongst local *giunte* was generally very low. Baldini shows that, between 1972 and 1989, of 904 *giunte* formed in 95 provincial capitals, less than 1 per cent lasted their entire five-year terms, most failing to survive more than a year. By contrast, between 1993 and 2001, there were only ten instances of municipalities being dissolved for reasons clearly associated with political conflict (as opposed, say, to personal reasons, like a mayor's decision to resign to seek higher office).[30] The indicator is not perfect, being built on data relating to provincial capitals only and, as Baldini himself notes, we lack information, for example, on the turnover of *giunta* members. The point is that the 1993 reform gives both mayor and council the possibility of getting their way by threatening each other's demise – though at the potential cost of their *own* demise. In such circumstances, unknown numbers of mayors, not resigning or being forced out, may have held on to their offices by 'blinking first', bowing to party pressures over the composition of their *giunte* rather than continuing to risk 'mutually-assured destruction'. Nevertheless, the seeming pre- and post-1993 contrast clearly demonstrates more *stable* mayoral leadership, which *may* reflect more *powerful* leadership with respect to political parties. Vandelli, by contrast, draws on data relating to municipalities generally to show that the number of dissolutions (429) in 1995 and 1996 were higher than before the reform in 1991 and 1992 (when their number was 312), concluding that 'the move from short-lived and permanently unstable executives

---

29   Bruno Dente, 'Sub-National Governments in the Long Italian Transition', pp. 176–93 in Martin J. Bull and Martin Rhodes (eds), *Crisis and Transition in Italian Politics* (London: Frank Cass 1997), p. 184.

30   Gianfranco Baldini, 'The direct election of mayors: an assessment of the institutional reform following the Italian municipal elections of 2001', *Journal of Modern Italian Studies*, vol. 7, no. 3 (2002), pp. 368–9.

to mayors able to deliver administrative continuity for a full term ... still remains, in an excessively large number of municipalities, a goal to be pursued, or perhaps, a myth'.[31] But these figures tell us little about change in the balance of power between mayors and parties: leaving aside our lack of information about why dissolutions occurred, one might expect *some* increase even with generally stronger mayors, simply because after 1993, there was no way to dispose of an unwanted mayor *other than* by votes of no-confidence and council dissolutions.

Arguably more telling are data concerning the fate of mayors who, having 'divorced' (or been divorced by) party coalitions supporting them in first-term elections, present themselves for re-election – but *against* the candidate chosen by the original coalition. Significant evidence of success by such 'renegade' mayors would suggest the creation of personal electoral followings had allowed them to become substantially autonomous of the parties. According to Baldini, between 1993 and 2002, only a few mayors – at least in provincial capitals – challenged their former parties in this way and all failed to be re-elected.[32] Again, however, caution is enjoined: aside from these few cases, other mayors could theoretically be *so* powerful that their supporting parties avoid divorce because they anticipate failure in any election contest. Moreover, even though mayors apparently cannot act in complete *disregard* of parties, they could, perhaps, bring *added value* to the political line-up running with them. In other words, it may be that the identity of mayoral candidates can make (significant) differences to the electoral fortunes of the parties and party coalitions with which they stand for election. If we had evidence of this, we might conclude they could draw on such political capital to increase their clout with party representatives when going about mayoral business after their election.

The choice of mayoral candidate clearly makes *some* difference to party fortunes. Indeed, *ex post facto* analysis suggests this difference is significant.[33] However, the difficulty about drawing any confident conclusions from this about mayoral power *vis-à-vis* parties is that the *conditions under which* it will make a difference are very difficult for actors to predict. For example, Baldini and Legnante show that, at the first municipal elections at which mayors elected after the reform could present themselves for re-election – the 1997 and 1998 elections – choosing the incumbent as mayoral candidate produced an 'added value' of about two votes in every ten cast for the parties, compared to only one in ten for non-incumbents.[34] The reasons why incumbents might make good choices are clear: incumbents necessarily have higher profiles in systems of political communication since, aside from their own propaganda activities, they feature in news reports about municipal activities; this means they have more time than competitors to establish public reputations; they can more easily influence the agenda of public debate than their competitors. But none of these opportunities *necessarily* confer electoral advantage and may even constitute significant *disadvantages* – where,

---

[31]   Vandelli, *Sindaci e miti*, p. 24, my translation.

[32]   Gianfranco Baldini, 'Eleggere I sindaci diece anni dopo', *il Mulino*, no. 402 (2002), pp. 658–67.

[33]   See, for example, Gianfranco Baldini and Guido Legnante, *Città al voto: I sindaci e le elezioni comunali* (Bologna: il Mulino, 2000).

[34]   ibid., p. 213–14.

for example, mayoral and municipal activities have been disappointing. Therefore the safest conclusion about the effects of the 1993 reform is that it has given mayors greater *potential* freedom from party dictates by conferring power resources previously unavailable to them. Most significant amongst these resources are threats of resignation; threats to stand for election against their supporting parties (which, though unlikely to produce mayoral victory, as we have seen, can cause the parties to *lose*); threatened refusals to stand, thereby depriving parties of any electoral 'added value' the mayor might have. These resources do not *inevitably* empower mayors, but under the right circumstances they *can* do so.

If direct election has altered mayoral relationships with political parties, it has clearly and obviously also affected mayors' relationships with constituents. Most straightforwardly, it has increased mayoral accountability for their municipalities' actions. This has empowered voters who, prior to reform, could only observe from the sidelines what effects their decisions might have on mayoral choices made by municipal councillors.[35] In the reform's immediate aftermath, several mayors tried taking advantage of their more direct exposure to public opinion to establish public profiles well beyond municipal boundaries (presumably with at least one eye on also strengthening their positions *within* their municipalities). This connected with the fact that many were non-party figures. With corruption scandals at their height, anti-party sentiment was running strongly and many mayoral candidates in 1993 were without previous party experience,[36] the parties themselves often opting for 'prestigious outsiders' in a search for presentable candidates. Once elected, the efforts of such candidates produced what after 1996 became known as the 'mayors' party' – a loosely organised cross-party structure surrounding Massimo Cacciari, the charismatic mayor of Venice, which campaigned for decentralisation on an explicitly cross-party basis.

All this has raised mayoral profiles in the public imagination. In so doing, it may have helped aggravate some of the problems in mayoral relationships with their constituents we alluded to earlier, particularly the unrealistic quality of constituents' expectations. Reflecting on his own mayoral experience in the Lombard city of Piacenza, Vaciago argues that 'Direct election has increased the mayor's authority, as a result of which voters, more than before, expect him to have the ability to solve their problems'.[37] Vandelli sees this as a real problem for mayors in the post-1993 world, arguing they risk being caught in an impossible position. On the one hand, in areas where resources are plentiful and with traditions of good local administration, they will be subject to 'Tocqueville's paradox' whereby improvements in the quality of government correspondingly increase citizens' demands and expectations leaving them as dissatisfied as before. On the other hand, in deprived areas the lack of the resources needed to allow local authorities to bring any significant improvement likewise generates dissatisfaction. In both cases, the result will be disappointment

---

[35]   The limit of two consecutive terms arguably weakens accountability somewhat and for this reason some – including Italy's president – have recently been calling for a change.

[36]   Baldini and Legnante, *Città al voto*, p. 123.

[37]   Giacomo Vaciago, 'Il sindaco uno e trino', *il Mulino*, no. 1 (1999), p. 98, my translation.

with the performance of new directly elected mayors.[38] If recent trends in turnout at municipal elections can be taken as at all revelatory – in provincial capitals it declined from 81.2 to 76.9 per cent between 1993 and 2002[39] – it seems as though Vandelli's pessimism is not entirely misplaced.[40] This could in turn point to difficulties being encountered by at least some mayors in utilising the additional administrative powers they acquired concomitantly with the 1993 reform, particularly those deriving from reversing the relationship between the competences of *consiglio* and *giunta* enacted by law number 142 of 1990: that is, removing general competence from the *consiglio*, by conferring on the *giunta* authority in all matters not expressly reserved to the *consiglio* (or mayor).

Finally, if reform has created what Trigilia has called '*l'illusione decisionista*'[41] (an expression essentially meaning the illusion, or vain hope, of mayors as 'quick decision-makers', able to get things done) then it has fundamentally altered the qualities and resources mayors require to exercise power and seek solutions to local problems. As we noted, in searching for support to modernise their communities, 'policy-broking' mayors were forced to try to circumvent bureaucratic obstacles by relying on clientelistic networks operating through the parties. This essentially meant that their most important assets were their political connections. With the collapse of the party-political networks accompanying the 1993 reform, this appears to have changed. First, it has been suggested that if, on the one hand, reform has heightened the salience of mayors in mobilising state resources for their communities, then, on the other, there has sometimes been 'a clear shift towards the sort of "administrative activism" Tarrow found to characterise French mayors in the early 1970s'.[42] 'Administrative activism', Tarrow explained, was connected less to party contacts than to a French mayor's involvement in 'an informal structure that follows the formal nexus between mayor and [higher level state officials] and opens up to him a number of pathways within the administrative system for the satisfaction of his community's needs'.[43] In this context, French mayors became 'managers', whose administrative abilities, *apolitisme* and ability to engineer communal consensus were the most important assets enabling them to capture state resources. What is striking is that it is precisely these kinds of 'leadership' qualities that now appear to be required by Italian mayors in the new position in which they find themselves after 1993.

Prior to reform, though mayors were *formally* heads of the local state, the opportunities they had to exercise leadership were heavily circumscribed by what

---

[38]   Vandelli, *Sindaci e miti*, pp. 61–4.

[39]   Baldini, 'Eleggere I sindaci diece anni dopo'.

[40]   Although clearly far more detailed analysis, drawing on survey data and information about the precise localities most effected by declining turnout would be needed before one could draw firm conclusions about this.

[41]   Carlo Trigilia, 'Conclusioni. Dalla politica alle politiche: comuni e interessi locali', pp. 579–602 in Raimondo Catanzaro, Fortunata Piselli, Francesco Ramella and Carlo Trigilia, *Comuni nuovi: Il cambiamento nei governi locali* (Bologna: il Mulino, 2002).

[42]   Fortunata Piselli and Francesco Ramella, 'Introduzione', pp. 7–44 in Raimondo Catanzaro, Fortunata Piselli, Francesco Ramella and Carlo Trigilia, *Comuni nuovi: Il cambiamento nei governi locali* (Bologna: il Mulino, 2002), p. 36, my translation.

[43]   Tarrow, *Between Center and Periphery*, p. 136.

we have seen was their dependence on short-lived and shifting party alliances within the *consigli*, which in turn reflected the operations of national-level informal power networks wherein mayors had fundamentally subordinate positions. With reform, alongside much higher levels of public accountability, mayors find themselves at the apex of local political networks, having acquired powers whose effective exercise requires skills that previously they did not require so much. Amongst these skills, management and consensus-building seem especially important. Thus, directly elected mayors, faced with the *illusione decisionista* amongst their constituents, can draw on their theoretically autonomous capacity to appoint members of their *giunta* to achieve policy successes. However, in so doing, they have to manage the reality that, with the 'return' of parties following the crisis of the early 1990s, their choices are increasingly subject to party-political pressures.[44] Having made his choices, or having been obliged to make certain appointments, the mayor then has to retain the trust and cooperation of members of his *giunta*, aware that public criticism of him by a *giunta* member undermines his capacity to act effectively as representative of the community.[45] In steering the *giunta* (as well as the *consiglio* and local bureaucracy) in developing and implementing policies, he has to win the cooperation of significant local interest groups whose attitudes can have major roles in determining success or failure. During their investigation of the effects of the 1993 reform, Catanzaro et al. conducted interviews with civil society leaders in a dozen municipalities across Italy.[46] They took as background the hopes that it would produce significant improvement in the efficiency and effectiveness of local-authority policy-making. In seeking to explain variation in the leaders' perceptions of improvement between one authority and another, the authors' concluded: 'The municipalities that appear … most innovative in terms of policies are above all those with mayors having high levels of leadership skills, both in terms of their personal qualities and in terms of previously acquired political experience'.[47]

Conclusion

What has apparently happened then is that, with the 1993 reform, mayors have at last become 'heads of the local state' in a sense with some real substance to it. Until then, party domination ensured a lack of overlap between formal and informal relations of power such that mayoral incumbents may or may not have been at the apex of local structures of influence in any real sense. Since 1993, with the institutional resources given to mayors, this is much more likely to be the case. Of course, conferring resources does not automatically mean the recipient will use them to good effect.

---

[44] Trigilia, 'Conclusioni', p. 583. In the 27 provincial capitals holding municipal elections in both 1993 and 1997, the percentage of mayoral candidates without previous party experience rose from 8.0 in 1998–1992 to 31.7 in 1993, while declining somewhat to 24.1 in 1997 (Baldini and Legnante, *Città al voto*, p. 121).

[45] Vaciago, 'Il sindaco uno e trino', p. 98.

[46] Raimondo Catanzaro, Fortunata Piselli, Francesco Ramella and Carlo Trigilia, *Comuni nuovi: Il cambiamento nei governi locali* (Bologna: il Mulino, 2002).

[47] Trigilia, 'Conclusioni', p. 596, my translation.

Almost everything depends on the personal and political skills of those wielding them and this, we may suggest, greatly helps explain the difficulty of generalising about how far mayors have been freed from their former subjection to political parties, as well as the contrasting assessments of the impact of reform upon the quality of Italian local governance. What is clear is that, in bestowing new power-resources on mayors, the reform has given them a set of opportunities which together constitute necessary, but not sufficient, conditions for them to make considerable difference to local policy-making. In the reform's immediate aftermath, when political parties were reeling, it was at least partly the desire to take advantage of these opportunities that attracted prestigious outsiders into mayoralty – people with real or fancied leadership qualities and hope that they could 'get things done'. The at least partial 'recovery' of parties since then has made leadership qualities appear even more essential. That incumbents with such qualities have in some highly publicised instances, notably Naples and Palermo in the poorer south, succeeded in bringing real improvements to their communities, has helped ensure that today's mayors are more well-known, more authoritative and more central figures in public political debate than they have ever been before – to Italian democracy's clear benefit.

CHAPTER NINE

From Party and State Domination to Putin's 'Power Vertical': The Subjugation of Mayors in Communist and Post-Communist Russia

Cameron Ross

Russian local government has until relatively recently been rather neglected by Russian and western scholars. Whilst there have been many scholarly works devoted to regional politics there have been relatively few studies of local-level politics and heads of local administrations.[1] Here, I focus on mayoral power and status in the Soviet and post-Soviet periods, from Gorbachev to Putin. I also examine the politics of local government reform and the problems of creating new municipalities based on the democratic principles of local self-governance.

Russia's Transition, Federalism and Local Politics

The new Russian Federation, emerging from the USSR's ashes in January 1992, was immediately beset by multiple political, economic and social problems. The Yeltsin leadership had the daunting task of simultaneously reforming both polity and economy. There were great fears that the hardships inevitably accompanying economic reform would turn the population against democracy. Moreover, after centuries of Tsarist autocracy and seven decades of Communist rule, civil society was feeble and political culture authoritarian.

As Theen notes, although Russia's history, both Imperial and Soviet:

---

[1]   T.H. Friedgut and J.W. Hahn (eds), *Local Power and Post-Soviet Politics* (Armonk, New York, 1994); V. Gel'man, S. Ryzhenkov, E. Belokurova and N. Borisova, *Avtonomiya Ili Kontrol'?* (Letnii Sad, St. Petersburg, 2002); Alfred B. Evans and Vladimir Gel'man (eds), *The Politics of Local Government in Russia* (Rowman and Littlefield, Boulder, New York 2004); V.B. Zotova (ed.), *Mestnoe Samoupravlenie v Rossii* (Os'-89, Moscow, 2003); Galina Kourliandskaya, Yelena Nikolayenko and Natalia Golovanova, 'Local Government in the Russian Federation: Developing New Rules in the Old Environment', in Victor Popa and Igor Munteanu (eds), *Local Government in Eastern Europe, in the Caucasus and Central Asia* (Budapest: LGI, 2001); Valery Tishkov, 'Local Self-Government Versus Local State Administration: Russia's Hybrid Experience', in V. Tishkov and E. Filippova (eds), *Local Governance and Minority Empowerment in the CIS* (Budapest: LGI, 2002).

is not completely devoid of elements of participatory government, for the most part the regions of Russia were administered not governed – let alone self-governed. In its historical evolution, the Russian Empire moved inexorably towards centralisation and bureaucratisation.[2]

Aside from the *Zemstvo* system, which provided limited local representation in the period 1864–1917, Russia had no experience of local self-government. During the Communist era, local government was part of a highly centralised, authoritarian, and hierarchical system of state administration, dominated at every level by the Communist Party. There were no nationwide multi-party elections; indeed, political parties were only legalised in 1990.

As I shall demonstrate, the legal and extra-legal powers of mayors in post-Communist Russia also vary significantly. These variations spring primarily from the development of high levels of constitutional, socio-economic and political asymmetry amongst Russia's 89 federal subjects (regions, republics and autonomies). The December 1993 Constitution granted the 32 ethnically-defined subjects far greater political and economy autonomy than the 57 territorially-defined regions (see Table 9.1). The 21 ethnic republics, in particular, were granted extensive powers, including rights to ratify their own constitutions and appoint their own chief executives.

Table 9.1   Federal Structure of the Russian Federation[3]

A. Ethnically defined subjects (32)
21 ethnic republics
10 Autonomous Okrugs
1 Autonomous Oblast
B. Territorially defined subjects (57)
6 Krais
49 Oblasts
2 Federal Cities (Moscow and St. Petersburg)

Constitutional asymmetry was further exacerbated during the Yeltsin era (1991–2000) with the development of 'contract federalism'. Between 1994 and 1998 Yeltsin, in return for political favours, signed bilateral treaties with 46 federal subjects. These granted the signatories extra-constitutional powers, including determination of their own forms of regional and local government. In many ethnic republics (for example, Adygeiya, Chechnya, Dagestan and Tatarstan), the chief executives were able to

---

    [2]   R.H.W. Theen, 'Russia at the Grassroots: Reform at the Local and Regional Levels', in I.J. Kim and J.S. Zacek (eds), *Establishing Democratic Rule* (Paragon House, St. Paul, Minnesota, 1993), p. 54.
    [3]   Cameron Ross, *Federalism and Democratisation in Russia* (Manchester University Press, 2002).

carve out personal fiefdoms and instigate highly authoritarian regimes. Local bodies were subordinated to republican administrations and mayors directly appointed by republican presidents. Before examining mayoral powers in the post-Communist period, we should first discuss Soviet local government.

Local Government and Heads of City Administrations in the USSR

As Campbell notes, the Soviet governmental system 'consisted of three parallel hierarchies: the representatives of legislative councils (soviets), the executive organs (which were nominally subordinate to the soviets at each level), and the communist party'.[4] Each level (union, republic, province, city, district and so on) possessed a local soviet, executive committee (*ispol'kom*) and party organisation. The work of the executive committees was guided by the principle of 'democratic centralism', whereby, all organs of state power and state administration formed a single system and worked on the basis of subordinating lower organs to leadership and control by higher organs. This was significantly reinforced by 'dual subordination', whereby each executive committee was directly accountable both to the soviet electing it and to higher executive and administrative bodies. Both principles of Soviet administration were deliberately designed to ensure high centralisation of decision-making within Soviet bureaucracies.

The city councils (soviets)

In 1982 2.3 million deputies were elected to 52,000 local soviets (at regional, city and district levels). At city level, 252,335 deputies were elected to 2,059 soviets averaging 137 deputies per assembly.[5] According to Article 95 of the USSR Constitution, soviet deputies were 'elected on the basis of universal, equal suffrage, by secret ballot'. However, until Gorbachev's late-1980s reforms, only the Communist Party could participate in elections and there were not even competing candidates. The Party selected the single candidate who stood unopposed in each constituency. As Smith notes:

> Because citizens had a duty to vote and well over 90 per cent of the local electorate regularly turned out to do so ... local election day itself was little more than a ritualised occasion for registering the supposed unity of the party-state and its citizenry.[6]

---

[4]   Adrian Campbell, 'Regional power in the Russian Federation', in Andrew Coulson (ed.), *Local Government in Eastern Europe: Establishing Democracy at the Grassroots* (Edward Elgar, Aldershot, 1995), p. 149.

[5]   E.M. Jacobs, 'Introduction', in E.M. Jacobs (ed.), *Soviet Local Politics and Government* (George Allen and Unwin, London, 1983), p. 9.

[6]   Graham Smith, *The Post-Soviet States* (Arnold, London 1999), p. 113.

The city executive committee (gorispol'kom)

At each hierarchical level, the chairman (mayor at city level) and executive committee were theoretically elected by, and accountable to, the soviets. Thus, according to Article 150 of the 1977 USSR Constitution, 'Executive committees of local soviets ... shall be directly accountable both to the soviet that elected them and to their executive administrative body'. But as Hahn notes, 'the soviets were in reality little more than ceremonial bodies ... charged with ratifying decisions already decided upon in advance by their executives and party organs'.[7] Members of the executive 'decided when to convene sessions of the soviets and which issues to introduce; they prepared the reports and the draft legislation; they established the list of speakers and even edited their speeches'.[8]

Executive committees and local councils were themselves dominated by party bodies at every level. Thus, whilst, according to Soviet law, the executive committee alone had the constitutional right, 'to make decisions ... binding on all enterprises, institutions and organisations located within a given territory, as well as officials and citizens',[9] in practice, the top city position was held not by the executive committee chair, but rather by the first secretary of the city party organisation (*gorkom*). Moreover, whilst party bodies were theoretically meant to provide only ideological guidance, and expressly prohibited from directly interfering in local councils' daily work, in practice party substitution (*podmena*) of local soviets was widespread.

Heads of city administrations were given their orders not only from higher-level state bodies but also by party officials at the local level and above. Not uncommonly, party officials also bypassed the soviets and city executive committee heads and gave direct orders to city officials. Thus, as a Communist Party Central Committee Resolution warned in 1971:

> In the practice of the district and city Party committees, there are still a good many instances of petty tutelage over the soviets and usurpation of their functions, as well as the adoption of Party decisions on questions that fall wholly within the jurisdiction of the soviets.[10]

The party also extensively used its powers of appointment (*nomenklatura*). Regional party organisations, for example, would play leading roles in appointing and dismissing key members of city administrations, including the chairs of executive committees. As Table 9.2 shows, the Communist Party and its youth-wing, the *Komsomol*, dominated city soviets and their executive committees.

---

[7]   Jeffrey Hahn, 'Developments in Soviet local politics', in A.J. Rieber and A.Z. Rubenstein (eds), *Perestroika at the Crossroads* (M.E. Sharpe, Armonk, New York, 1991), pp. 76–7.

[8]   N.G. Starovoitov, 'Sessii sovetov: teoriia, praktika, problemy', cited in Hahn, *Perestroika*, p. 85.

[9]   Law of the USSR, 25 June 1980, 'Ob Osnovnykh Polnomochiyakh Kraevykh, Oblastnykh Sovetov Narodnykh Deputatov', *Pravda*, 26 June 1980, p. 2.

[10]   Resolution of the Central Committee of the Communist Party of the Soviet Union, 12 March 1971, 'O Merakh po Dal'neishemu Uluchsheniyu Raboty Raionnykh i Gorodskikh Sovetov Deputatov Trudyashchikhsya', *Pravda*, 14 March 1971, p. 1.

Table 9.2   Communist Party and *Komsomol* Membership of City Soviets and their Executive Committees, Elected 1982[11]

Members	City Soviets (%)	Executive Committees (%)
Party	46.3	89.4
Komsomol	24.7	6.0
Total	70.0	95.4

There were also interlocking career structures for party and state functionaries, with officials regularly moving from one administrative hierarchy to another. Heads of city executive committees were also members of city party committees. Likewise, first party secretaries would also be members of city executive committees. Thereby the party could exercise direct control over heads of city administrations and the work of their executives.

As one might expect in such a situation and culture, the ceremonial and symbolic role of mayors as the personal embodiment of their localities was weak or non-existent during the Soviet era. Top party and state officials were deliberately moved from one region to another in order to prevent them from 'going native'. Mayors had few personal bonds of solidarity and loyalty with their cities. Leaders of local party bodies and soviets were seen more as enforcers of central power than defenders of local interests and there was widespread popular mistrust of all government and party bodies.

State enterprises

A third branch of power in Soviet cities were the directors of state enterprises, the most powerful of whom were also members of city party committees. In some 'one-company towns', where single giant enterprises dominated the economic landscape (e.g., Magnitogorsk), the factory boss was often the most powerful figure. Heads of city administrations depended on enterprises to provide their workers with housing, utilities and other public amenities. Indeed, most Soviet cities were planned to meet the interests of their enterprises rather than their citizens. Factory directors of large companies would take their orders directly from Moscow ministerial bosses rather than city mayors. Power relations between party officials and enterprise directors is well illustrated in a Russian novel where the director of a large factory explains to his wife that he had nothing to fear from the first party secretary of a city district party committee: 'He is afraid to fight [me], for he would not be able to take me on. His district is a poor one … all its economic base is in [my] hands.'[12] Thus, although the city executive committee chair was legally the most powerful single individual, it was actually the party first secretaries and enterprise directors who dominated city politics.

---

[11]   Cameron Ross, *Local Government in the Soviet Union* (St. Martin's Press, New York, 1987), p. 32.

[12]   V. Dudinstev, *Ne Khlebom Edinym* (Khuozh lit, Moscow, 1968), p. 27.

The Gorbachev reforms of the late-1980s

In 1985 Mikhail Gorbachev was elected head of the Communist Party, clearly mandated to lead the USSR out of economic and political stagnation. In 1988 he convened a special party conference where he put forward radical plans for democratisation. As Hahn notes, Gorbachev's reforms were primarily intended 'to shift the existing imbalance of power away from the party and ... executive branch in favour of the soviets, both nationally and locally'.[13] The 'role and powers of the soviets', Gorbachev stressed, were to be fully restored 'as sovereign organs of popular representation'.[14] In 1990, article 6 of the Constitution was repealed, allowing multiparty elections for the first time in Soviet history: throughout the country, members of local Party elites were swept from power. As Wollmann observes, in large cities like Moscow and Leningrad, 'reformist Communists and independents won the majority of seats in the soviets and immediately challenged the conservative Party *nomenklatura*, which was still well-entrenched in the local executive committees'.[15]

The April 1990 and July 1991 laws on local self-government

The first practical steps to reform local government came in the 9 April 1990 law *On General Principles of Local Self-Government and Local Economy in the USSR*.[16] Significantly, this was the first Soviet law to use the term 'local self-government'. As Kourliandskaya et al. note, it established:

> legal guarantees that local authorities were autonomous, independent and elected by popular vote; it codified the competence of local soviets, and it provided norms for the transfer of communal property to local soviets and the revenue sources of local soviets, including fixed shares of federal tax revenues, and a list of own taxes, levies and duties to be introduced at the discretion of the local soviets.[17]

However, whilst deputies to the soviets were to be popularly elected, heads of administration were still appointed from above. Direct mayoral elections were, however, allowed in Moscow and Leningrad on June 12 1991. In these, Anatolii Sobchak was elected Mayor of Leningrad and Yurii Popov Mayor of Moscow.

The first Russian law on local self-government, *On Local Self-Government in the Russian Soviet Federal Socialist Republic*, was passed a year later on 6 July 1991 while Russia was still part of the USSR. As Campbell notes, for the first time, appointments of key members of city executive committees, including mayors, were to be approved by

---

[13]   Hahn, 'Developments', p. 78.

[14]   B.A. Hazan, *Gorbachev's Gamble: The 19th All-Union Party Conference* (Westview Press, Boulder, San Francisco 1990), p. 88.

[15]   Hellmut Wollmann, 'Institution Building of Local Self-Government in Russia: Between Legal Design and Power Politics', in Alfred B. Evans and Vladimir Gel'man (eds), *The Politics of Local Government in Russia* (Rowman and Littlefield, Boulder, New York, 2004), p. 106.

[16]   'Ob Obshchikh Nachalakh Mestnovo Samoupravleniya i Mestnovo Khozyaistva v SSSR'.

[17]   Kourliandskaya et al., 'Local Government', p. 179.

city councils.[18] However, the 1990 and 1991 laws were never fully realised in practice, as local government reform was overtaken by the dramatic events of the 1991 'August Coup' and the USSR's subsequent collapse in December 1991.

Local Government Reform and Mayoral Powers Under Yeltsin 1991–2000

In the wake of the failed coup, the Russian Parliament in November 1991 reluctantly agreed to give President Yeltsin special powers, including rights to appoint and remove administrative heads regional soviets. In turn, these regional chiefs were granted rights to appoint and remove heads of city administrations, excepting those of regional capitals, which were directly appointed by the President.

The struggle over the December 1993 constitution

Between August 1991 and September 1993 there was a fierce struggle between the Russian Parliament and President. Each sought to impose their own draft constitution on the country. The deadlock only ended in October 1993 when Yeltsin sent the army to forcibly close down the Russian parliament and eject rebel parliamentarians. In the aftermath of these 'October days', Yeltsin vilified local soviets for supporting the parliamentarians. On October 7 1993, he stated on television:

> I will say in no uncertain terms that the majority of bodies of Soviet power bear direct responsibility for the extreme aggravation of the situation in Moscow. The system of soviets displayed complete disregard for the security of the state and its citizens, and so the soviets themselves wrote the final chapter of their political life.[19]

He ended by demanding the soviets be disbanded: 'I believe the soviets that took an irreconcilable position should ... make the dignified and courageous decision to dissolve themselves and leave the stage peacefully and decently, without upheavals and scandals. This is demanded by life itself.'[20]

After the October events, practically all soviets stopped their activities. A Presidential decree of 9 October 1993, *On the Reform of Representative Organs, the Powers and Organs of Local Self-administration*,[21] established that regional soviets' functions were to be temporarily taken over by their executives. In addition, Yeltsin's decree of 26 October 1993, *On the Reform of Local Self-administration in the Russian Federation*,[22] halted the activities of city and district soviets. New elections

---

[18]   Campbell, 'Regional Power', pp. 157–8.

[19]   Address by the President of the Russian Federation to the Citizens of Russia, *Rossiiskaya Gazeta*, 7 October 1993, pp. 1–2, translated in the *Current Digest of the Post-Soviet Press* (*CDPSP*), Vol. XLV, No. 40, 1993, p. 21.

[20]   *CDPSP*, p. 21.

[21]   'O Reforme Predstavitel'nykh Organov, Vlasti i Organov Mestnovo Samoupravleniya v Rossiiskoi Federatsii', *Rossiiskaya Gazeta*, 12 October 1993 (this was not operative in the 21 ethnic republics).

[22]   'O Reforme Mestnovo Samoupravleniya v Rossiiskoi Federatsii', *Rossiiskaya Gazeta*, 29 October 1993.

for much weaker local bodies were scheduled for early-1994. As Wollmann notes, the number of deputies and powers of the new local assemblies were significantly reduced. Henceforth, budgetary decisions would require the head of administration's consent. Moreover, 'the power of a local chief of administration was enlarged. That official now had the power to convene and preside over the sessions of the council'.[23] Between October 1993 and spring 1994, when new assemblies began being re-elected, mayors could rule their cities without any legislative check. As Gel'man et. al. note, with the Russian Constitution's ratification in December 1993, 'local self-government in Russia was proclaimed from above only two months after the conditions for its development had been destroyed from below'.[24]

Articles 130–133 of the Constitution provide the following guarantees:

> 1) Local communities possess autonomy in addressing issues of local importance, 2) local self-government may follow a diversity of organisational models, 3) regional authorities must take into account the preferences of the local communities when determining the boundaries of local government jurisdictions, 4) local governments possess financial autonomy (albeit limited), with discretion over the management of municipal property and the implementation of local budgets, 5) adequate funding is guaranteed for the performance of additional state functions delegated to the local governments by the decision of federal or regional state authorities, 6) local governments will be reimbursed for the costs of implementing federal mandates.[25]

Furthermore, Article 12 declares that, 'within the limits of its powers, local self-government is independent. Bodies of local self-government do not form part of the system of bodies of state power'. However, this is directly contradicted by Article 132(2) which declares that: 'Individual state powers can be vested in bodies of local self-government by law, with the transfer of the material and financial resources necessary to exercise them.' City governments have been overloaded by these obligatory state duties which both regional and federal bodies pass down and which they can monitor and control. Moreover, unfunded federal mandates have financially crippled most Russian cities. Nonetheless, Article 12 clearly states that local government is not simply a third tier of state power subordinate to federal and regional administrations.

The 1995 Russian law on local self-government

In 1995 a new Federal Law, *On Local Self-Government in the Russian Federation*, was adopted.[26] Finally ratified by the parliament in August 1995, this had to overcome two vetoes by the Federation Council (the Russian Parliament's Upper Chamber) before reaching the statute book. It was adopted at a time when all the

---

[23]   Wollman, 'Institution Building', p. 111.

[24]   Gel'man et al., *Avtonomiya*, p. 67.

[25]   Kourliandskaya et al., 'Local Government', p. 172.

[26]   Federal Law No 154-F3, 28 August 1995, 'Ob Obshchikh Printsipakh Organizatsii Mestnovo Samoupravleniya v Rossiiskoi Federatsii', in Predmety Vedeniya I Polnomochiya Mestnovo Samoupravleniya v Rossiskoi Federatsii (Moscow, Yuridicheskaya Literatura, 2001), pp. 21–31.

main power structures were gearing up for the December 1995 parliamentary and the 1996 Presidential elections. Implementing the 1995 law was therefore intricately linked with these events. Crucially, the centre wanted to gain the loyalty and support of the regions in these elections. They wished to block the law's implementation, particularly the section on popular election for heads of local administrations. Regions naturally wanted to retain the mayoral appointment powers Yeltsin had granted them in 1991.[27]

As Slider observes, the 1995 law:

> created for the first time the foundations for autonomous institutions of local government and gave local authorities wide ranging powers, including independent tax and budgetary authority, control over municipal property, and the right to make decisions in areas of competence that were binding on all organisations or enterprises that were located within its territory.[28]

Article 4 lays out federal bodies' rights regarding local self-government, whilst article 5 outlines the powers of the federal subjects in relation to local government and article 6 sets down the powers of local self-governments, listing 30 areas of local competence. The independence granted local self-government in the Constitution's article 12 is further developed in the 1995 law, article 17 forbidding organs of state power to independently creating local government bodies or appoint their personnel. Article 14 also forbids state organs and their personnel from carrying out local government functions.

Problems of implementing the 1995 law

As noted, the 1995 law was fiercely opposed by regional and republican heads who saw it as challenging their powers and prerogatives. Opposition had an economic and political basis. As Mitrokhin notes, 'The regional bosses, not without reason, saw local self-government as a force taking away from them large segments of their powers and finances … the very things they themselves had just wrested from the federal centre'.[29] If they could not block the passage of the law outright, then regional leaders did everything possible to minimise its impact. In several republics, local governments were illegally brought under direct control from chief executives and mayors were personally appointed and dismissed by republican leaders (for example, in Adygeya, Bashkortostan, Kalmykiya, Komi, Tatarstan, Tyva and Udmurtiya).

In April 1996 the Udmurtiya State Council, at the initiative of its Chairman, Alexandr Volkov, adopted a law replacing the republic's organs of local self-government with local government bodies directly subordinated to the Republican leadership. Only Anatolii Saltykov, Mayor of the capital city of Izhevsk, dared challenge this law. For his pains, Saltykov was soon put under surveillance by the Udmurtiya security forces and he and several colleagues in the city administration were subjected to blackmail and intimidation. Eventually, Volkov simply dismissed Saltykov, substituting one of his

---

[27] Gel'man et al., *Avtonomiya*, p. 78.

[28] Darell Slider, 'Governors versus Mayors', p. 147.

[29] Sergei Mitrokhin, 'It's a rare governor who doesn't dream of becoming a Khan', *Obshchaya Gazeta*, No, 44, 6–13 November 1996, p. 8.

own cronies. Appeals from the Russian Parliament to refer the matter to the Prosecutor General's office were unavailing. Thus 'before long, Izhevsk had two mayors: the democratically elected Saltykov and the personal appointment of Volkov'.[30]

In July 1996 President Yeltsin requested the Constitutional Court to check the legality of Udmurtiya's law. However, the Court's decision of 24 January 1997 was highly ambiguous. On the one hand, it sided with Yeltsin and declared Udmurtiya's attempts to abolish local self-government unconstitutional. The Court also ruled it obligatory that local government organs were elected. However, as Gel'man observes, 'the Court also declared that it was the right of subjects of the federation to create parallel organs of local state power in the capital cities and districts of federal subjects'.[31]

This ambivalent ruling, particularly its confirmation of the right of federal subjects to form their state institutions, allowed Udmurtiya's government to defend its actions and ignore Yeltsin's demands to reinstate local self-government. It was not long before other regions followed. For example, in Kareliya, Novosibirsk and Sverdlovsk regions, we have the ridiculous situation where there are local organs of state power, directly subordinate to regional leaderships, working alongside organs of local self-government. In other regions like Tatarstan, local self-government is confined to the lowest administrative levels, districts and rural settlements and does not operate in cities.

Municipal political institutions

Article 72 of the Constitution grants the Russian Federation and federal subjects joint jurisdiction in establishing 'general principles' for the organisation of local government. The rights and powers of municipal bodies are specified in municipal charters, varying considerably across the Federation. Under the 1995 Law, five basic types of local self-government may be created:

1.   a local legislature and a generally elected local administration head (a mayor); the latter also presides over the local legislature,
2.   a local legislature and a mayor elected by the legislature,
3.   a local legislature headed by a person who has no right to make decisions on his own, and a hired head of the local administration,
4.   a local legislature and a local administration formed out of the legislature's members who combine representative and executive functions; in this case, the head of the legislature is also the head of the local administration,
5.   a local community assembly (*skhod*) and local government head (occurs in small rural settlements).[32]

As of 1 September 2000, over 12,261 municipalities were registered in Russia, of which 11,691 had elected representative bodies. In approximately 7,000 (57 per

---

[30]   Mitrokhin, 'It's a rare governor', pp. 5–6.

[31]   Gel'man et al., *Avtonomiya*, p. 82

[32]   Armen Danielian, 'Local government in Russia: reinforcing fiscal autonomy', in Kenneth Davey (ed.), *Fiscal Autonomy and Efficiency: Reforms in the Former Soviet Union* (Local Government and Public Service Reform Institute, Open Society Institute, Budapest, 2002), p. 91.

cent) municipalities, mayors were elected directly by the citizenry by secret ballot. In 3,600 of these, mayors both head local administrations and chair local assemblies. In 4,519 of the municipalities (36.9 per cent), elected officials were chosen from among, and by, local council members, including nominees proposed by the regional government. In just 89 municipalities in five regions, councils hired local government heads on a contractual basis.[33]

Elections of heads of local administrations

By 2004 almost all Russian municipalities had successfully completed two or three cycles of mayoral elections. It is difficult to obtain up-to-date information on these. Here I provide data on the elections occurring between January 1994 and July 1998 (when there were more municipalities than noted above). During this election cycle, 13,734 local administration heads were elected in 87 of the 89 subjects of the federation. The vast majority of elections used the first-past-the-post system, with second-round runoffs for the two top candidates. Turnout in cities varied from 33 to 55 per cent. Of newly-elected mayors, 70 per cent were 30–50 years of age, 60 per cent had higher education, 24 per cent were female and 26 per cent had previously been mayors or deputy-mayors.[34]

Elections for local assemblies

Local councils are elected by universal, equal and direct suffrage. Numbers of deputies vary from just 4 in rural settlements to 30-plus in large cities. The vast majority of assemblies are elected for four years and usually meet at least six times a year.[35]

The following are the exclusive responsibility of local councils:

1) To adopt local laws; 2) approve the local budget and report on its execution; 3) adopt plans and programmes of local development and approve reports on their implementation; 4) establish local taxes and fees; 4) establish procedures for the management and disposal of local property; 5) monitor the activities of local governments and officials.[36]

Between January 1994 and July 1998, 12,942 municipalities held elections. 380,000 candidates competed, averaging two to five per constituency, and 113,300 were elected. The vast majority of constituencies (70 per cent in 81 of the 89 federal subjects) used the first-past-the-post system. In 30 per cent, elections were conducted using proportional representation with two to 20 candidates competing in multi-member districts. The vast majority of deputies are part-time, a factor undoubtedly weakening their ability to scrutinise the work of the executive and hold administrative heads to account.

---

[33]   Kourliandskaya et al., 'Local Government', p. 197.

[34]   A.V. Ivanchenko, A.A. Veshnyakov, V.I. Vasil'ev and V.I. Lysenko (eds), *Vybory v Rossiiskoi Federatsii* (Moscow, VELTI, 1998), p. 122–4.

[35]   11 per cent were elected for just two years and 7 per cent for five years.

[36]   Kourliandskaya et al., 'Local Government', p. 85.

Political parties

Clientelism, not party politics, dominates Russian local government. Parties played only very minor roles in elections to local assemblies and heads of administrations. 'The main criteria for electing mayors and local council members are personal characteristics, such as the occupation of the candidate or past experience in government administration. Teachers, doctors and directors of enterprises are prolific'.[37] Thus only 3 per cent of local assembly candidates stood on party platforms and, of these, only 5 per cent won seats in the 1994–1998 round of elections.[38] The vast majority of mayors are independents. Just 1 per cent of those standing on party tickets for the mayoralty over the period 1994–1998 were victorious.[39]

When democratic institutions are weak and inchoate, their role is soon taken by informal practices, like clientelism, patrimonialism and corruption.[40] The chronic weakness of parties has left open the door for other groups to enter local politics. Two of the most powerful are industrial executives and state bureaucrats. In a new post-Communist corporatist alliance, regional economic and political elites (many of whom were former Soviet *nomenklatura*) have joined forces to plunder the wealth of their regions and cities. Key members of the Soviet economic and administrative elites now dominate and control the work of Russia's local assemblies. Thus, for example in 1998, representatives of large business concerns won 20 of 30 seats in the Izhevsk City Assembly.

> The new members of the legislature controlled two of the largest banks in the city, all the private television stations, 90 per cent of private newspapers, two thirds of the market for oil products, all three large construction companies, and the two trading companies. Among the winners was the Chairman of 'Udmurtneft', which extracts 80 percent of the oil in the Udmurtiya region. No political party member was elected.[41]

Mayoral power and responsibilities

Both the scope of mayoral responsibilities and the terms of office are established by municipal charter. Most cities follow what is known as the 'strong mayor/weak council' model. A classic version is when a popularly elected mayor also chairs the local council. Thus the charter of the city of Cheliabinsk states that the mayor 'has the status of a deputy, is chair of the city assembly (*duma*) and head of the city executive'. Large municipalities where the mayor is also the chairman of the legislative assembly include Izhevsk, Orenburg, Orsk, Irkutsk, Bratsk, Astrakhan, Belgorod, Kostroma, Kurgan, Rostov-on-Don, Samara, Stavropol, Khabarovsk and Cheliabinsk.[42] Here, mayors have the right to

---

[37]   ibid, p. 182.

[38]   Slider, 'Governors versus Mayors', p. 148.

[39]   Kourliandskaya et al., 'Local Government', p. 124.

[40]   G. O'Donnell, 'Delegative Democracy', *Journal of Democracy*, Vol. 5, No. 1, January 1994, pp. 55–69.

[41]   'Mayor, Businessmen Win Local Elections in Izhevsk', *Russian Regional Report*, Vol. 3, No. 16, 23 April 1998, p. 382 (no author noted).

[42]   A, Kouznetsov, A. Shanin and G. Vetrov, 'Conflict of Interest in Russian Local Government: Challenges for new legislation', in Babara Kudrycka (ed.), *Combating Conflict of*

organise council work, preside over its sessions, sign and promulgate acts adopted by the council and *veto* its decisions. Councils can overturn mayoral vetoes only by a two-thirds majority – very difficult in assemblies where parties are weak or non-existent. Mayoral powers in such places can be very extensive indeed, as is evident in Table 9.3.

Table 9.3   Powers Granted to the Mayor of Cheliabinsk[43]

1.	Guarantees the implementation of federal and other legal acts on the territory of the city.
2.	Represents the city and organs of self-administration in international relations and signs treaties and agreements.
3.	Convenes and leads sessions of the city assembly (Duma), and signs its decisions and other documents.
4.	Reports to the assembly about the state of affairs within the city's boundaries.
5.	Coordinates the activities of the Duma's deputies and standing commissions, assists commission members in carrying out their powers.
6.	Adopts measures for open and transparent government.
7.	Guarantees and establishes procedures for carrying out referendums and elections.
8.	Establishes the structures of the city administration (Housing and Communal Services; Transport; Communications; Development of Enterprises and Small Business; Trade; Health; Education; Culture, Fitness and Sport; City Planning and Architecture; Social Security; Law and order; Administration of Municipal Property; Economic Planning, Budget and Finance; Land Use and Environmental Protection; Labour and employment; Youth affairs; Civil Defence).
9.	Draws up and places before the Duma draft plans for the complex development of the city.
10.	Organises the complex economic and social development of the city and ensures the implementation of the budget in correspondence with the decisions of the Duma.
11.	Takes prime responsibility for managing the city budget, finance and credits. Opens and closes the administration's bank accounts; signs and approves financial documents.
12.	Establishes stabilisation and development funds and distributes grants to the city's urban districts.
13.	Adopts resolutions and orders and can rescind legal acts of subordinate organs of the city administration.
14.	Draws up plans, and confirms staffing, for city and district administrations. Adopts resolutions on the structure of city administration. Appoints and dismisses administrative personnel, chiefs of district and settlement administrations, in agreement with the city assembly: appoints and dismisses leaders of municipal enterprises and organisations.
15.	Organises the work of the administration in dealing with citizens' appeals and requests.

Interest in Local Government in the CEE Countries (Open Society Institute, Budapest, 2004), p. 258.

43   Source: E.M. Koveshnikov, *Munitsipal'noe Pravo* (Norma, Moscow, 2002), pp. 144–7.

16.   Takes charge of civil defence during emergencies.
17.   Presents to the population of the city and the city assembly a yearly report about the activities of the city administration.
18.   Defends and promotes the interests of the population, and organs of the city administration in courts and organs of state power.
19.   Makes necessary provision for the implementation of legislation adopted by the city assembly in accordance with the city charter. Within the areas of his/her competence adopts resolutions and orders.

The 'weak mayor/strong council' model is much less common, encountered mainly in smaller cities and rural areas. Here, mayors are elected by council members, who can keep a much closer check on their activities. Such mayors, as in western democracies, have to rely on the support of the deputies to remain in power.

In sharp contrast to the Soviet era where mayors often came from outside and were imposed on the localities from above, popularly elected mayors today are much more likely to have been born and made their careers in their cities. Many mayors are now viewed much more positively as advocates and defenders of local interests and many have now built up strong reservoirs of local support and solidarity.

Mayors versus regional governors

Conflict between mayors and governors is widespread in Russia. As Domnysheva notes, 'The interests of mayors, who are primarily concerned about their own city, rarely coincide with the broader views of governors who are responsible for their entire region'.[44] Thus, when things go wrong, 'governors blame everything on mayors and mayors blame everything on governors'.[45] Often the primary reason for such conflicts are economic: 'the unwillingness of regional leaders to share the instruments of powers such as property, taxes and other financial resources as well as decision-making authority in areas of business and economics.'[46]

Battles between governors and mayors of regional capitals have been particularly intense. According to Russian law, corporate taxes are paid at an enterprise's place of registration. Capital cities of regions are thus major centres for the 'accumulation of tax revenues, rent payments and most other kinds of payment'.[47] Not surprisingly, mayors will seek to keep these finances to help fund hard-pressed municipal services. The struggle over local government

[44]   Yelizaveta Domnysheva, 'Congress of Municipalities – The Kremlin's Long Awaited Child', *Noviye Izvestia*, June 20, 1998, p. 2. Translated in *CDPSP*, Vol. 50, No. 25, 1998, p. 11.
[45]   Besik Pipia, 'Divide and rule', *Nezavisimaya gazeta*, 3 March 1998, p. 10. Translated in *CDPSP*, Vol. 50, No. 9, 1998, p. 15.
[46]   Wollmann, 'Institution building', p. 110.
[47]   Pipia, 'Divide and rule', p. 15.

reform in Udmurtiya, discussed above, was closely connected with the battle to control the spoils of privatisation, also part of a bid by the republic's leadership to take control of funds going to Ishevsk, the capital city. Conflicts between mayors and governors have intensified as local government finances have been squeezed under President Putin's administration. For example, over the period 1999–2002, 'the average share of tax revenues in local budgets dropped from 27.6 per cent to 18.7 per cent while the average share of subsidies from federal and regional budgets increased from 26.7 per cent to 40.5 per cent'. Moreover, as Shvetsov notes, whilst municipal budgets were responsible for 32 per cent of overall expenditure in Russia's consolidated budget, they received less than 22 per cent of total revenues.[48] As a result, 'over 75 per cent of Russia's local councils have to rely on financial support from federal or regional governments'.[49]

Political as well as economic factors help explain conflicts between mayors and governors. As Wollmann notes, regional leaders 'tend to be ardent decentralisers whilst dealing with central government', but 'adamant centralisers in relation to local organs'.[50] Furthermore, as Slider notes, mayors and governors serve different electorates. 'Rural voters, who in the Russian context have tended to be among the most hostile to reform and turn out to vote in the highest numbers, [have] sometimes been decisive in electing regional executives and legislatures.' Thus, for example, the struggle between the Mayor of the city of Krasnoyarsk and the Governor of Krasnoyarsk region was intensified by the fact that the governor won much of his support from rural voters, while a majority of those in the capital city voted against him. Mayors tend to be 'more pro-market and to favour more radical political reforms'.[51] In addition, mayors are often the main opposition candidates to governors in regional elections. Hostility between governors and mayors was also encouraged by the Yeltsin administration, which adopted a policy of divide and rule in the regions and often sought the support of mayors in its struggle against governors.

As membership of national parties is very low, governors and mayors quite often form their own political machines to fight local elections. Thus, for example, the Governor of Sverdlovsk, Eduard Rossel had his own political movement in the region (the 'Transformation of the Urals') and his own newspaper *Oblastnaya Gazeta*. Likewise, the Mayor of the capital city Ekaterinburg, Chernetskii', headed his own political movement (Our Home-Our City) and controlled a newspaper of the same name.[52] In Pskov region, the regional newspaper, *Pskovskaia Pravda*, is controlled by the governor, whilst the city newspaper, *Novosti Pskova*, backs the mayor.[53]

Governors are also not averse to using extra-legal or illegal means to maintain their power base. As Gel'man stresses:

---

[48]   Vladimir Gel'man, 'The Politics of Local Government Reform in Russia: From Decentralisation to Recentralisation', paper presented to the Conference, 'The Fall of Communism in Europe: Ten Years On', The Hebrew University of Jerusalem, 14–17 May 2001, p. 3.

[49]   ibid., p. 9.

[50]   Wollmann, 'Institution building', p. 110.

[51]   Slider, 'Governor's versus Mayors', p. 154.

[52]   Sergei Pushkarev, 'The Conflict between the Sverdlovsk Governor and Yekaterinburg Mayor', East West Institute, *Russian Regional Report*, 17 July 1998, p. 5.

[53]   Slider, 'Governors versus Mayors', p. 161.

while the first regional elections held in the early 1990s were an important step on the path to democratising political life in the regions, in the beginning of this decade we are witnessing movement in the other direction, a 'de-democratisation' of Russian political life. The formal elections are nothing more than a smoke screen for uncompetitive voting, hiding the informal practice in which leaders are simply appointed, as happened during the Soviet era.[54]

Governors and mayors command significant 'administrative resources', which have 'often included compliant regional assemblies, courts and electoral commissions'.[55] The outcomes of Russian local elections are now, more than ever, decided in courtrooms, and election-commission headquarters rather than in polling stations.[56]

Federal level officials have taken up the cry of regional dictators like Rakhimov in Bashkortostan and Shaimiev in Tatarstan – 'It is not so important how the votes are cast but rather how they are counted'. What Pribylovskii calls 'Bashkir Electoral Technology' is one of the favorite methods employed by regional leaders to manipulate elections. Here opposition candidates are prevented from competing by decisions of regional electoral commissions or local courts, or they are expelled from the elections during the campaign itself. Sometimes, compromising materials may be collected by regional police forces to 'persuade' incumbent mayors to voluntarily withdraw from elections.[57] Thus Viktor Cherepkov ran for mayor or other office 26 times in the city of Vladivostok, 'but in every case he was either removed by the regional [governor] Nazdratenko, or the elections were overturned. The region's courts and election commission were firmly under the governor's control'.[58] In Krasnodar region, over 30 mayors were forced from office during 2002–2004, after being charged with trumped-up criminal offences.[59] In 2003–2004, refusals to register candidates, or their enforced withdrawal, was implemented in mayoral elections for Novosibirsk (March 2003), Norilsk (April 2003), Vladivostok (July 2004), to name but a few.[60] As we shall now see, new legislation on local self-government adopted under Putin gives regional governors greater powers to dismiss local administrative heads without need of such illegal methods.

Putin's Radical Reform of Local Government and the Power of Mayors 2000–2005

Putin's reform of local government must be seen in light of his wider federal reforms and his attempts to instigate what he calls a 'power vertical' in Russia. Since coming to power in 2000, he has re-centralised power under the Kremlin and weakened the powers of both regional and local governments. In October 2004 Putin pushed legislation through the Russian Parliament giving him new powers to directly

---

[54]   Vladimir Gel'man, 'Democratic Gains Reversed in Regional Elections From Moscow to Sakha', East West Institute, *Russian Regional Report*, Vol. 7, No. 5, 6 February 2002.

[55]   Slider, 'Governors versus Mayors', p. 157.

[56]   Nikolai Petrov, 'Regional Elections under Putin and Prospects for Russian Electoral Democracy', *Ponars Policy Memo* 287, February 2003, p. 2.

[57]   Petrov, 'Regional Elections', p. 2.

[58]   Slider, 'Governors versus Mayors', p. 158.

[59]   *Russian Regional Report*, Vol. 9, No. 15, 31 August 2004, p. 1.

[60]   ibid, pp. 8–9.

appoint regional governors, and plans are afoot to give regional chief executives similar rights to appoint mayors.

In October 2003, the Russian Parliament ratified Putin's Law *On Local Self-Government in the Russian Federation*.[61] This challenges the independence of local self-government, granting regional bodies new powers to control municipalities. For many critics, the new law seeks 'the etatization (*ogosudarstvlenie*) of local government'. It focuses much more on local self-government's accountability to the state than its accountability to the public.[62] Thus, although Article 34(4) reaffirms that, 'bodies of local self-government shall not be a part of the system of bodies of state power', it also stresses that, 'bodies of state power and state officials' in certain circumstances 'may participate in the formation of local self-governments, and the appointment and release of local officials'. Furthermore, the new law specifies numerous instances where regional governments can legally take over the functions of local self-governments and regional governors can impeach heads of municipalities. Thus, according to Article 75, local governments may be temporarily taken over by regional governments if they accumulate debts exceeding 30 per cent of their own locally-generated budget revenues. Article 74 (1) states that heads of local administrations may be impeached if they adopt measures producing 'violations of human and citizens rights and freedoms' or presenting 'a threat to the unity and territorial integrity of the Russian Federation', or the 'national security of the Federation and its military efficiency'. Article 74 (2), further provides for impeachment of municipal heads if they fail to rescind legal acts, a local court order has declared to infringe the Russian Constitution or federal or regional laws. As Lankina notes, 'It is not difficult to imagine how the regional authorities may use any of these provisions to penalise politically disobedient municipalities'.[63]

The Law creates a two-tier system of local government with upper-level municipal districts and lower-level settlements and cities. The legislative assemblies of the municipal districts are not to be elected by the population but instead composed of the heads of administrations under their jurisdiction. Most large cities will be granted the special status of 'city districts' and not subordinated to municipal districts. However, regional administrations will have sole power to decide whether particular towns or cities are classified as city-districts, thereby increasing regional governors' leverage over uncooperative mayors.

Election of the heads of municipal districts

As under the 1995 law, mayors can be elected by popular vote or indirectly by city councils. However, the new law states that a municipality head 'may not concurrently hold the positions of a chairperson of the representative body of the municipality and

---

[61]   Federal Law, 6 October 2003 No 131-F3, 'Ob Obshchikh Printsipakh Organizatsii Mestnovo Samoupravleniya v Rossiiskoi Federatsii' (Moscow, Omega-L, 2003).

[62]   *NGO Newsletter*, Issue 55, April 23, 2003, p. 7.

[63]   Tomila Lankina, 'The Kozak commission's local government reforms', paper presented to the 36th Annual Conference of the American Association for the Advancement of Slavic Studies, Boston, USA, December, 2004.

the head of the local administration'. Moreover, the head of the executive branch of these new bodies is to be an 'executive manager', hired by contract.[64] One third of the members of the panels charged with appointing these new managers are to be chosen by regional administrations thereby giving governors key influence over such appointments. Under the new system, mayors will be left with largely ceremonial duties, real power being placed in the hands of city managers. Meanwhile, Putin's latest policy initiative to grant governors power to directly appoint mayors clearly violates article 32 of the Russian Constitution, which states that, 'Citizens of the Russian Federation shall have the right to elect and to be elected to bodies of state governance and to organs of local self-government'.[65]

In conclusion, Russia's mayors continue to work under a highly centralised and politicised system of state administration where informal extra-legal rules of the game dominate formal constitutional and legal norms. Parties play only a minor role in city politics and patron-client relations dominate the political landscape. Putin's new law on local self-government has left mayors at the mercy of regional governors, and as Malyakin stresses, the President's federal reforms have instigated:

> the construction of a rigid vertical of power in which regional law conforms to federal law, the president enforces federal standards on the governors through the federal districts, and the governors in turn control local government through the municipal districts.[66]

---

[64]   Gel'man, 'The Politics of Local Government', pp. 15–16.
[65]   Robert Coalson, 'Mayoral elections: democracy's last stand? RFE/RL', *Russian Political Weekly*, Vol. 5, No. 9, 4 March 2005, p. 1.
[66]   I. Malyakin, 'Putin against the regions: round two', *Russia and Eurasia Review*, Vol. 1, No. 2, June18, 2002, p. 4.

CHAPTER TEN

The Mayor in American Local Government

Benjamin A. Lloyd, Donald F. Norris and Thomas J. Vicino

An enduring and intriguing debate about the impacts of local government structure on public policy has dominated American academic interest for decades.[1] From Progressive Era reformers advocating 'good, honest government' to their modern-day counterparts promoting 'efficient service delivery', politicians and practitioners alike have experimented with structure as a means to achieve these and other lofty goals. Accordingly, a plethora of academic studies have examined the impacts of such reforms. Our purpose here is to describe the American mayoralty, and examine whether differences in structure involving that office matter to the public management and policy choices of American cities. We first explore mayoralty's historical development from colonial times through the reform movement, which gave the impetus for structural change. Next, we describe the structural characteristics of American local government at the start of the twenty-first century, including different forms of mayoral power. Then, we review the scholarly literature and finally try to gauge what we know about the impact of structure upon local government performance and policy.

We believe this study is important for at least four reasons. Firstly, the sheer number of general-purpose local governments in the U.S.A – nearly 40,000, of which approximately half are municipal governments – suggests that knowing whether structure matters could be useful both academically and practically. Secondly, citizens, advocates and governmental officials demonstrate repeatedly their belief that local government structure matters. Whether true or not, such convictions motivate numerous efforts around the country each year to change that structure. Thirdly, the issue has been prominent in American academic discussion and debate for over 100 years. Finally, in recent years, perceptions of the American mayoralty have informed or misinformed the debate about both local government performance and the viability of adopting American style mayors in other countries, especially Britain.[2]

---

[1]   J. Edwin Benton, 'The Impact of Structural Reform on County Government Service Provision', *Social Science Quarterly*, 84, no. 4 (2003), p. 858.

[2]   Steve Leach and Donald F. Norris, 'Elected Mayors in England: A Contribution to the Debate', *Public Policy and Administration*, 17, no. 1 (2002), pp. 21–38.

Municipal Government and the Mayor in Early America

Ernest S. Griffith's four-volume *History of American City Government* provides a detailed and comprehensive history of American municipal government from the Colonial Era through the Progressive Era of 1900–1920.[3] According to Griffith, the administrative structure for American municipalities evolved from the English model imposed on the early colonists.[4] Colonial mayors served as nominal heads of municipal corporations, and often held other offices, such as tax collector or coroner.[5] Typically, the colonial governor appointed the mayor for a one-year term and, in most cases, he could be reappointed.[6]

After the United States gained its independence, it became common practice for members of the municipal council (typically known as the Board of Aldermen) to select the mayor. However some municipalities utilised more innovative means. For example, Baltimore's charter of 1797 decreed that the mayor be selected by electoral college, a method deliberately imitating the process of electing American presidents. Eligible voters elected 16 electors, two from each of the city's eight council districts (or wards), who in turn chose the mayor.[7] The charter imitated the federal constitution in other ways too. It provided for a bicameral municipal council, an institution that Baltimore's nearby commercial rival Philadelphia had adopted the year before.[8] Baltimore was also the first municipality to grant the mayor the power to *veto* legislation passed by the council.[9] To this day, Baltimore's mayor is considered to wield particularly high levels of power compared to other American mayors.

Direct election of mayors did not begin to emerge until the 1820s. Until then, only a few municipalities allowed eligible voters to elect the mayor.[10] Between 1820 and 1840, many cities and towns began adopting direct mayoral elections, including St Louis (1822), Boston (1822), Detroit (1824), New York (1834) and Philadelphia (1839). Baltimore discarded its electoral college for elections in 1833. Griffith partially attributes this movement to the emergence of Jacksonian Democracy in the 1820s, which held that the common man should have more influence on his government.[11] This period also saw the emergence of ethnically- and geographically-based political power in larger cities as immigrant populations from Europe began settling in concentrated neighborhoods. The first politically empowered immigrant

---

[3]   Griffith's first volume, *The Colonial Period*, was originally published in 1938, and reprinted in 1972. The other three were published between 1974 and 1976. Griffith co-authored the second volume, *The Formation of Traditions, 1775–1870*, with Charles Adrian. See footnote 5 below.

[4]   Charles R. Adrian and Ernest S. Griffith, *A History of American City Government: The Formation of Traditions, 1775–1870* (New York: Praeger Publishers, 1976), p. 177.

[5]   ibid; and Ernest S. Griffith, *History of American City Government: The Colonial Period* (New York: Da Capo Press, 1972): p. 186.

[6]   Griffith, *History of American City Government: The Colonial Period*, pp. 172–3.

[7]   Adrian and Griffith, *History of American City Government: 1775–1870*, pp. 177–8.

[8]   ibid., p. 158.

[9]   ibid., p. 190.

[10]   New Haven (1784), Nashville (1806), New Orleans (1812) and Annapolis (1819).

[11]   Adrian and Griffith, *History of American City Government: 1775–1870*, pp. 178–9.

group was the Irish, followed by the Italians, Poles and Jews. Until this time, urban political power had been confined to cadres of mostly Protestant economic elites.[12]

During this early period of mayoralty, it was quite common for the local executive to have certain legislative and judicial powers. Typically, he served as presiding officer of the local council with full voting privileges.[13] He was also a justice of the peace just as in colonial times.[14] However, while his functions were broad, the administrative powers of most mayors were not extensive. They had only minor roles in influencing the process of selecting municipal officials, since appointments were usually the council's responsibility.[15]

As the nineteenth century progressed, political leaders and citizens alike demanded that the separation of powers principle be structurally applied to municipal government as it had been to federal and state government. Many city charters were amended to remove some mayoral legislative and judicial powers. At the same time, charters often added mayoral *vetoes* and legislative overrides to provide checks between the two branches.[16]

The 1850s and 1860s saw both the emergence of 'professional municipal politicians' and the rise of political machines in many large cities.[17] Machines were essentially clubs that dominated the operations of a particular political party within a city or portion of a city. Although partisan organisations, their purpose was not to advance a particular political ideology. Rather, it was to acquire, exploit and preserve political power. Fred I. Greenstein identified four main elements of machine politics:

1. A disciplined party hierarchy that runs the machine;
2. Party control of the process of nomination to public office;
3. A party leadership that usually does not hold public office;
4. A group of loyal party workers and core of voters, which are maintained through the dispersal of both material rewards (for example, patronage, jobs, contracts) and 'non-ideological psychic rewards' (e.g., personal and ethnic recognition, camaraderie).[18]

According to Harrigan and Vogel, the emergence of ethnic-based community politics facilitated political machines. They generated support within ethnic neighborhoods by offering recently arrived immigrants services, jobs, government contracts and, perhaps most importantly, friendship and support.[19] City residents, job-seekers and

---

[12]   John J. Harrigan and Ronald K. Vogel, *Political Change in the Metropolis* (New York: Longman, 2003), pp. 61–76.

[13]   Adrian and Griffith, *History of American City Government: 1775–1870*, p. 189.

[14]   ibid., pp. 190–91.

[15]   Jon C. Teaford, *The Unheralded Triumph: City Government in America, 1870–1900* (Baltimore: Johns Hopkins University Press, 1984), p. 43.

[16]   Adrian and Griffith, *History of American City Government: 1775–1870*, p. 196.

[17]   ibid., p. 180.

[18]   Fred I. Greenstein, 'The Changing Pattern of Urban Party Politics', *Annals of the American Academy of Political and Social Science*, 353 (1964), pp. 1–13.

[19]   Harrigan and Vogel, *Political Change in the Metropolis*, pp. 80–83.

businesses not friendly to the machine were at a clear disadvantage, as the distribution of resources was more commonly based on loyalty to the machine than capability or merit. During the early-twentieth century, various political leaders wielded control over city governance by abusing the powers of office for personal gain. For instance, Gilbertson's early work emphasised such abuses. The New York County sheriff pocketed some $60,000 in fines in 1917 and the Cook County treasurer left his four-year term $500,000 richer in 1916.[20] Scholars have attributed instances like these to a weak political structure that did not provide accountability or professionalisation for government officials. In other words, the spoils system was all too commonplace during this era. Particularly contemptuous of machines were the upper class and elites of cities, who felt that the machine system limited their influence in city politics and empowered the lower classes.

At the machine's head was typically a 'boss' who selected the individuals to represent the party in elections for municipal offices (for example, mayors, city councilors, judges). Political power within cities, therefore, was rooted in the machine rather than in city government. Given the community-based nature of their operations, machines exerted considerable influence over the membership of a city's legislative body, which was typically elected from districts. Nonetheless, mayors who did not do the bidding of the machine leadership risked losing at least the support, and at most the re-nomination, of their party in the next election. One of the more famous machines was Tammany Hall, the powerful Democratic Party apparatus for New York City. It dominated city politics for most of the period from the 1850s to 1934, when anti-Tammany reformer Fiorello LaGuardia won the mayoralty. Likewise, the remnants of the reign of the Daley Machine in Chicago still persist. Richard J. Daley was elected mayor of Chicago in 1955 and served until his death in 1976. His pro-growth agenda, centering on building city infrastructure, was ripe for a patronage system to award city contracts and jobs in return for votes. In 1989, Daley's son was elected mayor and still serves at the time of writing.

Scholars have mixed perceptions of the 1870–1900 period, during which machines governed virtually every large city.[21] Griffith refers to these decades as a period of 'conspicuous failure', borrowing from an 1888 statement by British observer John Bryce who found the corruption associated with machine politics in American cities a major defect in the governance of the young country. This line of thinking produced the reform movement that generated considerable support at around the turn of the century. However, Teaford counters that 'late nineteenth century urban government was a failure not of structure but of image'.[22] Calling this period a time of 'trumpeted failures and unheralded triumphs', he notes the effectiveness of the machine system in delivering quality services and maintaining fiscal stability.[23]

---

[20]   Henry S. Gilbertson, *The County: The 'Dark Continent' of American Politics* (New York: National Short Ballot Organisation, 1917).

[21]   Harrigan and Vogel, *Political Change in the Metropolis*, p. 81.

[22]   Teaford, *The Unheralded Triumph*, p. 10.

[23]   ibid., p. 6.

The Reform Movement

Justly or not, political machines were (and remain) widely perceived as corrupt and undemocratic. Thus a government reform movement arose in the late-nineteenth and early-twentieth centuries calling for the restructuring of municipal institutions in ways that weakened the power of machines. The changes advocated by the 'progressive reformers' were designed to remove machine bosses from the electoral process and ensure government was administered more efficiently and honestly.[24]

Samuel Hays' historical analysis of the early Progressive reform movement demonstrates that city business elites and upper classes typically supported structural change in local government for two main reasons. First, they favored changes they argued would make government more efficient and less costly, inasmuch as they were the source of a sizeable portion of municipal revenue. Second, elites favored any change that would potentially weaken the machine's political power.[25] According to Hays, these reform measures:

> constituted an attempt by upper-class, advanced professional, and large business groups to take formal political power from the previously dominant lower- and middle-class elements so that they might advance their own conception of desirable public policy.[26]

Examples of reform are given below, along with their intended consequences:

- *At-large elections* requiring that city-council members be elected through a citywide vote. In other words, each citizen was to have the opportunity to vote for council members representing the entire city. By contrast, single-member districts facilitated machine precincts, which encouraged council members to attend only to their own district's needs and not citywide issues.
- *Nonpartisan elections* removing party affiliations from local elections. This supposedly limited the machine's ability to nominate and elect its own candidate. Reformers held that cities were in the business of delivering public goods and services. A neutral, apolitical environment was therefore desired.
- *Strong mayors* providing local governmental executives with 'centralised responsibilities' and allowing greater roles for policy formulation and implementation, making it difficult for the machine to assume too much power.
- *Council-manager forms of government* promoting apolitical governing environments because professional managers headed up local government. The city was to be run in a 'business-like manner' and the council made public policy. (The reformers came to favor the council-manager after they became disillusioned about the actual performance of strong mayors in the late 1900s.[27])

---

[24]   Harrigan and Vogel, *Political Change in the Metropolis*, p. 86.

[25]   Samuel P. Hays, 'The Politics of Reform in Municipal Government', *Pacific Northwest Quarterly* 55, no. 4 (1964), p. 157.

[26]   ibid., p. 165.

[27]   Russell D. Murphy, 'The mayoralty and the democratic creed: the evolution of an ideology and an institution', *Urban Affairs Quarterly*, 22 (September 1986), pp. 3–23.

The reformers sought to change the existing mayor-council structure for several reasons. Foremost, the reformers wanted city administrative functions to be carried out in politically neutral environments that would remove patronage and partisan favoritism from the provision of public service delivery.[28] Also, many Machine-Era cities had 'weak mayors', who had limited roles in the administration of city services.[29] Administrative units, or departments, reported to the council, not the mayor. The council had budgetary and general policy power in the local political system. This form of government reflected an early American mistrust of centralised government.[30]

The progressive reformers promoted strong mayor-council structures because the political machine often dominated weak mayor-council cities.[31] Under the weak mayors of the Machine Era, mayoral powers were limited in areas where power was most needed, like budget formulation, and the nomination and removal of city officials. Duvall even asserts: 'the mayor was chief executive in name only.'[32] Under the strong-mayor form, the mayor would have centralised authority over the bureaucracy and would be the city's chief administrator.[33] Strong mayor's powers included the ability to *veto* council legislative measures, nominate and terminate appointed city officials and craft public policy. Accordingly, the strong mayor's office, as the reformers argued, would be strengthened by centralising local government authority in one individual whom voters could hold accountable.[34]

However, by the early-twentieth century, the strong mayor form fell out of favor with the reformers who then began to advocate for the council-manager form of government. Under the idealised version of this form of municipal government, the city council would be chosen in a non-partisan election from an at-large (the city as a whole) constituency and would function as a sort of corporate board of directors. The council would also appoint a professional manager to run the day-to-day affairs of the city. Roger Kemp captures the essence of this reform in stating that this governmental form 'provides the best answer to effective leadership by the mayor and city council, and a professional approach to solving city's problems'.[35] He further notes that, while slow to develop (it is only 80 years old), it grew directly out of the Progressive Era and its ideals.

Specifically, four factors influenced the growth and popularity of the council-manager form. First, urbanisation dramatically impacted on the urban landscape by

[28]   Harrigan and Vogel, *Political Change in the Metropolis*, p. 87.

[29]   Julianne Duvall, 'Contemporary Choices for Citizens', in Roger L. Kemp (ed.), *Forms of Local Government: A Handbook for City, County, and Regional Options* (Jefferson, NC: McFarland and Co., 1999), p. 66.

[30]   Charles R. Adrian, 'Forms of Local Government in American History', in Roger L. Kemp (ed.), *Forms of Local Government: A Handbook for City, County, and Regional Options* (Jefferson, NC: McFarland and Co., 1999), p. 57.

[31]   ibid.

[32]   Duvall, 'Contemporary Choices for Citizens', p. 63.

[33]   ibid., p. 66.

[34]   ibid.

[35]   Roger L. Kemp, 'The Council-Manager Form of Government', in Roger L. Kemp (ed.), *Forms of Local Government: A Handbook for City, County, and Regional Options* (Jefferson, NC: McFarland and Co., 1999), p. 69.

placing demands on local government to deliver services and public facilities.[36] As cities and counties grew into metropolitan areas, residents demanded basic infrastructure resources like water, roads and schools. Second, many local governments have adopted business and corporate ideals, which determine public values and governance. Economy and efficiency (business principles), Kemp holds, are the foundations of the council-manager form.[37] Third, the Progressive movement advocated an apolitical and professional manager to ensure competent public decision-making and nonpartisan elected officials. 'Progressive values, which favored impartiality and looked down upon personality politics and favoritism' provided the foundation for this form of government.[38] Last, the public administration movement – spearheaded among others by political scientist and former president Woodrow Wilson – was influential for this plan because it argued for a distinction between politics and administration. Therefore, under this form of government, the elected officials craft public policy, and the manager implements the policy and oversees daily government activity.[39]

Since the Progressive Era reforms, the distribution of the principal forms of municipal government structure has gradually changed, as cities increasingly have opted for council managers. The following section details the structural characteristics of American municipal government at the beginning of the twenty-first century.

The American Mayor at the Dawn of the Twenty-first Century

The USA has nearly 20,000 municipalities, serving populations ranging from zero to over 8 million. Two-thirds of American municipalities serve populations of less than 2,500.[40] Municipal governments can be classified as cities, towns, townships, villages, boroughs, districts and plantations. Similarly, local-elected executives in the U.S. can be labelled by various titles, including mayor, president, executive and board chair. 'Mayor' is used most commonly and, quite frequently, elected executives will be referred to as 'mayor' even when their official titles are something else. But the differences between American municipal governments go far beyond population size and simple labelling. There are measurable differences in both governmental structure, and in the roles of elected executives. And, as we will demonstrate, these differences have implications for both politics and policy.

The International City/County Management Association (ICMA) surveys municipal governments quinquennially to examine and identify trends in the structural characteristics of American municipal governments. The 2001 *Form of Government Survey* was based on responses to questionnaires sent to all municipalities with populations of 2,500 and above and to a sample of municipalities with populations of fewer than 2,500. Since ICMA used a different methodology for surveying the smallest municipalities, our analysis includes only those serving populations of 2,500 and above. Over half (54 per cent) returned the questionnaires and the survey results reflected the fact that there are many more small municipalities than larger ones (see Table 10.1).

---

[36]   ibid., 71.
[37]   ibid.
[38]   ibid.
[39]   ibid., p. 72.
[40]   United States Bureau of the Census, *2002 Census of Governments*.

Table 10.1   Survey Response, ICMA Form of Government Survey, 2001 (municipalities with populations over 2,500 only)[41]

	No. of municipalities	No. of responses	Response Rate
Total	6,967	3,759	54%
Population group			
Large (250,000 and above)	66	35	53%
Medium (50,000–249,999)	560	330	59%
Small (2,500–49,999)	6341	3394	54%

The survey found that the elected executive's job was officially full-time in only 17 per cent of the municipalities that responded. However, mayoralty was full-time in 68 per cent of large cities (i.e., with populations of 250,000 or more).

In three-quarters of municipalities, voters directly elected the mayor. In another 22 per cent, the council selected mayors from amongst their own members. The remaining three per cent selected their mayor in some other way, like rotating the office among council members, or granting the office to the council member with the most votes in a general election. The mayor was directly elected in all the responding large cities.

The commonest term-length for American mayors was four years (45 per cent), and one-third had two-year terms (33 per cent). Four-year terms were the clear choice in large cities (80 per cent). Only 9 per cent of municipalities limited the number of terms mayors could serve, with two-term limits being most common. More than half (51 per cent) of large cities imposed term-limits on their mayors. Regardless of the election method, in more than two-thirds of municipalities (69 per cent) mayors sat as city-council members. Thirty per cent of all mayors, including two-thirds (66 per cent) of large-city mayors, could *veto* council legislation.

A key indicator of mayoral power is whether he or she has budgetary authority. In only a few municipalities (12 per cent) is developing the budget the mayor's sole responsibility. More commonly, the budget is the sole responsibility of a non-elected appointee like the city manager or finance director (68 per cent). But in nearly half of large cities (49 per cent), the mayor has independent authority over the budget.

Aside from illuminating the characteristics of the mayor's role, the survey also provided data on how municipalities conduct governmental functions. ICMA recognises five different forms of municipal government, defined as follows (see also Table 10.2):

1. *Mayor-Council* – 'Elected council or board serves as the legislative body. The chief elected official is the head of government, with significant administrative authority, generally elected separately from the council.' *Nearly four in ten of*

---
[41]   Adapted from Susan A. MacManus and Charles S. Bullock III, 'The Form, Structure, and Composition of America's Municipalities in the New Millenium', in *Municipal Year Book 2003*, (Washington, DC: International City/County Management Association, 2003), p. 5.

all municipalities (38 per cent) have this form of government, including 60 per cent of large cities.

2. *Council-Manager* – 'Elected council or board and chief elected official (e.g., mayor) are responsible for making policy. A professional administrator appointed by the board or council has full responsibility for the day-to-day operations of the government.' *This form is found in over half (54 per cent) of all municipalities and 40 per cent of large-city governments.*

3. *Commission* – 'Members of a board of elected commissioners serve as heads of specific departments and collectively sit as the legislative body of the government.' *This form is hardly used at all today, having lost favour since the turn of the twentieth century. It is found in 1 per cent of cities and no large city uses it.*

4. *Town Meeting* – 'Qualified voters convene to make basic policy and to choose a board of selectmen. The selectmen and elected officers carry out the policies established by the government.' *This form is found in 6 per cent of all municipalities and no large cities.*

5. *Representative Town Meeting* – 'Voters select citizens to represent them at the town meeting. All citizens may attend and participate in debate, but only representatives may vote.'[42] *This form is found in 1 per cent of all municipalities and no large cities.*

To summarise, council-manager government has been adopted in most American municipalities, but the mayor-council form is still used in nearly four out of ten municipalities with populations above 2,500 and 60 per cent of large cities. Very few use the commission, town meeting or representative town meeting forms and the town meeting or representative town meeting forms are rarely found outside New England.

Table 10.2   American   Municipal   Forms   of   Government,   2001 (municipalities that offered a response)

	All municipalities		Large municipalities only*	
	No.	%	No.	%
Mayor-Council	1401	38	21	60
Council-Manager	2013	54	14	40
Commission	44	1	0	-
Town Meeting	208	6	0	-
Representative Town Meeting	37	1	0	-
Total	3703	100	35	100
* Cities with populations of 250,000 and above.				

[42]   The definition of each form was quoted directly from the questionnaire that ICMA distributed to potential respondents to the 2002 survey.

Not only can form of government characteristics differ by city population, but also by location. The council-manager form is the overwhelming government of choice for municipalities on America's West Coast, while municipalities in the Midwest and Mid-Atlantic prefer the mayor-council form. Most common in New England is the town meeting, followed by the council-manager. Form of government figures for the Southeast, Great Plains, and Rocky Mountain regions are similar to the national figures.

MacManus and Bullock compared the form of government figures from the 2001 survey to those conducted in 1981, 1986, 1991 and 1996. Considering only municipalities with populations of above 2,500 and discarding those using town-meeting forms, they found the council-manager form surpassed the mayor-council form as the most used governmental type at some point in the early-to-mid 1980s. In 1981, mayor-council governments outnumbered council-manager governments 52 per cent to 46 per cent. By 1986, the council-manager form had overtaken the mayor-council form, 53 per cent to 44 per cent. Since then, use of the council-manager form has been rising, while use of both the mayor-council and commission forms has declined.[43]

Mayoral Forms

Since our subject is the American mayor, we should discuss the distribution of mayoral forms among U.S. municipalities. By mayoral form we mean whether a city has a strong or a weak mayor. Much of the literature about U.S. mayors and much of the recent debate about adopting the mayoral form in the U.K. presumes the existence of what is known as the 'strong mayor'. Mayors can be said to be weak or strong in at least two ways: structurally or non-structurally.

Leach and Norris examined data from the 1996 ICMA Survey to determine whether American municipalities had strong mayors. They established three categories of strong mayor, based on the extent to which mayors had certain legal powers and structural characteristics: for example, control over the budget and personnel appointments; whether the mayor was full- or part-time; was directly elected; had a four-year term; was a member of the city council; and whether the mayor had *veto* power. Mayors with more of these powers and characteristics were stronger structurally and legally than those with fewer – that is, they had more 'formal' power. Depending on the extent that these formal powers inhered in the office, Leach and Norris characterised it either as a very strong mayor, a moderately strong mayor, or a weak strong mayor.[44]

Their principal finding was that very few American municipalities had strong mayors of any kind and fewer still had very strong mayors. For example, they found that 0.6 per cent of all cities and 1.8 per cent of mayor-council cities had very strong mayors; 2.5 per cent of all cities and 6.9 per cent of mayor council cities had moderately strong mayors; 6.3 per cent of all cities and 17.9 per cent of mayor-council cities had weak strong mayors. Cumulatively, only 9.4 per cent all cities and 25.2 per cent of mayor-

---

[43]   MacManus and Bullock, 'The Form, Structure, and Composition of America's Municipalities in the New Millenium', p. 6.

[44]   Leach and Norris, 'Elected Mayors in England', pp. 28–32.

council cities had strong mayors of any sort. This means that, whether in terms of legal powers or the structural characteristics of mayoral offices, over 90 per cent of all cities and three quarters of mayor-council cities (74.8 per cent) have weak mayors.[45]

It is beyond our purview here to examine in detail the non-structural factors affecting mayoral power and performance. Suffice to say that much has been written about this subject and seems to suggest that even structurally weak mayors can exercise power like structurally strong mayors through such mechanisms as political machines (e.g., Richard J. Daley of Chicago, *termed 'the American Pharaoh' by one writer*[46]), governing regimes (various Atlanta mayors[47]) and the personal abilities of mayors themselves (e.g., the mayors of San Francisco and Boston,[48] Philadelphia[49] and Baltimore[50]).

A reasonable conclusion that can be drawn from these and other works is that, although cities are truly limited in what they can do by a variety of both internal and external forces (e.g., demographics, wealth, local economy, legal structure, political culture, intergovernmental relations and others), mayors can make a difference in both the internal management of cities and their policy outputs. Mayoral leadership in turn is contingent on a variety of factors, circumstances and conditions (including mayoral personalities and abilities) affecting how far mayors can and cannot make a difference in their cities and citizens' lives.[51] However, the persona of the mayor himself or herself is seen as important to mayoral achievement.

Impacts of Governmental Structure

Regardless of the debate over mayoral leadership, a perennial and important question about local government structural reform is whether it has produced the impacts the Progressive reformers desired. Greater efficiency and increased accountability are two expected outcomes of structural reform. For example, are reformed cities and counties more economically efficient and less corrupt? Do reformers overstate or understate the impacts of political structural change? Do these structural changes in government impact upon the types of public policy (like service delivery and taxation) cities or counties pursue? Scholars have asked questions like these to determine what impact, *if any*, government structure has on desired reform outcomes. Here, we briefly review the

---

[45]   ibid.

[46]   Adam Cohen and Elizabeth Taylor, *American Pharaoh: Mayor Richard J. Daley: His Battle for Chicago and the Nation* (Boston: Little, Brown, 2000).

[47]   Clarence N. Stone, *Regime Politics: Governing Atlanta, 1946–1988* (Lawrence, KS: University of Kansas Press, 1988).

[48]   Barbara Ferman, *Governing the Ungovernable City: Political Skill, Leadership and the Modern Mayor* (Philadelphia: Temple University Press, 1985).

[49]   Buzz Bissinger, *A Prayer for the City* (New York: Random House, 1997).

[50]   C. Fraser Smith, *William Donald Schaefer: A Political Biography* (Baltimore: The Johns Hopkins University Press, 1999).

[51]   See Melvin G. Holli, *The American Mayor: The Best and Worst Big City Leaders* (University Park, PA: Pennsylvania State University Press, 1999); and Lana Stein, 'Mayoral Politics', in John P. Pelissero (ed.), *Cities, Politics, and Policy: A Comparative Analysis* (Washington, DC: CQ Press, 2003).

major scholarly contributions to answer these and similar questions about the impacts of changing government structure on public policy and management.

Early work on political restructuring focused on two basic elements: municipal government differences and policy expenditure differences. Lineberry and Fowler's classic 1967 study spurred decades of research on this theme. They drew a random sample of 200 cities (from the 309 cities with populations over 50,000 in 1960) to determine the impact of city political structure on taxation and public expenditures (public policy outputs). Overall, they found that reformed governments taxed their residents less and spent less than their unreformed counterparts.[52] Specifically, council-manager governments with at-large and nonpartisan elections taxed 7–13 per cent less and spent 12–13 per cent less than mayor-council cities with district and partisan elections.[53] They also found that socio-economic variables (i.e., race, income and household size) are positively related to public-policy outputs. In other words, unreformed cities tended to be more responsive to citizens' demands for public goods and services and therefore spent more on their residents. Most subsequent empirical studies have considered similar socioeconomic variables to determine whether structure matters for policy outputs.

However, several successive studies, using similar methodologies, reported conflicting results to Lineberry and Fowler's. For instance, Clark's study of 51 cities showed reformed city structures were associated with higher levels of aggregate spending than unreformed cities.[54] Clark was interested in the impact of community structure and government structure on budgetary-expenditure patterns. He correctly hypothesised that 'large, more economically diversified communities with government structures favoring citizen participation had more decentralised patterns of decision-making … which in turn, led to a higher level of community budget expenditures'.[55] His benchmark for budget expenditures was the adoption of urban renewal programs. He found that reformed structures were more likely to adopt such programs and thus had higher spending levels. By controlling for an array of variables like population, poverty, industrial activity, economic diversification, education, religion and community volunteerism, he found that reformed cities actually spent more than traditional governments.

Confusing the issue even more is Liebert's challenge to the methodology employed by others. He challenges previous work on linking expenditure policy to political structure. Liebert studied 675 cities (with populations over 25,000), and classified cities by the types of public policies they are responsible for carrying out. Cities either have total control, partial control, or no control over what they spend. For example, cities with high levels of poverty and minorities may have little control over spending whereas a wealthier jurisdiction may have more discretion. Specifically, education and welfare expenditures account for most of the variation in budgetary patterns. He found

---

[52]   Robert L. Lineberry and Edmund P. Fowler, 'Reformism and Public Policies in American Cities', *American Political Science Review*, 61, no. 3 (1967), p. 707.

[53]   ibid., p. 708.

[54]   Terry N. Clark, 'Community Structure, Decision-Making, Budget Expenditures, and Urban Renewal in 51 American Communities', *American Sociological Review*, 33, no. 4, (1968), p. 591.

[55]   ibid., p. 576.

that, controlling for the functional inclusiveness (meaning 'the scope of functions combined within a government') of municipalities, the relationship between political structure and policy outputs disappeared.[56] He held that, when studying expenditure levels, research must only consider what the local jurisdiction is responsible for spending (and not what higher levels of government mandate in spending). So, Liebert argued, research must focus on determining what city government is responsible for in its own capacity rather than overall spending levels.

Subsequent research partially confirms and partially refutes Lineberry and Fowler's findings. Several longitudinal studies in the late-1970s and early-1980s contradict each other. For example, Lyons studied unreformed cities between 1962 and 1972, and found that, as citizens demanded more public resources, unreformed cities spent money at higher rates than reformed cities.[57] He concluded reformed cites were thus better equipped to contain public spending within their fiscal means, confirming Lineberry and Fowler's initial findings suggesting political structure does matter in this area. Yet more recent research contradicts Lyons' findings. For instance, Morgan and Pelissero analysed 11 reformed cities with populations over 25,000 (and 11 control cities) from 1948 to 1973 and found that municipal fiscal behavior was unaffected by changes in political structure, contradicting both Lineberry and Fowler as well as Lyons.[58] They employed a quasi-experimental time-series design to test the impacts of municipal reform on policy expenditures. It was the first study of its kind to explore city expenditures over a long period of time. The study considered a wide variety of forms of public expenditures, including general revenue, general expenditures, police, fire and sanitation expenditures, parks expenditures and highway expenditures. In all cases, reformed cities did not spend or tax less than unreformed cities. The authors argue that structure accordingly does *not* matter for policy outputs and suggest political culture or governing ideologies may be better indicators for fiscal decisions.

These mixed findings suggest there may be methodological problems with the studies scholars conduct. Farnham and Bryant raise several important methodological issues about such studies.[59] First, most only explore the impacts of structural change on cities. There is a deficit of scholarly activity in relation to county government. As counties modernise and assume large policy roles, it will be important to test the hypotheses on them. Second, studies largely focus on large central cities (50,000 or more). Structure may matter more or less for smaller cities. Incorporating medium and small cities into empirical studies would therefore begin answering this question. Third, the limited scope of the types of cities studied may not be very representative of overall municipal trends. For instance, studies have considered Northeastern

[56]   Roland J. Liebert, 'Municipal Functions, Structures and Expenditures: A Reanalysis of Recent Research', *Social Science Quarterly*, 54, no. 1 (1974), p. 771.

[57]   William E. Lyons, 'Reform and Response in American Cities: Structure and Policy Reconsidered', *Social Science Quarterly* 59, no. 2 (1978), p. 130.

[58]   David R. Morgan and John P. Pelissero, 'Urban Policy: Does Political Structure Matter?', *American Political Science Review*, 74, no. 4 (1980), p. 1005.

[59]   Paul Farnham and Stephen Bryant, 'Form of Local Government: Structural Policies of Citizen Choice', *Social Science Quarterly*, 66, no. 2 (1985), p. 390.

and Rustbelt cities, which tend to decline, while Sunbelt cities experience growth. Therefore, Farnham and Bryant convincingly argue for expanded research of more diverse geographic samples of governments.

Conclusion

Two distinct movements have shaped the debate over American local government structure. First, during the late-nineteenth and early-twentieth centuries, at the height of the big-city political machine, Progressive reformers sought to clean up government by changing the municipal structure to a strong-mayor form and later to the council-manager form. Second, during the post-World War II decades, the persistence of suburbanisation led city and county governments to become increasingly important players at the local level. Demands for new services and calls to end corruption motivated reformers to change governmental forms to manager/administrator structures. Overall, reform measures were more successful in municipal than county governments. More than half of all municipalities are reformed, while only one-third of counties are in this category. Reform movements can be broadly characterised as measures to increase both the responsiveness and efficiency of American local government.

At the turn of the twenty-first century, we find significant structural differences between all municipalities and those with large populations (250,000 or greater). The council-manager form predominates in all municipalities but 60 per cent of large cities have adopted the mayor-council form. Most mayors are part-time, although 68 per cent of large-city mayors are full-time. Most mayors regardless of city size are directly elected and serve four-year terms. Most large cities (51 per cent versus 9 per cent of all cities) limit mayoral terms. Most mayors, regardless of city size, are members of their respective city councils. However, only one-third of all mayors have *veto* power *versus* two thirds of large-city mayors. Finally, there has recently been a discernable trend for cities to switch from the mayor-council form to the council-manager form (except among large cities).

The distribution of mayoral forms – that is, whether cities have strong or weak mayors – clearly shows that few American cities have strong mayors, even when the bar for determining 'strong' is lowered considerably. Less than 10 per cent of all cities and only about a quarter of mayor-council cities had very strong, moderately strong, or weak strong mayors.

Regardless of the structural characteristics of the mayor's office, however, the literature shows that individual mayors can overcome structural weaknesses and govern strongly. At the same time, mayors in structurally strong offices can fail to use their powers effectively, and consequently govern poorly. Two examples from our backyard are instructive.

From 1971 to 1987, William Donald Schaefer was mayor of Baltimore and by all accounts a strong mayor.[60] Of course, it helped that the office of Baltimore's mayor is structurally one of the strongest in the nation. The incumbent is elected for a four-year

---

[60] See Fraser Smith, *William Donald Schaefer: A Political Biography* (Baltimore: Johns Hopkins University Press, 1999).

term without term limits. The mayor appoints and alone can remove nearly all top city officials. He has exceptionally strong executive budgetary power and writes the budget. The council can only reduce it. The council cannot add or move money among line items, departments, or programs. Finally, the mayor has a majority of the votes on the Board of Estimates, the body that approves all city expenditures and purchases. Schaefer used all his formal powers as well as the enormous power of his personality and his exceptional ability to command media and public attention to govern strongly, and according to most observers, effectively during his 15-year tenure.

Kurt L. Schmoke, Baltimore's first elected African-American mayor, followed Schaefer. The circumstances Schmoke inherited in 1987 were hardly as favorable as those facing Schaefer in 1979. The city and the nation were just climbing out of severe economic recession. Federal policy toward major cities was changing from grudging support to outright hostility, and federal funds for cities were drying up dramatically. A crack-cocaine epidemic was beginning to impact on Baltimore and crime rates, especially rates of violent crime, were skyrocketing. The results of years of neglect of the city's school system were becoming sadly evident. And, Baltimore was haemorrhaging jobs and residents to the suburbs. About the only bright spot in the city was its downtown Renaissance focused on the revitalised Inner Harbor. However, a 1986 study of its problems claimed the rest of the city represented the 'rot beneath the glitter' of the Inner Harbor.[61] Thus, Schmoke took office with several serious problems facing Baltimore. Twelve years later when he left office, most local observers felt little had improved during his tenure and much had gotten worse, particularly schools, crime, drugs and continuing losses of jobs and residents. Furthermore, most argued that the quality of city services and the management of city government itself had declined under Schmoke.

Yet, at the same time, in a somewhat larger city faced with similar problems 90 miles northwards, Mayor Ed Rendell was given mostly favorable ratings for his eight years in office. Rendell's city of Philadelphia (Pennsylvania), like Baltimore, had continued in these years to lose population, jobs and tax base. But Rendell was viewed as having made a good fight to save the city against strong odds. As one writer said:

> He had inherited a city that was reeling ... and he had nursed it back to a semblance of health. He had infused hope ... He had restored the budget. He had restored the faith of Wall Street [the municipal bond market] in a place that had been a laughing stock.[62]

Clearly, there are differences in mayoral leadership not solely attributable to structure alone. Some mayors in weak-mayor cities (for example, Richard J. Daley in Chicago) govern strongly despite their office's structural weakness. Others, like Schaefer of Baltimore, govern strongly partly because of the structural and legal tools available to them. Still others, like Schmoke in Baltimore, by most accounts, govern ineffectively despite having one of the strongest mayoral offices in the country.

Studies of structural impact, employing a variety of methodologies and analytical techniques, have produced, at best, diverse findings. In the end, there seems some

---

[61]   Peter L. Szanton, *Baltimore 2000: A Choice of Futures* (Baltimore: Morris Goldseker Foundation, 1987), p. 12.

[62]   Buzz Bissinger, *A Prayer for the City* (New York: Random House, 1997), p. 342.

evidence that reformed cities do spend less. However, variation in findings depends, in part, on whether or not researchers control for 'functional inclusiveness', or the number and extent of functions provided by local governments. Finally, structure is clearly not the only determinant of city performance and policy-outputs. Political ideology and local civic engagement trends may also be determinants. For example, as Hanson shows in his political analysis of Dallas, local civic and political cultures were important in determining education reform and economic development.[63] Also, tax and service preferences may play important roles in the type of local government citizens prefer. Finally, the wealth (e.g., as measured by median household income) and socioeconomic status of residents seem to play a role in both structure and outputs.[64]

We have therefore come full circle. The question provoking this chapter – whether mayors and local government structure matter – remains unresolved. Intuitively and anecdotally, it appears that mayors can matter. Some mayors, even without benefit of structurally strong offices, govern strongly. Others, even with structurally strong offices, fail to do so. The evidence about whether other structural attributes matter is less clear. This is perhaps because of the differing methodologies and data sources the many studies of structural impacts have employed, producing inconsistent and even contradictory findings. Thus, there is ample room in American scholarship for continuing research into the impacts of mayors and local governmental structure on cities.

---

[63]   Royce Hanson, *Civic Culture and Urban Change: Governing Dallas* (Detroit: Wayne State University Press, 2003).

[64]   See Lineberry and Fowler, 'Reformism and Public Policies in American Cities'.

Index

Note: Bold page numbers indicate the most significant occurance of the entry.

For Product Safety Concerns and Information please contact our EU
representative GPSR@taylorandfrancis.com
Taylor & Francis Verlag GmbH, Kaufingerstraße 24, 80331 München, Germany

www.ingramcontent.com/pod-product-compliance
Lightning Source LLC
Chambersburg PA
CBHW070407270326
41926CB00014B/2732